# MERRILL
# Health
## Focus on You®

## Linda Meeks, M.S.
Associate Professor of Health Education
College of Education
The Ohio State University
Columbus, Ohio

## Philip Heit, Ed.D.
Professor and Chairman of Health Education
Professor of Allied Medicine
College of Education      College of Medicine
The Ohio State University, Columbus, Ohio

**Cover Photograph**
Enjoying the company of others when ice skating can be both fun and healthful. These young people are not only improving their social health by participating in an activity with their friends, but are also improving their physical fitness.

# MERRILL
**PUBLISHING COMPANY**

# A Merrill Health Program

Health: *Focus on You*®, K Big Book (with TE)
Health: *Focus on You*®, Student Editions, 1–8
Health: *Focus on You*®, Teacher Editions, 1–8
Health: *Focus on You*®, Teacher Resource Books, K–8 (Reproducible Masters)
Transparency Package (K–8)
Health Directory

**Linda Meeks** and **Philip Heit** are the coauthors of Merrill Publishing Company's K to 12 health program. Ms. Meeks and Dr. Heit conduct workshops in health science, curriculum design, and health methodology, in addition to the courses they teach at The Ohio State University. Both have taught health education in public schools and have individually authored articles and texts. Ms. Meeks is coauthor of *Toward a Healthy Lifestyle Through Elementary Health Education*. Ms. Meeks and Dr. Heit are the coauthors of *Teaching Health in Middle and Secondary Schools*.

## Editorial Review Board

*Project Editor:* Robin P. Mahaffey; *Editors:* Linda McLaughlin, Shelle Thraen, David Mielke; *Production Editor:* Helen Mischka; *Project Designer:* Jeff Kobelt; *Series Artist:* Kenneth E. Stevenson; *Project Artist:* David L. Gossell; *Photo Editors:* Aaron Haupt, Mark Burnett; *Cover Photo Editor:* Barbara Buchholz; *Illustrators:* Nancy A. Heim; Intergraphics; Don Robison, Jim Shough

*Cover Photo Credit:* George Anderson

ISBN 0-675-03256-3

Published by

**Merrill Publishing Company**

# Preface

If you were to describe yourself, think what qualities you would include. Would you be able to describe yourself as a young, healthy person? Do you feel good about yourself? The first step to becoming your best is to focus your attention on your health. Your health is influenced by what you think and do. *Health: Focus on You*® will help you determine which actions to take to develop a healthy you.

*Health: Focus on You*® is designed to provide you with health knowledge in ten areas of health; Mental Health, Family and Social Health, Growth and Development, Nutrition, Exercise and Fitness, Drugs, Diseases and Disorders, Consumer and Personal Health, Safety and First Aid, and Community and Environmental Health. Good physical, mental, and social health that are needed for a balanced lifestyle will also be described.

*Health: Focus on You*® emphasizes using your knowledge to take actions that promote health for you, others, and the environment. You will study life management skills that will contribute to the quantity and quality of the years throughout your life.

*Health: Focus on You*® also emphasizes using your knowledge to make responsible decisions. You will study how to make decisions that are healthful, safe, legal, that show respect for yourself and others, and that follow parental guidelines. You will have confidence in the decisions you make.

*Health: Focus on You*® provides an enjoyable approach to studying health. You will become more aware of the many health choices open to you and how they affect your life. You will see how a healthful lifestyle can enrich your life in many ways.

# Table of Contents

## Unit 7   Diseases and Disorders . . . . . . . . . . 212

## Unit 8   Consumer and Personal Health . . . 244

# Mental Health

Did you know . . .

▶ making responsible decisions helps you like yourself and have good health?

▶ knowing how to express emotions and handle stress improves health?

# Achieving a Healthful Lifestyle

Making decisions regarding your health is like building your own kite. You choose the colors and the design. The behaviors you choose for your health will not only be a reflection of you, but will determine the quality of your life.

- *describe healthful behaviors, risk behaviors, and risk situations.*
- *use the responsible decision-making model and refusal skills.*

There is a saying "Always give your best efforts in what you do and the best will return to you." Maybe you have heard this saying before. What does it mean to you? How is it related to having a healthful lifestyle? What does it mean to be at your best?

## Knowing About Health

Part of being at your best is examining the quality of the life you lead. To examine the quality of your life, you will need to know what it means to be healthy. You will want to learn more about health.

### 1:1  A Healthful Lifestyle

Your **lifestyle** is the way in which you live. Think about the opening statement in this chapter. One way to live a healthful lifestyle would include making your best effort to have good health. **Health** is the state of your body and mind and how you get along with others.

When you make your best effort to have good health, you must work on three kinds of health. These are physical health, mental health, and social health.

*What are the three kinds of health needed for a healthful lifestyle?*

**FIGURE 1-1**. Family members care for and help one another.

*What are two important ways to achieve high level wellness?*

**Physical health** is the state of your body. Your best effort for physical health should include eating a balanced breakfast each morning, getting plenty of exercise, rest and sleep, and keeping your body well-groomed.

**Mental health** is the state of your mind and the way you express your feelings. To make your best effort for mental health, plan ways to sharpen your thinking. Know how to express your feelings and solve problems. Your best effort for good mental health also will be helped by increasing strengths, changing a weakness to a strength, and keeping a positive attitude.

**Social health** is the state of your relationships with others. Your best effort for social health will be to work so that your family will care for each other. This might mean talking and listening to family members and helping with household chores. Good social health also means making an effort for healthful relationships with others. This might include friends, teachers, and other adults in your community. Using good manners and following the rules at school and at home will help you achieve good social health.

When you give your best effort to have good physical, mental, and social health, you will improve your self-concept. **Self-concept** is what you think and how you feel about yourself. A good self-concept is an important part of good health. You will study more about self-concept in Chapter 2.

## 1:2 Wellness

**Wellness** is the highest level of health you can reach. Wellness includes good physical, mental, and social health. You may want to rate your efforts and your level of health. As you give your best efforts in all three kinds of health, you achieve a higher level of wellness. The Wellness Scale helps you define the level of health you have achieved. See Figure 1-2 on page 7. There are two important ways that help you reach a high level of wellness.

**1.** Choose healthful behaviors.

**2.** Avoid risk behaviors and risk situations.

**Healthful behaviors** are actions that increase the level of health for you and others. Healthful behaviors also are called wellness behaviors. Examples of healthful behaviors include exercising, eating healthful foods, working puzzles, reading interesting books, and using manners. These actions promote physical, mental, and social health. They help you rate your level of health at the high end of the Wellness Scale.

**Risk behaviors** are actions that might be harmful to you or to others. These actions may harm your physical, mental, and social health. Eating snacks high in sugar and salt is a risk behavior. Other examples of risk behaviors are smoking, not doing your homework, not brushing your teeth, and riding double on a bike.

*What are risk behaviors and risk situations?*

**Risk situations** are conditions that may harm your health. Imagine you are riding in a car. The driver drives faster than the speed limit. The driver's action threatens your health and safety. Suppose you are with young people who gossip about your best friend. Later, you feel badly for having listened. By being in risk situations, your physical, mental, or social health may be harmed.

When you choose risk behaviors or are involved in risk situations, your rating on the Wellness Scale will be affected. Your rating will be toward the lower end. Your chances of becoming ill, getting hurt, or having an accident increase.

**FIGURE 1–2.** Where would you rate your level of health on the Wellness Scale?

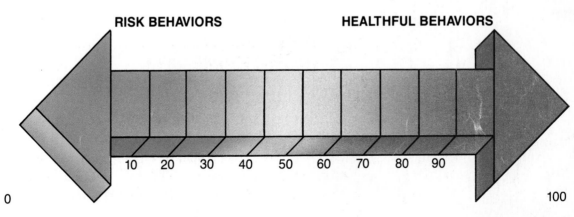

RISK BEHAVIORS        HEALTHFUL BEHAVIORS

10   20   30   40   50   60   70   80   90

0            100

Poor Health        Good Health

## 1:3 Health Knowledge and Behavior ____

Your level of health is related to your behavior. You are aware, or should be aware, that YOU are responsible for many decisions that affect your level of health. Studying about health will help you gain health knowledge. **Health knowledge** is an awareness of facts about health. When you know the facts about health, you are able to know the difference between healthful behaviors and risk behaviors. You are able to tell the difference between healthful and risk situations. You will be able to make healthful decisions.

Suppose you learn that frequently eating foods that contain fiber helps reduce the risk of colon cancer. You learn that there is fiber in whole wheat bread but very little in white bread. You may not have known these facts previously. You share what you have learned about bread with your family and decide to buy wheat bread instead of white bread. Your use of health knowledge influenced your behavior which, in turn, influenced your health and the health of your family.

This textbook contains facts about ten different areas of your health. See Table 1–1 on page 9. In each area, you will study about healthful and risk behaviors and risk situations. A behavior or situation in any one of the ten areas of health may affect other areas of health. Just one behavior choice may have an effect on your total health.

For example, eating a balanced breakfast is a healthful behavior. Your body gets the food it needs to grow. You have enough energy to think clearly and play. Breakfast is a time you might be with your family. Eating a healthful breakfast is an example of one behavior that affects physical, mental, and social health.

Smoking is a risk behavior. The ingredients in smoke can seriously harm your lungs and other body organs. Cigarette smoke may reduce your ability to think clearly. Your breath might smell like smoke. Your teeth might become yellow. Smoking affects your total health. Even if you do not smoke cigarettes, smoke from others may harm your health. Being around others who are smoking is a risk situation.

*Why is it important to have health knowledge?*

**FIGURE 1–3.** How can a healthful behavior affect your total health?

Table 1-1

| Ten Areas of Health | |
|---|---|
| Mental Health | ways to think clearly, express feelings, make responsible decisions, say NO, and handle stress |
| Family and Social Health | family relationships including changes, skills for getting along with friends, communication skills, and peer pressure |
| Growth and Development | physical, mental, and social changes that occur during your life from birth until death |
| Nutrition | nutrients needed for optimum health and disease prevention |
| Exercise and Fitness | health benefits of exercise, the components of physical fitness, and the design of physical fitness plans |
| Drugs | responsible decision making in the use of medicine and in the prevention of the misuse and abuse of chemicals |
| Diseases and Disorders | prevention, causes, signs, symptoms, and treatment of communicable and noncommunicable diseases and disorders |
| Consumer and Personal Health | personal habits, products, services, medical and dental care, consumer protection agencies, and health careers |
| Safety and First Aid | prevention, care, and treatment of injuries and illnesses resulting from accidents, emergency situations, and crimes |
| Community and Environmental Health | ways to maintain and promote the health of the people and places around you, and services available for health care |

**Think About It**

1. How does giving your best effort to the three kinds of health influence your self-concept?
2. How do risk behaviors influence your health?
3. What is the difference between a risk behavior and a risk situation?

## Making Decisions and Contracts

You can feel certain that the choice to have a healthful lifestyle can be yours. Responsible decision-making skills will help you. Also, using life skills will help you maintain a healthful lifestyle.

### 1:4  Responsible Decisions ─────────

**Responsible decisions** are decisions that result in actions that promote health for you and others. How can you know if your decisions are responsible? The **responsible decision-making model** is a list of steps you can use to help you make decisions. Think about the steps that follow.

1. Identify the situation about which a decision must be made.
2. Identify the different decisions you may make to resolve the situation. There may be more than one way to deal with the situation.
3. Ask yourself questions about each possible decision.

There are five questions that can be used to identify responsible decisions. They will help lead you to responsible actions. For some decisions, all five questions would not apply.

- Would the results of my decision be healthful?
- Would the results of my decision be safe?
- Would the results of my decision be legal?
- Would the results of my decision show respect for myself and others?
- Would the results of my decision follow my parents' or guardian's guidelines?

4. After you have applied the five questions to each possible choice, make a responsible decision and act on it.
5. Judge your actions. Review your decision to confirm that it was a responsible decision.

When you make responsible decisions, you increase your chances of having good health. This gives you a

*What is the responsible decision-making model?*

**FIGURE 1–4.** You can choose to have a healthful lifestyle.

feeling of confidence. You feel good about yourself and your efforts. Because you have given your best efforts to have good health, you have improved your self-concept.

Sometimes people your age try to change the decisions you make. **Peer pressure** is the influence that people your age try to have on your decisions. When you choose friends who are concerned about their health, they may encourage you in healthful ways. These friends may help you make responsible decisions and choose healthful behavior. You will learn to have confidence in your own ability to act responsibly.

Other people may pressure you to make decisions that result in risk behaviors or risk situations. Think of an example of a time when this may have happened to you. How did you handle the situation? You work toward good health by saying NO when you are pressured to do something that is harmful, unsafe, or illegal. You say NO when you are pressured to do something that shows disrespect for yourself and others. You say NO when you are pressured to do something that does not follow your parents' or guardian's guidelines. When you say NO to risk behaviors or situations, you say YES to good health. You feel good about yourself when you make responsible decisions about your health.

*How might peer pressure influence you in positive ways?*

**FIGURE 1--5**. Say NO to behaviors that are harmful, unsafe, or illegal.

## 1:5  Refusal Skills

*What are refusal skills?*

**Refusal skills** are ways to say NO to risk behaviors. These skills are helpful if peer pressure is being used to influence your decision. Suppose someone tries to encourage you to smoke a cigarette. Here are some refusal skills you can use to say NO.

- Look directly at the person.
  When you make eye contact, the person will know you mean what you say.
- Say NO clearly and firmly.
  "No, I do not want to smoke."
- Give a reason.
  "I do not want to harm my lungs with cigarette smoke."
- Let your actions show that you mean what you say.
  Do not accept a cigarette.
- Do not change your mind.
- Encourage the person to choose a healthful behavior.
  "Let's play soccer instead."
- Leave if the person continues to pressure you.
- Always tell an adult you trust if you are continually pressured to take part in a behavior that is not legal.

You may also be able to use these refusal skills to say NO to a risk situation.

# ACTIVITY

## The Broken Record

Make a record like the one in the picture. Think of a risk behavior in which your peers might pressure you to engage. On your record, state the risk behavior and write two or three reasons why you would say NO to this behavior. Use the broken record approach when you are asked to do something harmful, unsafe, or illegal. Repeat your reasons for saying "NO" over and over. You will sound like a broken record.

**FIGURE 1–6.** Following a plan to practice a life skill will improve your health.

## 1:6   Health Behavior Contracts ————

A **life skill** is a healthful behavior to learn and practice throughout your life. At the end of each chapter in this textbook is a list of life skills. Each list reminds you of healthful behaviors about which you have just gained health knowledge. Life skills will help you reach goals you set for good health.

One way to practice each life skill is to design a health behavior contract. A **health behavior contract** is a written guide that helps you make a plan to follow a life skill for good health. Look at the Health Behavior Contract, Table 1–2 on page 14. The life skill you want to follow is to eat healthful snacks. Your plan describes what healthful snacks you might enjoy. It helps you be certain that the snacks belong to a healthful food group. There is a place on the health behavior contract to write down the snacks you chose to eat. There is also a place to write how well the plan worked for you. You can make a health behavior contract for other life skills that are listed at the end of each chapter. When you design and follow health behavior contracts, you are more likely to practice life skills for the rest of your life.

*What is a health behavior contract?*

4. How can you know if a decision is a responsible one?
5. What are some refusal skills you can use to say NO?
6. Why might you make a health behavior contract?

**Think About It**

Table 1–2

## Health Behavior Contract

**GOAL:** My goal is to follow a healthful diet.

**LIFE SKILL:** I will eat healthful snacks.

**MY PLAN:** I will select snacks from the four healthful food groups and the combination group. The following is a list of healthful snacks.

| Milk | Fruit-Vegetable | Grain | Meat | Combination |
|---|---|---|---|---|
| milk | banana | cereal | chicken | peanut butter sandwich |
| cheese | apple | bread | boiled egg | pizza |
| yogurt | carrot sticks | crackers | peanuts | taco |
| cottage cheese | celery | plain popcorn | peanut butter | cheese and crackers |

**HOW I FOLLOWED MY PLAN:**

| Day | Snacks I chose to eat   A * is placed by my healthful snacks. |
|---|---|
| **Sunday** | *milk, *carrot sticks |
| **Monday** | *banana, *graham crackers |
| **Tuesday** | cake, cola |
| **Wednesday** | *peanut butter sandwich, *milk |
| **Thursday** | six cookies, *apple |
| **Friday** | *cheese sandwich |
| **Saturday** | brownie |

**HOW MY PLAN WORKED:** I made healthful choices on Sunday, Monday, Wednesday, Thursday, and Friday. This plan will help me choose healthful snacks.

## Life Skills

▶ Choose healthful behaviors that promote a good self-concept and good physical, mental, and social health.

▶ Use health knowledge to avoid risk situations.

▶ Use the responsible decision-making model to promote healthful behavior.

▶ Use refusal skills to say NO to harmful peer pressure.

**Summary**

1. You are at your best when you have good physical, mental, and social health and a good self-concept. *1:1*
2. Good health is achieved by choosing healthful behaviors and avoiding risk behaviors and risk situations. *1:2*
3. Health knowledge helps you choose among healthful behaviors, risk behaviors, and risk situations *1:3*
4. The responsible decision-making model can help you make decisions that result in actions that promote your health and the health of others. *1:4*
5. Refusal skills can be used to help you say NO to risk behaviors and risk situations. *1:5*
6. A health behavior contract can be used to help you make a plan to practice a life skill. *1:6*

**Words for Health**

*Complete each sentence with the correct word.*
*DO NOT WRITE IN THIS BOOK.*

health
health behavior contract
health knowledge
life skill
lifestyle
mental health
peer pressure
physical health
refusal skills

responsible decision-making model
responsible decisions
risk behaviors
risk situations
self-concept
social health
wellness

1. _____ are conditions that may harm your health.
2. _____ is the highest level of health you can reach.
3. _____ is the influence that people your age use to try to encourage you to make the decisions that they want you to make.
4. A(n) _____ is a written guide that helps you make a plan to follow life skills for health.
5. The _____ is a series of steps you apply to a situation to help you make decisions.

6. _____ are actions that might be harmful for you or others.
7. Your _____ is the way you live.
8. _____ is the feeling you have about yourself.
9. _____ are ways to say NO to risk behaviors and risk situations.
10. A(n) _____ is a healthful behavior to learn and practice throughout your life.
11. _____ is the state of your relationships with others.
12. The state of your body and mind and how you get along with others is _____.
13. Decisions that result in healthful actions are _____.
14. The state of your body is _____.
15. _____ is an awareness of facts about health.

**Reviewing Health**

1. What three kinds of health are needed for total health?
2. How might you improve your self-concept?
3. How can you use the Wellness Scale to determine your level of wellness?
4. What are three possible consequences of choosing risk behaviors or being in risk situations?
5. Why do you need health knowledge?
6. What are the ten areas of health?
7. In which area of health do people promote the health of their community?
8. How does one behavior choice affect your total health?
9. What five questions might you ask yourself to make a decision that results in responsible actions?
10. How might peer pressure affect the decisions that you make?
11. What are eight refusal skills you can use when you experience peer pressure?
12. How can the broken record approach help you avoid risk situations?
13. Why is it important to follow life skills throughout your life?
14. What are the parts of a health behavior contract?

*Use the life skills from this chapter to respond to the following questions.*

*Situation:* You have stayed after school to watch a game. You live a mile from the school and have told your parents that you will be walking home. You are to call them when you begin to walk home. After the game, a friend's older brother offers you a ride. He usually drives too fast.

1. Apply the questions from the responsible decision-making model to each choice to decide which choice results in a responsible action.

2. Why is it important to avoid risk situations?

*Situation:* Your friend invites you to stop over after school. Your friend's parents are not home. You say NO because it is against your parents' guidelines for you to be at a friend's home without parents being there. Your friend begins to pressure you saying, "They won't know. We will only be there for fifteen minutes. Other boys and girls are stopping by without their parents' approval."

**1.** Why is your decision responsible?
**2.** How might you use refusal skills to reinforce your NO decision with your friend?
**3.** Why is it unimportant that others are stopping at the house?

*Situation:* Your friend you walk to school with is late today. She tells you not to worry about getting to school on time. She will save time by not eating breakfast.

**1.** Why is her decision not responsible?
**2.** What would you tell your friend about eating breakfast?

---

**Extending
Health**

1. Have each family member use the Wellness Scale on page 6 to rate their wellness. Have each family member share some healthful behaviors they have chosen and what risk behaviors and situations they have avoided.
2. Share a health behavior contract such as the one on page 14 with your family. Ask each family member what life skill they believe contributes the most to good health. Make a sample health behavior contract for one of the life skills your family identifies.

# Achieving Good Mental Health

This disabled artist has discovered a means of self-expression. Her abilities grew from good feelings about herself and the self-confidence she has to try new things. What are your hidden talents?

# Chapter 2

**STUDENT OBJECTIVES:** *You will be able to*

- *explain how self-concept, personality, and philosophy of life influence health.*
- *express emotions in healthful ways and manage stress.*

Imagine you are sitting in a chair with "Director" written on the back. Instead of directing a play, you are in charge of directing your mental health. Just as a director of a play has learned the details of directing plays, you need to learn information about directing your mental health.

## Self-Examination

Several years ago there was a television show called *This Is Your Life.* Each show described important details about the life of a special person. The audience enjoyed knowing even the smallest details. For good mental health it is important to be able to describe details about yourself. You need to learn what your characteristics are, your likes and dislikes, your strengths and weaknesses, and your special skills.

## 2:1  Positive Self-Concept

In Chapter 1, you learned that your self-concept is the way you feel about yourself. A **positive self-concept** is the good feeling you have about yourself most of the time. You feel confident and enjoy trying new things. You do not worry about making mistakes.

*How do you feel when you have a positive self-concept?*

19

When you have a positive self-concept, you have a good feeling about being unique (yoo NEEK). Being unique means that there is no one else just like you. You are special. You accept the ways in which you are different from others. For example, you accept the fact that you might be short or tall or have curly or straight hair. You are aware of your talents and know what tasks are difficult for you.

When you feel good about yourself, you are more likely to feel good about others. You more quickly accept the differences of others. You are not jealous when someone can do something better than you. Likewise, you are not critical when someone is not as capable as you. You understand that each person is unique.

*What are two ways to improve your self-concept?*

One way of improving your self-concept is to become aware of your strengths. Your **strengths** are the areas in your life in which you do well. For example, playing the piano might be one of your strengths. You feel good because you play the piano well. When you receive applause at your piano recital, you feel good about the honor. **Weaknesses** are the areas in your life in which you are not strong. Everyone has weaknesses. It is healthful to recognize your weaknesses. Working to improve weaknesses helps improve your self-concept.

Suppose you are uneasy when you have to speak in front of your classmates. You would like to have more confidence in this situation. You decide to work on changing this weakness. One way to change is to offer to answer questions in small groups. Then try this in larger groups. You might feel awkward at first, but with practice you will gain confidence. Soon it will become easier to speak in front of others. You will feel good about being able to overcome this weakness.

## 2:2  Healthful Personality

**Personality** is the way a person feels, thinks, and acts. Suppose you were to write a theme about yourself. You would tell about your personality. You would include how you respond to situations. Your self-concept is how you feel about yourself. When you have a positive self-concept, you are more likely to have a good feeling about yourself. Others like to be around you.

Other factors influence your personality. **Heredity** (huh RED ut ee) is the passing of traits from one generation to another. Maybe you have overheard someone say that a child's smile or laugh is just like that of one of his or her parents. A similar statement may have been said about you and a trait you share with a family member. The traits you are born with will affect your personality.

The **environment** is everything that is around you and its influence upon you. The environment in which you are raised influences your personality. Suppose you grow up in a family in which you receive a great deal of love and affection. Your personality is likely to reflect these qualities. You are more likely to have a positive self-concept.

Your **culture** is a blend of the influences on your life by people in your home, city, state, and nation. The people with whom you spend the most time influence the way you act. They may influence the way you speak and the expressions that you use. Celebrations and traditions may be a part of your culture. These patterns of acting and expressing yourself become part of your personality.

*How does your self-concept affect your personality?*

**FIGURE 2–2.** Your personality is influenced by your culture.

**FIGURE 2–3.** Working toward getting high grades may help you achieve a long-term goal.

## 2:3 Philosophy of Life

A **philosophy** (fuh LAHS uh fee) **of life** is a view of life or an attitude toward life and its purpose. Examples are "always give your best" or "do something to serve others." Your philosophy of life reflects your values. A **value** is anything that is desirable or important to you. For example, your values might include honesty, loyalty, family, friends, and education.

Your values serve as guidelines to help you choose actions. When you value education, you study to get good grades in school. When you value honesty and loyalty, you tell the truth and you are a faithful friend. When you value your family, you spend time with family members. Your values are influenced by your family. Your parents' or guardian's attitudes about life influence their actions. You learn from what they say and do. You may form similar values.

Your philosophy of life and your values influence your goals. Goals are desired achievements toward which you work. **Long-term goals** are goals to be achieved in the future. **Short-term goals** are goals that are achieved in order to reach long-term goals. You may have a long-term goal to graduate from college or vocational school. Your short-term goals might include

- maintaining high grades for acceptance into school.
- saving money to help with expenses.

You are never too young to begin setting goals and making plans for the future. In this textbook, you will study about many health careers. Striving for one of these careers might become a goal for you. Your parents or guardian can help you set realistic goals. Goals that you cannot achieve may discourage you. However, setting goals that are too easy will not challenge you to be at your best.

**Think About It**

1. How do you feel about others when you have a positive self-concept?
2. How might the culture in which you live influence your personality?
3. How do short-term goals differ from long-term goals?

## A Plan for Good Mental Health

How would you describe someone with good mental health? People with good mental health are able to meet the demands of life. They respect themselves and others. However, people with good mental health are not perfect. They feel anger, sadness, and stress. People with good mental health are able to effectively handle whatever happens in their lives.

### 2:4 Expressing Your Emotions

**Emotions** are the feelings you have in response to events and life situations. Because your life is full of a variety of situations, you experience many different emotions. To achieve good mental health, you need to learn to understand your emotions and express yourself in healthful ways. There are four questions you might ask yourself when you experience emotions.

1. What emotion am I feeling?
2. Why do I feel this way?
3. What are some ways I might express my feelings?
4. Which ways of expressing my feelings are healthful?

*What might you ask yourself when you need to understand your emotions?*

**FIGURE 2–4.** A person who has good mental health expresses emotions in healthful ways.

23

## Expressing Anger

Suppose a friend promises to go to a movie with you. Your friend then decides to go shopping with someone else instead. When your friend calls to tell you about the change in plans, you feel anger. **Anger** is a strong, unfriendly feeling that usually occurs when a person's feelings are hurt. Your friend has hurt your feelings by changing the plans you made. How might you express your anger?

- While you were still talking to your friend you might hang up the phone. You might not speak to your friend when you see him or her.
- You might wait and get even by doing the same thing to your friend the next time you get together.
- You might yell at one of your family members.
- You might tell your friend why you are angry.

You think about each of these possible ways to express your anger. You decide that telling your friend you are angry is the most healthful choice. You express your feelings without causing harm to your friend or being insulting. You do not direct your feelings at someone who is not involved. Finding a healthful way to express your feelings even when you are angry is important for your health and the health of others.

FIGURE 2–5. You might express your love by preparing something special for someone else.

## Expressing Love

Suppose your sister makes you something for your birthday. She has kept the present a big surprise. When you open it, you find something that is special. You know how long she worked to make the gift. You are grateful and love your sister. How might you express your feelings?

- You might hug your sister.
- You might write her a note and tell her you love her.
- You might tell her how much you love her.

In this situation, each of the actions is healthful. Each action shows your sister how you feel. You choose one of these healthful ways to express your feelings.

# ACTIVITY

### Expressing Emotions in Healthful Ways

Divide a paper into five columns like the one shown. In the first column, there is a list of emotions. Find the definition for each emotion in a dictionary. In the second column, describe an event or situation in which you experienced this emotion. In the third column, describe the way you expressed this emotion. In the fourth column, tell if your choice was healthful. In the fifth column, list other ways to express this emotion. *Do not write in this book.*

| EMOTIONS | EVENT OR SITUATION | WAY I EXPRESSED | HEALTHFUL? | OTHER WAYS THIS EMOTION MIGHT HAVE BEEN EXPRESSED |
|---|---|---|---|---|
| Anger | | | | |
| Excitement | | | | |
| Worry | | | | |
| Love | | | | |
| Sadness | | | | |

## 2:5 Experiencing Stress

Each day you are challenged with many demands on your time and efforts. You may have a difficult test in school. Someone may call you for the first time on the phone and ask you to go someplace special. The championship soccer or basketball game might be today or your teacher may ask you to give a report in front of the class.

*What are three types of stressors?*

**Stress** is the body's reaction to any physical, mental, or social demand. A **stressor** is anything that causes stress. A stressor might be a person, an event, or an assignment. Your response to a stressor depends on your ability to cope or deal with the stressor.

People often respond differently to the same stressor. Let's use an example to understand how you might respond to a stressor. Suppose a championship game is about to begin. This is a stressor for you. Your body reacts to this stressor. Your adrenal glands produce adrenaline (uh DREN ul un). **Adrenaline** is a hormone that raises blood pressure and causes the liver to release sugar into the bloodstream to provide extra energy. Your heart begins to beat faster. You breathe more often each minute. Additional blood flows to your muscles to help them do more work. Muscles may become more tense. Less blood flows to your stomach. Your mouth may become dry and your hands moist.

These changes may be helpful or harmful depending upon your reaction to the changes. **Eustress** (YOO strus) is a helpful response to a stressor in which body changes help a person's performance. In this case, the extra sugar gives you energy for the game. The increased blood flow delivers oxygen to your cells for the extra effort. The muscle tenseness goes away when the game starts. You perform well. After the game, you no longer experience these body changes and you relax.

**Distress** is a harmful response to a stressor in which a person is unable to cope and to perform well. Suppose you became so tense during the game that your tenseness interfered with your normal skills. You began to make mistakes. After the game, you continued to respond to this stressor. You were upset about your performance and unable to sleep.

When you experience distress, your body changes may last for a period of time. Your heart rate may remain higher than normal. Your liver may continue to release more sugar than usual. Your breathing rate increases. These changes cause your body to become tired. You are unable to perform well in other areas of your life. You are more likely to become ill or have an accident.

**FIGURE 2–6**. Your body may react to a stressor such as playing in a baseball game.

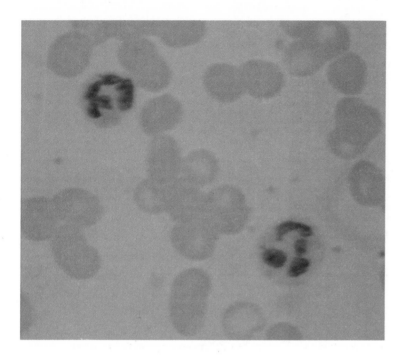

**FIGURE 2-7.** White blood cells in the immune system are less able to fight disease when the body has periods of frequent stress.

## 2:6  Distress and Disease ⎯⎯⎯⎯⎯⎯

Many diseases are related to being unable to express emotions or manage stress. Periods of frequent stress affect the body's immune system. The immune system is made up of white blood cells and other substances in the blood that destroy pathogens. Frequent stress lessens the body's ability to fight disease. Some communicable diseases, such as colds, canker sores, and flu, are more common when a person experiences frequent stress.

Headaches, stomachaches, and lack of sleep also can be linked to too much stress. In middle aged persons, some other diseases are linked to prolonged stress. Because the heart works harder during stress, prolonged stress is linked to both high blood pressure and other kinds of heart disease. Continued stress may keep the immune system from fighting cancer cells; thus, cancer is more common.

Frequent stress also is related to an increase in accidents. It is difficult to concentrate if something is bothering you. You might make careless mistakes that result in accidents. When you are tired, you are more likely to make mistakes resulting in accidents.

*Why do people who are experiencing stress have more accidents?*

## 2:7 Managing Stress

Whenever you experience stress, ask yourself three questions.

**1.** What is causing me to feel stress?

**2.** What can I do about the cause of the stress?

**3.** What can I do to keep my body strong and healthy?

Most of the time you will be able to do something by yourself about the stress you feel. In order to do this, first try to identify the cause of your stress. When you understand the cause, think about ways to change the stressor. You might use the responsible decision-making model to decide which way would be best. Eating healthful foods and getting plenty of rest will help to keep your body strong and healthy. Also, you will be able to think more clearly.

You may not be able to do something by yourself about the cause of your stress. Your parents or guardian, your teacher, or your school counselor might be able to help you.

*What are stress management skills?*

During times of stress, you can use stress management skills. **Stress management skills** are ways to reduce the harmful effects of the body changes caused by stress. Some stress management skills help you feel good about yourself. Use the suggestions in Table 2–1.

Table 2-1

## Stress Management Skills

**To Feel Good About Yourself**

Make a time management plan. Plan for each hour of the day by listing a time for each task to develop a feeling of accomplishment.

Talk with parents or other trusted adults.

Spend time with friends who encourage and support you in healthful activities.

Use the responsible decision-making model to rate the actions you might take. Feel in control.

Keep your appearance neat and clean.

**GOOD MENTAL HEALTH**

100

Perform Well

Possible Accidents and Illnesses

Perform Poorly

0

**POOR MENTAL HEALTH**

**To Keep Your Body Healthy**

Exercise regularly. Regular exercise uses the sugar in the blood. It reduces muscle tenseness. You sleep well. Exercise causes a natural hormone, that increases your feeling of well-being, to be released into the bloodstream.

Eat well-balanced meals.

Reduce sugar. Too much sugar uses up vitamins in the body. Vitamin B is needed to have healthy nerves and to help you relax.

Reduce salt. Too much salt increases heart rate and blood pressure.

Avoid caffeine. It raises heart rate.

Get plenty of sleep and rest.

---

4. When might you feel angry?
5. Why might you have more colds when you experience stress?

**Think About It**

## Life Skills

▶ Change weaknesses to strengths to improve self-concept.
▶ Develop short-term and long-term goals that reflect your philosophy of life and values.
▶ Express emotions in healthful ways.
▶ Make and follow a plan to manage stress.

## Suicide Prevention Hotline

Each year thousands of young people who have problems think about suicide. Suicide is the intended taking of one's own life. Many suicide attempts can be prevented. At those times, a troubled young person has found someone to talk with about problems. Matt Fotos is a volunteer at a mental health center. He takes calls on the suicide prevention hotline. Matt received special training at the center before he was ready to take calls on the hotline.

One of the training sessions taught volunteers how to watch for certain signs in a person who is thinking about suicide. These signs include:

- having a drastic personality change.
- withdrawing from family and friends.
- losing interest in personal care and appearance.
- losing interest in schoolwork.
- having problems getting along with others.
- using drugs, such as marijuana or alcohol.
- changing sleeping and eating habits.
- giving away valued possessions.
- talking about getting even with friends or parents.
- talking about suicide.
- asking questions about death.

Another training session focused on talking with young persons who are de-pressed and thinking about suicide. Matt learned how to listen and give support until help arrives. At first he practiced these skills during the sessions. Later, after the training was over, he began to answer the hotline.

Training also focused on talking with friends of the depressed young person. Matt learned about suicide prevention strategies. Suicide prevention strategies are actions to take when someone shows signs of deep depression. A friend of such a person may call the suicide prevention hotline. He or she is told to stay with the person until help arrives. Listening and showing support for the person helps. A depressed person should be encouraged to talk. Any talk about suicide should always be taken seriously. A responsible adult should always be notified.

**Summary**

1. When you change weaknesses to strengths, you improve self-concept. *2:1*
2. Personality is influenced by your heredity, environment, and culture. *2:2*
3. Your philosophy of life and your values influence your goals. *2:3*
4. To achieve good mental health, you need to learn to understand your emotions and express yourself in healthful ways. *2:4*
5. Eustress is a helpful response to a stressor while distress is a harmful response to a stressor. *2:5*
6. Many diseases are related to not being able to manage stress or express emotions healthfully. *2:6*
7. When you experience stress, identify the cause and use stress management skills to reduce the effects. *2:7*

**Words for Health**

*Complete each sentence with the correct word.*
*DO NOT WRITE IN THIS BOOK.*

adrenaline
anger
culture
distress
emotions
environment
long-term goals
personality

philosophy of life
positive self-concept
strengths
stress
stress management skills
stressor
value
weaknesses

1. _____ is the combination of the way a person feels, thinks, and acts.
2. _____ is a strong, unfriendly feeling that usually occurs when a person's feelings are hurt.
3. A(n) _____ is an overall view of life or an attitude toward life and the purpose of life.
4. _____ is a harmful response to a stressor in which a person is unable to cope and to perform well.
5. _____ are ways to reduce the harmful effects of the body changes caused by stress.

6. _____ are the areas in your life in which you do well.
7. A(n) _____ is anything that causes stress.
8. _____ are goals to be achieved in the future.
9. _____ are the feelings you have in response to events and life situations.
10. A(n) _____ is the good feeling you have about yourself most of the time.
11. _____ is everything around you that influences you.
12. Anything that is desirable or important to you and that helps you choose actions is a(n) _____.
13. The body's reaction to any physical, mental, or social demand is _____.
14. _____ is a hormone that causes body changes in response to a stressor.
15. The areas in your life in which you are not strong are _____.

**Reviewing Health**

1. How does feeling good about yourself influence your feelings toward others?
2. What is the difference between your strengths and your weaknesses?
3. What are three influences on your personality?
4. What are values and how do they influence you?
5. How are short-term goals related to long-term goals?
6. What are four questions you might ask when you experience an emotion?
7. What should you remember in order to express anger in a healthful way?
8. What three things might act as stressors?
9. What bodily changes occur as a result of stress?
10. How is eustress different from distress?
11. How do frequent periods of stress affect the immune system?
12. What diseases in middle-aged persons have been linked to prolonged stress?
13. What are some stress management skills that help you feel good about yourself?
14. What are some stress management skills that keep your body healthy?

*Use the life skills from this chapter to respond to the following questions.*

*Situation:* You are at a camp for three weeks this summer. Unfortunately, one of your cabinmates at camp is someone with whom it is difficult for you to get along. This person sneaks out of the cabin almost every night. This practice is against camp rules and interrupts your sleep. You have had very little sleep for the last few nights and you are quite angry about the actions of this person.

1. What are four questions you might ask yourself about the emotions you are feeling?
2. How might you express your emotions?
3. Why is it important to express emotions to this person in a healthful way?
4. If you continue to room with this camper, what are some stress management skills you might use?

*Situation:* You are going to give a speech at school tomorrow. You have practiced several times and are well prepared. You are excited about doing a good job. Yet, you still feel nervous about getting up in front of your class to speak. You are having difficulty sleeping. You keep waking up and have trouble going back to sleep.

1. What three questions might you ask yourself about the stress you are feeling?
2. What stress management skills will you use to help you sleep?

*Situation:* You are concerned about your best friend. He is very depressed. He does not seem to care about his appearance anymore. His grades in school are falling.

1. What can you do to help your friend?
2. Where might your friend go to receive help?

**Extending Health**

1. Find out what a psychosomatic illness is. Write a report about one of these illnesses. Share your report with the class.
2. Interview an adult who you believe shares emotions in healthful ways. Discuss how this person expresses emotions healthfully.

# Family and Social Health

Did you know . . .

▶ the ability to give and receive love is often the key to happiness and a feeling of well-being?

▶ talking to parents is helpful when there are family changes?

# Family Relationships

Your family is the source of many of your memories. Family members often help you to remember forgotten details of your life and learn about the past of other family members. What new information have you discovered in recent family gatherings?

# Chapter 3

**STUDENT OBJECTIVES:** *You will be able to*

● *describe kinds of families, family roles, and ways to show family love.*

● *discuss ways to adjust to family changes.*

The family is celebrating the grandparents' anniversary. Each family member has a special relationship with the grandparents. They have shared many experiences. You belong to a family too. You will share many experiences with your family.

## Belonging to a Family

Family relationships are important. Your family provides you with a feeling of belonging. Your family helps you learn about relating with others. The adults in your family help you learn about your role in your family.

### 3:1  Kinds of Families

A **family** is a group of people who are related. There are many kinds of families. Think about the families of your classmates.

Some of your classmates may live in traditional families. A **traditional family** is a family that consists of a mother and father and their child or children. This mother and father may have their own children; they may have adopted children; they may have foster children.

*What is a traditional family?*

An **adopted child** is a child who permanently lives with parents in a family but who has different natural parents. There are many reasons why children are adopted. The natural parents may not be able to care for the child or they may have died. A **foster child** is a child who temporarily lives with a family other than his or her own. There are many reasons why a child might live in a foster home. One reason might be the child's natural parents may not be able to take care of him or her.

Some of your classmates may live in single-parent families. A **single-parent family** is a family that consists of a child or children living with either their mother or their father. A child whose parents divorce might live in a single-parent family. When one parent dies, a child might live in a single-parent family.

Some of your classmates may live in stepfamilies. Parents who divorce often remarry. If one parent dies, the other parent might remarry. When a parent remarries, a stepfamily is formed. A **stepfamily** is a family that consists of a mother or stepmother, a father or stepfather, and one or more stepchildren. Table 3-1 describes the family members that might belong to a stepfamily.

*What is a single-parent family?*

Table 3–1

| Possible Stepfamily Members | |
|---|---|
| **Stepfather** | Man married to a person's mother who is not his or her natural father. |
| **Stepmother** | Woman married to a person's father who is not his or her natural mother. |
| **Stepson** | Son of a person's husband or wife from a former marriage. |
| **Stepdaughter** | Daughter of a person's husband or wife from a former marriage. |
| **Stepbrother** | Son of a person's stepmother or stepfather. |
| **Stepsister** | Daughter of a person's stepmother or stepfather. |

**FIGURE 3-1.** Older family members help teach about family values.

Some of your friends may live in extended families. An **extended family** is a family in which members from three generations live together. Another way to describe the extended family is that one or more grandparents live with the family. There are many reasons for the extended family. In many cultures, parents usually live with their married children and grandchildren. It is believed that the oldest members of the family have a very positive effect on younger members. The older members help teach about family values.

*What is an extended family?*

## 3:2  Family Roles

Your family helps you learn accepted ways of interacting with others. It teaches you about the roles of family members. For example, your parents or guardian work to earn income for the family. One of their roles is to make enough money to provide the family with a place to live, food to eat, and clothes to wear.

In most families, everyone helps with household chores. Preparing dinner, cleaning dishes, cutting grass, raking leaves, walking the family pet, taking out the trash, dusting, and vacuuming are chores that must be done. If you live on a farm or your family has some type of family business, you may have a role in the work.

There is another type of role that is influenced by your family. Your **sex role** is the way you act as a result of your attitude about being male or female. The adults in your family or other adults you admire help develop your sex role. If you are a female, your sex role is feminine. You copy the behavior of your mother, stepmother, or other women whom you respect. You learn from observing how the men you like view women.

A woman might be feminine and act in many different ways. A woman might be a lawyer and be very feminine. She might enjoy homemaking, gardening, playing tennis, or playing softball. Another woman you admire might enjoy working with small children. A woman can be feminine in anything she chooses to do.

If you are a male, your sex role is masculine. You copy the behavior of your father, stepfather, or other men whom you respect. You learn from observing how the women you like view men.

A man can be masculine and act in many different ways. He is masculine when he does chores that were once usually done by women. A man is masculine when he expresses his feelings to others. A father or stepfather is masculine when he goes fishing, mows the grass, teaches young children, or becomes a nurse. A man can be masculine in anything he chooses to do.

Boys and girls and men and women like to do many of the same activities. They may enjoy the same kinds of hobbies, sports, and careers. Men and women share many of the same feelings and needs.

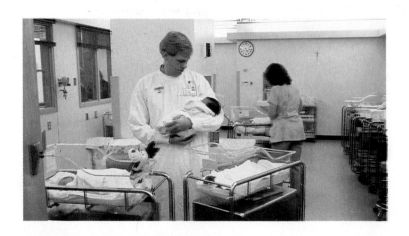

**FIGURE 3–2.** Men and women may enjoy the same kinds of careers.

## 3:3  Family Love

In Chapter 2, you studied about emotions and healthful ways to express them. Persons who are experts in mental health agree that the most important emotion is love. The ability to give and receive love is often the key to happiness and a feeling of well-being. The first place that you learn about love is within your family.

Certain skills must be practiced over and over in loving family relationships. You began learning about love when you were a small child. You began learning about being a loving person from the way you were treated. A **loving person** is someone who is respectful, understanding, responsible, and self-disciplined.

To be **respectful** is to think other people are worthwhile. You listen to their ideas even when they are different from your own. When adults are talking, it is respectful to listen without interrupting.

To be **understanding** is to be aware of how another person feels or thinks. Suppose your father has a difficult day at work. Your father might have a headache and request some quiet time. You are being understanding when you keep the radio or television volume low. You allow your father some time alone even though you might want to talk.

*What are four qualities that describe a loving person?*

**FIGURE 3–4.** A responsible family member is trustworthy and reliable.

To be **responsible** is to be trustworthy. This is very important in all relationships, especially within a family. Parents fulfill many responsibilities to keep family life running smoothly. They expect you to do the same. There are rules you must obey. There are chores you are expected to do. When you are responsible, parents know they can count on you. If you say you will be home at a certain time, you are responsible when you arrive home on time.

*How do you show that you are self-disciplined?*

*Son control your actions*

To be **self-disciplined** is to be able to control your actions. When you are self-disciplined, you work at what must be done until it is completed. Perhaps you promised to cut the grass. A friend stops by and asks you to go to a movie. You continue to cut the grass even though you would rather go to the movie. You show you are self-disciplined when you finish the task you promised to do.

Practicing the skills of being a loving person will help you in many areas of your life. This will improve your self-concept and level of wellness.

**Think About It**

1. Why do some cultures favor the extended family?
2. Who influences a boy's sex role?
3. How does a loving person act?

# Adjusting to Family Change

An adjustment is a way of coping or dealing with a changing situation. There are many changes that might take place within a family. There might be separation or divorce. Other changes might include a serious illness or the death of a family member. At times such as these all family members make adjustments.

## 3:4  Separation and Divorce

All married couples struggle at times to keep a good relationship with each other. In most cases, the marriage is maintained and usually becomes stronger. However, sometimes the problems create so much stress that married partners decide to separate. A **separation** is an agreement between a married couple to live apart but remain married while seeking to work out their problems. Some married couples solve their problems during the separation. They then may choose to live together again.

Other couples are not able to work out problems. They may decide to legally end their marriages. A **dissolution** is a legal way to end a marriage in which the couple decides the details of the agreement. A **divorce** is a legal way to end a marriage in which a judge decides the details of the agreement.

Separation, dissolution, and divorce are stressful for all family members. Children whose parents are going through these changes may have many different feelings. They may feel angry that their family life has changed. They may feel guilty and wonder if they caused the problem. They may feel sad or depressed because their parents are not together. As a result of their feelings, it may be hard to concentrate at school.

These children need to know that their parents' problems are not their fault. Talking with parents about feelings helps. Knowing that they are loved by both parents helps. Friends can help by listening and showing concern.

*What feelings might children have when parents separate or end their marriage?*

angry, guilty
depressed

**FIGURE 3–5.** Talking with parents helps children understand their feelings.

There may be other changes to which children must adjust. The family may need to move. Each family member may need to help more around the house. Again, talking about these changes helps. Classmates can be friendly and include new students who move into their neighborhood and school.

## 3:5  Family Illness or Death

Changes in the health of a family member may require adjustments. Suppose someone in a family suffers a long illness. Family members may need to give extra time to caring for or visiting this person. Friends can help. There are many ways they can assist a family that is adjusting to such an illness.

At some time, every family experiences the death of a family member. Death may happen suddenly and without warning or it may be expected after a long illness. When a grandparent has grown old and is dying, extra care is needed from family members. The ill or dying grandparent needs love, reassurance, and support.

When a family member dies, others in the family experience grief. **Grief** is the expression of sorrow. Grief may be expressed in different ways. Some family members may feel sad and cry; some might be angry; some

*How might family life change when a family member has a long illness?* ~~GAgrg~~

~~gartg~~

extra time with person

**FIGURE 3-6.** Every family experiences the death of a family member.

might want to be alone. It is normal to have changing feelings and behavior. Eventually a person feels less grief and is better able to cope with the loss.

Talking, showing, and sharing feelings with other family members and friends are helpful. Speaking with a trained counselor or a teacher also may help a person deal with his or her feelings of grief. It is important to remember the good times shared with the person who has died and to talk about these memories. Talking and showing emotion are healthful ways to deal with grief.

You can help a person who has lost a close friend or family member. Let that person know that you care and will help in any way you can. Be a good listener. Encourage the person to show emotions, not hide them.

 ## ACTIVITY

### Helping a Grieving Friend

Pretend that your friend's pet has been hit by a car. Your friend is feeling very sad about it. You are going to call your friend and express your sympathy. What might you say to your friend? Why is it helpful for your friend to share feelings?

**4.** Why should children of divorced parents talk to both parents about their feelings?

**5.** What changes might occur in a family when a grandparent is seriously ill?

**Think About It**

## Life Skills

- ▶ Develop a healthful sex role.
- ▶ Practice being respectful, understanding, responsible, and self-disciplined.
- ▶ Discuss adjustments to family changes with parents, guardians, and other trusted adults.

# Health Highlights

## Research in Discipline and Child Abuse

Dr. Charles Johnson is a physician who works with children at a children's hospital. Dr. Johnson has a special interest in children who have been victims of child abuse. Child abuse is the maltreatment of children. "Mal" means bad. Maltreatment means bad or harmful treatment. Young people often ask Dr. Johnson why an adult might harm a child. He explains that there are different reasons.

- Most adults who harm children were victims of child abuse when they were children.
- Sometimes adults do not know how to use healthful ways to discipline children.
- Often adults who abuse children have unrealistic expectations. They feel that the child should be able to do very difficult tasks.
- Most adults who abuse children have other stressors in their lives. For example, the adults may have difficult marriages or job situations. They may abuse drugs. Teenage parents are more likely to abuse their children than older parents.

Regardless of the reasons adults abuse children, Dr. Johnson stresses there are two important facts. First, no child deserves abuse. Second, adults who abuse children need help.

Dr. Johnson educates parents, teachers, school nurses, and other physicians to recognize the signs and symptoms of child abuse. Children who have been abused are reassured that they do not deserve maltreatment. Dr. Johnson helps them to feel worthwhile and to improve their self-concepts.

Adults who abuse children also are helped through counseling. Often, they suffer from a poor self-concept. They need to feel better about themselves and less frustrated. Dr. Johnson is committed to making changes in situations where a child is being abused.

Dr. Johnson feels a special commitment to his research into preventing child abuse. He is currently developing programs to educate young people in schools about effective parenting.

# Chapter 3 Review

**Summary**

1. There are many different kinds of families. *3:1*
2. Your sex role is learned by observing the behavior of your parents and other adults whom you respect. *3:2*
3. A loving person is someone who is respectful, understanding, responsible, and self-disciplined. *3:3*
4. Children whose parents separate or divorce need to discuss their feelings and adjustments. *3:4*
5. Changes in the health of a family member or a death in the family may require adjustments within the family. *3:5*
6. Discussing and showing feelings are healthful ways to deal with adjustments. *3:5*

## Words for Health

*Complete each sentence with the correct word.*
*DO NOT WRITE IN THIS BOOK*

| | |
|---|---|
| adopted child | responsible |
| dissolution | self-disciplined |
| divorce | separation |
| extended family | sex role |
| family | single-parent family |
| foster child | stepfamily |
| grief | traditional family |
| loving person | understanding |
| respectful | |

1. A(n) _____ is a child who permanently lives with parents in a family but who has different natural parents.
2. A(n) _____ is someone who is respectful, understanding, responsible, and self-disciplined.
3. Your _____ is the way you act as a result of your attitude about being male or female.
4. _____ is sorrow or sadness.
5. A(n) _____ is a family that consists of a mother and father and their child or children.
6. A(n) _____ is an agreement between a married couple to live apart but remain married while seeking to work out the problems.

7. To be _____ is to think other people are worthwhile.
8. A(n) _____ is a family that consists of a mother or stepmother, a father or stepmother, and one or more stepchildren.
9. A(n) _____ is a legal way to end a marriage in which the couple decides the details of the arrangement.
10. To be _____ is to be able to control your actions.
11. A(n) _____ temporarily lives with a family other than his or her own.
12. A group of people who are related is a(n) _____.
13. A person who is _____ is aware of how another feels or thinks.
14. A(n) _____ is a legal way to end a marriage in which a judge decides the details of the agreement.
15. A(n) _____ is a family in which members from three generations live together.

**Reviewing Health**

1. What are the different kinds of families?
2. How does an adopted child differ from a foster child?
3. What are some possible members of a stepfamily?
4. What is an advantage of living in an extended family?
5. Why is it important for family members to have roles?
6. Who helps you develop your sex role?
7. What does it mean to be feminine or masculine?
8. Why is love a very important emotion?
9. Where is the first place most persons learn about love?
10. What are four skills needed to be a loving person?
11. How are dissolution and divorce similar, yet different?
12. What are some of the different feelings of children who experience the separation, dissolution, or divorce of parents?
13. What are some ways that children of parents who are separated or divorced might be helped?
14. How might a family need to adjust when a family member suffers a long illness?
15. Define grief and list ways that grief may be expressed.
16. How might you help someone who is experiencing grief?
17. What are healthful ways for a person to express grief?

*Use the life skills from this chapter to respond to the following questions.*

*Situation:* Your friend went to an activity after school and then over to a friend's house. He did not tell his parents where he was going. They were very worried when he did not come home at his usual time. When your friend did arrive home, his parents were relieved that he was safe but angry that he had not called to tell them where he was. Now, he is grounded for a week. He thinks his parents are being unfair. He thinks a week is too long to be grounded.

1. What skills should your friend work on to be a loving person to his parents?
2. How would you explain to your friend why his parents took the actions they did?
3. Why is it important that your friend be responsible?

*Situation:* Your friend's parents are divorced. Her father recently remarried and now has a stepdaughter living with him. Your friend has mixed feelings about having a stepsister.

1. What are positive feelings that your friend could have about the situation?
2. What would be a healthful way for your friend to adjust to the changes in her life?
3. How might you act in a loving way to help your friend accept her stepsister?
4. What can your friend do to help her stepsister adjust to this family change?

1. Interview someone who has a grandparent living with them. Discuss the benefits of an extended family.
2. Write a short report that describes the characteristics of family life in a foreign country.
3. Interview a guidance counselor. What does a guidance counselor do? Why is this an important career? How can a counselor help young people your age?

# Healthful Relationships

Many opportunities exist for us to develop meaningful relationships. Friends share ideas and feelings. They support each other through happy as well as difficult times. Have you been a friend to anyone today?

# Chapter 4

**STUDENT OBJECTIVES:** *You will be able to*
- *have good relationships, spend quality time alone, and choose friends wisely.*
- *use manners and good communication skills.*

A line from a song says that the luckiest people in the world are people who need people. We might change the line to say that people who get along well with people are some of the healthiest people in the world.

## The Importance of Relationships

Some young people your age were asked to list five behaviors or five attitudes they felt were important for good health. They mentioned behaviors such as exercising, eating breakfast, and getting plenty of rest. They might have included many other behaviors. Other choices include having good relationships, spending quality time alone, and choosing friends wisely. These choices also are important to your health.

## 4:1 Knowing About Healthful Relationships

A **relationship** is the connection you have with another person. You form different kinds of relationships with different people. Some of the people with whom you

**FIGURE 4–1.** You form relationships with friends.

*What is the difference between destructive and healthful relationships?*

form relationships are members of your family, friends at school, people in the community, and yourself. You have relationships with people of both sexes and of different ages.

Look at the Relationship Scale on page 53. Some relationships are healthful and add to balanced health and personal satisfaction. They promote a good self-concept. Some relationships are destructive. They may cause poor health and unhappiness. They may lead to a poor self-concept.

A list of skills that promote healthful relationships is included in Table 4–1. You have already studied some of these skills in the first three chapters of this book. In Chapter 1, you studied the importance of liking yourself and having a good self-concept. You also studied responsible decision-making skills and how to use refusal skills. In Chapter 2, you studied healthful ways to express emotions. In Chapter 3, you studied that a healthful relationship requires respect and understanding. Being responsible and self-disciplined are covered in this chapter. You will study about good manners and communication skills. When you develop healthful relationships, you feel good about yourself.

Table 4-1

## Relationship Scale

0                                                                100

| **Destructive Relationships** | **Healthful Relationships** |
|---|---|
| • Poor health | • Balanced health |
| • Unhappiness | • Personal satisfaction |
| • Poor self-concept | • Good self-concept |

Some relationships are healthful and contribute to balanced health and to personal satisfaction. Other relationships are destructive. They contribute to poor health and unhappiness. You can learn traits and skills to help you be at the high end of the Relationship Scale and to have healthful relationships with others.

| | |
|---|---|
| • like yourself. | • show respect for others. |
| • spend some time alone. | • be understanding. |
| • make responsible decisions. | • be responsible. |
| • use refusal skills when needed. | • use good manners. |
| • express emotions in healthful ways. | • practice communication skills. |

## 4:2 Spending Time Alone

It takes time and energy to get to know yourself and to have a good self-concept. Having some quiet time each day allows you to think about your feelings.

Being comfortable when alone is part of good social health. It is a sign that you like yourself and would be a good friend to others. When you spend time alone you discover there are activities you enjoy. You might read a book or work a puzzle. You might write a letter. Sometimes you need some "thinking time." You can think about what is going on around you.

*Why is it important to have quiet time each day?*

Being alone is different from being lonely. Being alone means being by yourself. You can be satisfied and happy by yourself. Being lonely means being unhappy because you are not with others. Everyone is lonely at times. However, it is not healthful to feel lonely every time you are alone.

Spending time alone gives you time to consider your behavior. **Self-loving behavior** is behavior that shows concern and liking for oneself. For example, enjoying reading a book alone is self-loving behavior. Saying NO when someone offers you a cigarette is self-loving behavior. Being well-groomed is self-loving behavior. Each of these actions show you care about yourself.

*What is self-loving behavior?*

**Self-centered behavior** is selfish behavior. It stresses one's needs and wishes with no concern for others. Suppose you always want to do what you would like to do rather than what a best friend would like to do. Your behavior is self-centered. If you always talk about yourself and never ask questions when talking with others, your behavior is self-centered. Self-centered behavior does not contribute to forming healthful relationships.

Usually, people who choose self-centered behavior do not have a good self-concept. They want to be the center of attention in order to feel better about themselves. People do not enjoy being around someone who is self-centered.

**FIGURE 4–2.** Spending time alone is healthful.

## 4:3  Forming Healthful Friendships ———

**Friends** are the people you know well and like. You can have friends of all ages. You can have friends of both sexes. You can have friends you see often. You can have friends you see very seldom.

People your age were asked what qualities they liked most in a good friend. They responded that they like friends

- who are trustworthy.
- who are honest.
- who listen when I talk.
- with whom I can share fun times.
- who will help when I have a problem.
- who act in ways that I can be proud.
- who are thoughtful.
- who encourage me to try new things and to be my best.
- who have a good sense of humor.
- who get along with my family.

It may surprise you to learn that persons of the opposite sex value the same qualities that friends of the same sex value. You are beginning to pay more attention to your sex role and the changes in your body. You may have more interest in the opposite sex. You are experiencing new feelings. These feelings are natural and healthy. They are part of maturing.

When you are older, you may begin to date. **Dating** is the sharing of social activities and time with members of the opposite sex. Dating is really an extension of friendship. The same qualities you find desirable in a friend will be desirable in a date.

**FIGURE 4–3.** You can have friends of all ages and both sexes.

1. Explain three skills you feel are important for healthful relationships.
2. How are self-loving and self-centered behavior different?
3. How are good friendships and good dating relationships similar?

**Think About It**

## Good Manners and Communication

Ideas, information, and feelings are communicated by what you say and how you act. Your skill in communicating affects the quality of your relationships with others.

### 4:4  Using Manners

Everyone likes to be treated in a considerate way. Having manners is an important part of relationships. **Manners** are thoughtful ways of behaving. Most likely your family has guidelines concerning manners. Manners are skills to be developed according to those guidelines.

One way to practice these skills is to have an attitude of gratitude. Do you know what this means? When you are grateful, you appreciate what others do for you. You are thankful for what you have. Suppose your parents buy you a new sweater. If you are grateful, you tell them you appreciate the sweater. You show them you are grateful by taking good care of it. Suppose your grandparent sends you a birthday gift. Writing a thank-you note or telephoning your grandparent shows you are grateful. When you show your appreciation to others, it strengthens your relationship with them.

*Why is it important to have an attitude of gratitude?*

There is another way to practice the skill of using manners and being polite. For example, you might be having a snack with friends. You could say "Pass the ketchup" or "Please pass the ketchup." Sometimes you work on a school project with a friend. It is more polite to say "Please hand me the scissors" than "Hand me the scissors."

When you have manners, you admit your mistakes to others. Suppose you interrupt someone who is talking. You say "Excuse me" and allow him or her to continue.

## 4:5  Telephone Manners

Manners are very important when using the telephone. The phone is a valuable tool for communication. It is especially important for your parents to get their phone calls and messages. Ask your parents how they would like your home phone to be answered. Always answer the phone in this way.

When you are calling someone to the phone, be polite to the caller. You might say, "Just a moment please," and go get the family member. It is rude for the caller to hear you yelling. If someone is not home, follow your parents' directions. If a parent or guardian is not home, you might say that this person is not able to come to the phone. Ask if you can take a message. Write down the message including the name and phone number of the person who called.

*How might you call someone to the phone in a polite way?*

**FIGURE 4–5.** Taking messages correctly is an important part of good telephone manners.

**FIGURE 4–6.** Be responsible when you use the phone.

Be respectful of others when you use the phone. Remember, others in your family need the phone too. Limit your number of calls and the length of time you talk. Check with your parents or guardian about appropriate times to use the phone. Do not call others very early in the morning or after a certain time at night. It helps to know the phone rules of your friends' families as well as those of your family.

Do not make prank phone calls. They are illegal. A prank call you think is funny could be very frightening to the person receiving the call. Remember, respect for others includes using the phone in a polite way at all times.

## 4:6 Communication Skills

When you talk, you communicate not only by the words you use but also by the tone of your voice. When you use only behavior and no words to communicate, you share with others in a nonverbal way. **Nonverbal behavior** is conduct without using words. Nonverbal communication is the use of behavior rather than words to express yourself. Nonverbal communication might include shaking your head, smiling, laughing, or patting someone on the back. In each case, you are giving a message without using words.

*What are some ways to show nonverbal behavior?*

There are three kinds of behavior you may use to communicate. You may use words, actions, or both. Let's examine these three kinds of behavior. **Aggressive behavior** is the use of words and/or actions that show disrespect toward others. Calling someone a name, interrupting frequently, and pushing or shoving another person are examples of aggressive behavior. This kind of behavior does not promote good relationships.

**Passive behavior** is the practice of not expressing ideas, opinions, and feelings. You may be afraid to say what you think or feel. You may look for ways to avoid revealing your true feelings. These are examples of passive behavior. Passive behavior can be harmful when you are in a situation in which you should say NO and do not.

**Assertive behavior** is the practice of expressing your thoughts and feelings honestly. This kind of behavior is not threatening to others. You are able to look directly at the person and say NO when necessary and with confidence. Assertive behavior is healthful. It is healthful because others know exactly what you think and feel.

*Why is assertive behavior healthful?*

Assertive behavior helps you when you experience peer pressure. Let's use an example. Suppose a friend asks you to come over after school but neither of your friend's parents are home. If you used aggressive behavior, you might say "What a dumb idea."

**FIGURE 4–7.** There are different kinds of behavior you may use to communicate.

If you used passive behavior, you might say you had something else to do and look away. You had nothing else to do, but you were uncomfortable telling your friend the real reason.

If you used assertive behavior, you might say, "Sorry, I can't come over. Neither of your parents will be home." When you used the assertive behavior, you did not say something nasty to your friend. You also did not avoid your real reasons or feelings. Assertive behavior helps you communicate well with others. You are able to express your thoughts honestly without being threatening.

## ACTIVITY

### Practice Using Assertive Behavior

Act out a make-believe scene with your classmates. Pretend you are in a restaurant with your parents. You are seated in the nonsmoking section. Someone at the table next to you lights up a cigarette and begins to smoke. Show how you might act with 1) aggressive behavior, 2) passive behavior, 3) assertive behavior. Now think of another scene to act out with classmates. Show the three kinds of behavior.

**Think About It**

4. How might you show an attitude of gratitude?
5. How might you show respect when using the phone?
6. What is the difference between aggressive behavior and assertive behavior?

## Life Skills

▶ Choose healthful relationships that contribute to balanced health, personal satisfaction, and a good self-concept.
▶ Spend time alone.
▶ Choose self-loving behavior rather than self-centered behavior.
▶ Use manners and be respectful when using the telephone.
▶ Choose assertive rather than passive or aggressive behavior.

# Chapter 4 Review

**Summary**

1. Healthful relationships contribute to balanced health, personal satisfaction, and good self-concept. *4:1*
2. Practicing the ten skills that promote healthful relationships will add to balanced health and personal satisfaction. *4:1*
3. Spending time alone helps you consider whether your behavior is self-loving or self-centered. *4:2*
4. Persons of the opposite sex value the same qualities that friends of the same sex value. *4:3*
5. Having manners is an important part of relationships. *4:4*
6. Having manners includes being grateful, polite, and able to admit your mistakes. *4:4*
7. Respect for others includes using the telephone in a polite way at all times. *4:5*
8. Taking complete telephone messages is an important part of good telephone manners. *4:5*
9. Nonverbal communication is expressing yourself without using words. *4:6*
10. It is best to use assertive behavior to communicate with others. *4:6*

**Words for Health**

*Complete each sentence with the correct word.*
*DO NOT WRITE IN THIS BOOK.*

aggressive behavior
assertive behavior
dating
friends
manners

nonverbal behavior
passive behavior
relationship
self-centered behavior
self-loving behavior

1. ＿＿ is selfish behavior.
2. ＿＿ is conduct without using words.
3. A(n) ＿＿ is the connection you have with another person.
4. ＿＿ is the practice of expressing your thoughts and feelings honestly.
5. ＿＿ are thoughtful ways of behaving.
6. ＿＿ is the use of words and/or actions that show disrespect toward others.

7. _____ are the people you know well and like.
8. _____ is the sharing of social activities and time with members of the opposite sex.
9. _____ is behavior that shows concern and liking for oneself.
10. _____ is the practice of not expressing ideas, opinions, and feelings.

## Reviewing Health

1. Why are healthful relationships important to good health?
2. What are ten skills that promote healthful relationships?
3. What are some advantages to spending time alone?
4. How is being alone different from being lonely?
5. How are self-loving behavior and self-centered behavior different?
6. What are ten qualities young people admire in friends of both sexes?
7. How is dating related to friendship?
8. What is an attitude of gratitude?
9. What are some ways to admit your mistakes to others?
10. What are some ways to be polite when using the phone?
11. Why is it responsible to avoid making prank calls?
12. What are some ways to communicate using nonverbal behavior?
13. What are three kinds of behavior that can be used to communicate?
14. How is assertive behavior a healthful means of communicating with others?

## Using Life Skills

*Use the life skills from this chapter to respond to the following questions.*

*Situation:* You are working on homework with a friend after school. Your friend picks up a page of your completed homework to copy it. You are annoyed that your friend does not do his or her own homework.

1. How might you show your feelings if you have aggressive behavior? passive behavior? assertive behavior?
2. Which is the healthiest way to behave? Why?

*Situation:* Marla and Beth decide to make prank phone calls to a classmate's house. At school the next day, they overhear their classmate telling about the prank calls. She had been alone and the calls made her very scared.

1. How did Marla and Beth show disrespect for their classmate?
2. What should Marla and Beth do?

*Situation:* You have a friend who always wants to do things his way. You let him plan and decide everything. You are angry because he is so bossy but you never say anything.

1. What different kinds of behavior are you and your friend showing?
2. Is this a healthful relationship? Explain.
3. How might you and your friend change to make this a better friendship?

*Situation:* You and your best friend planned to order pizza on Saturday night and have a sleepover at your house. Your friend forgot that he had promised to babysit for his little sister that night.

1. How would you express your disappointment to your friend?
2. What might you suggest you do instead?

---

1. Read a book on manners. Summarize what you have learned. Share at least one finding with the class.
2. Investigate a career in which the telephone is a primary means of communication.
3. Interview someone who has a job involving communicating with people. Ask what skills are necessary for a career in communication.
4. Write a want ad for a friend. Include all the qualities you would expect of a friend. Then answer the question, "Would you hire yourself?"
5. Write a letter to someone. You might choose a family member, friend, or teacher. Express your gratitude for something that person has done for you.
6. Set aside a certain period of time each day to be alone. Keep a diary of how you spend your time and how you felt after your "alone time."

**Extending Health**

# Growth and Development

Did you know . . .

▶ your body systems must work well together to keep you healthy?

▶ each stage of the life cycle has special characteristics?

# Unit 3

# Your Body Systems and Health

Like a racing team, your body systems function as a unit. Each system contributes toward a successful performance. The failure of one affects the others. Can you recall a time when you were injured or ill and your abilities suffered?

# Chapter 5

STUDENT OBJECTIVES: *You will be able to*

- *describe the structure, function, and care of the body systems for support and control.*
- *describe the structure, function, and care of the body systems for energy and transport.*

The driver is ready for an automobile race. To prepare for this kind of race, the racing team practiced together. Some members of the team care for the car's engine. Other members are responsible for changing tires and pumping fuel during pit stops. The driver's responsibility is to control the car while going as fast as possible around the track. To be a winning team, all members must work well together. If one member of the team does not perform effectively, the entire effort of the team can fail. Each team member depends on the other.

## Support and Control Systems

Like a racing team, your body systems function as a team. Good health depends on body systems working together. If one body system does not work well, other body systems may be affected.

Just as a car has a framework to support it and an electrical system for control, your body has support and control systems. The body's support systems are the skeletal and muscular systems. The body's control systems are the nervous and endocrine systems.

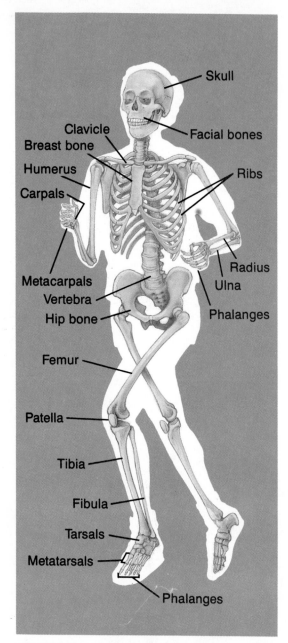

Skull

Clavicle
Breast bone
Humerus
Carpals

Facial bones

Ribs

Metacarpals
Vertebra
Hip bone

Radius
Ulna

Phalanges

Femur

Patella

Tibia

Fibula

Tarsals
Metatarsals

Phalanges

**FIGURE 5–1.** The skeletal system is made of long, short, and flat bones.

*What are the main purposes of the skeletal system?*

## 5:1   The Skeletal System ———

The **skeletal system** is the body system made up of all the bones in the body. This system has two main purposes. It holds the body together and it protects many inner body parts. For example, the ribs protect the lungs; the skull protects the brain.

Bones also play a role in movement. They bend at joints so that different body parts can move in different directions. A **joint** is a place where two bones meet. There are different types of joints in your body. Hinge joints allow bones to move up and down in one direction. Your elbow is an example of a hinge joint. Ball-and-socket joints allow your bones to move in circles. Your shoulder is a ball-and-socket joint that allows your arm to move in circles. Fixed joints allow no movement. The skull is composed of fixed joints.

There are three types of bones in your body. These are long bones, short bones, and flat bones. An example of long bones are the bones between your knee and hip. Long bones help large body parts, such as the leg, move. Short bones are the bones in the wrists and the ankles. These bones are made of soft material. They are covered with a thin layer of harder bone. The ribs are an example of flat bones. Flat bones protect body parts such as the heart.

There are ways to keep your skeletal system healthy. Eating a balanced diet, including foods that contain calcium, helps keep bones strong. Regular exercise also helps keep bones strong. Wearing protective equipment, when needed, helps prevent injuries. For example, a safety helmet protects the skull, and pads protect the elbows and knees.

## 5:2 The Muscular System ——

There are three kinds of muscles in the body. They are smooth, cardiac, and skeletal. Different kinds of muscles have different functions in the body. Smooth muscles line some internal organs; cardiac muscle forms the heart; skeletal muscles are attached to bones. The **muscular system** is the body system made up of all the muscles in the body. **Voluntary muscles** are the muscles over which you have control. Suppose you are standing. The muscles used when standing are voluntary muscles. **Involuntary muscles** are muscles that you do not control. Your heart is an involuntary muscle. Your heart muscle works without your control.

Skeletal muscles work in pairs to help you move. When one muscle contracts or shortens, the other extends, or straightens. Hold your arm out straight. Place your other hand around the muscle above your elbow. Then bend your arm at the elbow. Which muscle contracted? How could you tell? Which muscle relaxed? How could you tell?

Throughout your life, your muscles work to help keep you healthy. Your muscles help you breathe and move. Your heart muscle pumps blood through your body. For your muscles to work at a high level, they need care.

There are ways you can care for your muscles to help keep them healthy. Regular exercise helps keep muscles strong. However, when starting a new exercise, such as jogging, it is best to start gradually. If you begin by jogging a long distance you may overuse your muscles. This may cause them to become sore. Stretching the muscles before using them for short quick movements will help prevent muscle pulls.

*What are the three kinds of muscles in the body?*

**FIGURE 5–2.** Regular exercise helps keep the muscular system healthy.

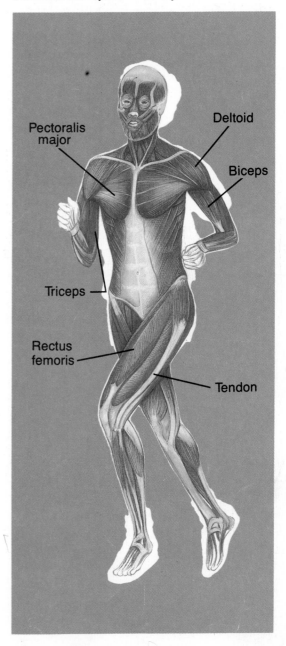

Pectoralis major

Deltoid

Biceps

Triceps

Rectus femoris

Tendon

## 5:3 The Integumentary System ─────

The **integumentary** (ihn teg yuh MENT uh ree) **system** is the body system made of parts that cover the body. Skin, hair, nails, and glands in the skin are parts of this body system.

The skin is the largest organ in the body. It has many important functions. It protects body parts against injury. It serves as a protective layer that keeps microorganisms from entering the body. The skin also helps the body maintain a certain temperature. For example, when your body is very warm, your sweat glands produce perspiration. As the water in sweat evaporates from your skin, your body is cooled.

*What is melanin?*

The skin contains melanin. **Melanin** (MEL uh nun) is a substance that gives skin its color. The greater the amount of melanin in the skin, the darker the skin. Melanin also helps protect the skin from the ultraviolet rays of the sun. These rays are harmful because they can cause skin cancer.

You can help keep your skin healthy. Using soap to wash your skin breaks down the oils on the surface. This helps remove the dirt during washing.

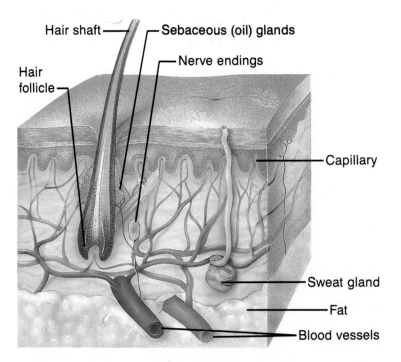

**FIGURE 5–3.** Skin, hair, nails, and glands make up the integumentary system.

## 5:4 The Nervous System _____

The **nervous system** is the body system for communication and control. It is composed of special cells called neurons (NOO rahnz). The brain, spinal cord, and nerves that branch off the cord, are the major parts of the nervous system. The nervous system controls every activity in your body.

Suppose someone throws a ball to you. Neurons in your eyes react and a message is sent to your brain. Your brain interprets the message and you see the ball. To actually catch the ball, other parts of your body must react. Messages are carried from your brain to your muscles. The result is that you move your body into position to catch the ball.

Catching a ball is only one example of an activity controlled by the nervous system. The nervous system controls all of your senses. Your senses allow you to experience everything around you. Senses include seeing, hearing, touching, tasting, and smelling. Nerve endings in taste buds in your tongue help you tell the difference between sweet, sour, bitter, and salty. Nerve cells in the upper part of your nose help you notice different odors.

*What are the different senses?*

71

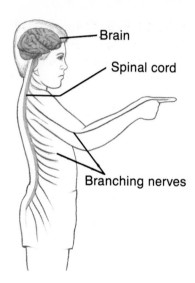

**FIGURE 5-5**. The nervous system controls every activity in your body.

*What are hormones?*

Your nervous system also helps protect you. Suppose you touch something hot. You would move your hand away immediately. This is called a reflex. A **reflex** is an involuntary response to changes inside or outside the body. When you touch something hot, messages travel from neurons in your skin to your spinal cord. Messages are sent from the neurons in the spinal cord to the muscles in your hand to pull away from the hot object. At the same time, messages are sent along neurons to the brain and you are aware that the object is hot. All this activity occurs within a split second after touching the hot object.

It is important to keep your nervous system healthy. Wearing a helmet when riding a bike or playing certain sports will help protect your brain. Regular exercise will help your nervous system work at its best.

## 5:5 The Endocrine System

The **endocrine** (EN duh krun) **system** is the body system made up of glands that produce hormones. **Hormones** are chemicals that act as messengers to regulate body activities. Each gland produces a different hormone. Each hormone has a certain function.

Endocrine glands control many of the changes in the body. For instance, the rate of growth is controlled by the hormone produced by the pituitary (puh TEW uh ter ee) gland. A person's response to an emergency is affected by the adrenal (uh DREEN ul) glands. Adrenaline (uh DREN ul un) is a hormone produced by the adrenal glands that helps the body react to an emergency. This hormone will cause an increase in heart rate, blood pressure, and blood sugar. These temporary changes help a person handle emergencies.

The ovaries (OHV reez) and testes (TES teez) are parts of the reproductive systems. They are also endocrine glands. The **ovaries** are female glands that release ova. **Testes** are male glands that produce sperm cells. Ova, or egg cells, and sperm cells are reproductive cells.

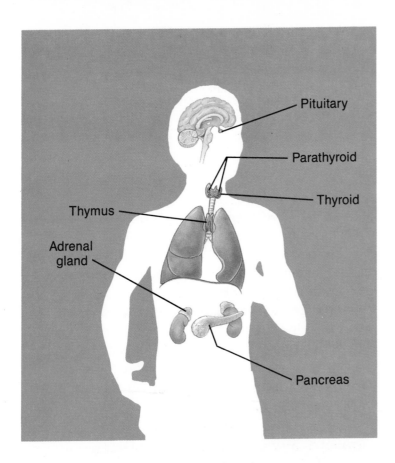

**FIGURE 5–6**. The endocrine system controls many changes that take place in a person's body.

Both testes and ovaries are influenced by the pituitary gland. Pituitary hormones stimulate the ovaries to produce two hormones, progesterone (proh JES tuh rohn) and estrogen (ES truh jun). Pituitary hormones stimulate the testes to secrete a male hormone called testosterone (teh STAHS tuh rohn). Both female and male hormones are responsible for body changes that take place just before and during the teenage years. You will study more about these changes in Chapter 6.

*What are the names of the female hormones?*

1. What kind of joint is your knee joint?
2. Why should you stretch the muscles in your legs before running fast?
3. Why is sweating healthful?
4. How does the nervous system affect sense organs?
5. Why is adrenaline important for your health?

**Think About It**

73

# Energy and Transport Systems

During a race, a car needs a source of energy to finish the race. This energy comes from burning fuel. Special tires help transport the car and its driver safely to the finish. Your body also has an energy system that helps you perform and complete activities. It also has a system that transports important products throughout your body.

## 5:6  The Digestive System

Your body needs a source of energy to perform everyday tasks. The source of your energy is the food you eat. One system in your body changes the food you eat into a form your cells can use.

*What is the digestive system?*

The **digestive system** is the body system made of parts that help your body use food. Food provides your body with nutrients (NEW tree unts). A nutrient is a substance in food that helps your body produce and repair new cells and gives you energy to perform everyday tasks.

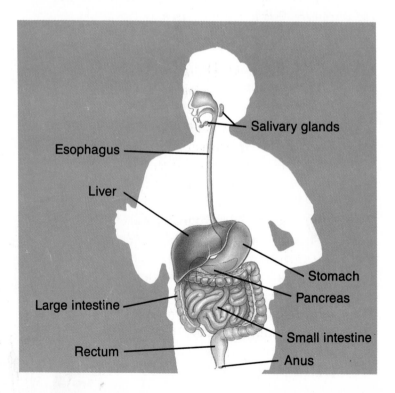

**FIGURE 5–7.** Your digestive system helps your body use food.

The organs of the digestive system perform many different tasks. The action of chewing food moistens the food and breaks it into smaller pieces. A substance produced by the salivary (SAL uh ver ee) glands changes the chemical nature of some types of food. Figure 5–7, on page 74, shows the main organs in the digestive system. They form a continuous tube through which food is moved.

There are ways to help keep your digestive system healthy. Drink several glasses of water each day. Eat fruits, vegetables, and other foods with fiber. Fiber is a natural substance found in foods from plants. Fiber and water help food move through the digestive system.

## 5:7  The Circulatory System ——

The **circulatory system** is the body system that consists of blood, blood vessels, and the heart. Oxygen, other gases, and nutrients are moved throughout the body by this sytem.

Look at Figure 5–8 and notice the difference among arteries, veins, and capillaries. Arteries are the largest blood vessels. They transport blood from the heart to the lungs to pick up oxygen. Veins return this blood to the heart. The heart then pumps the blood through arteries to body cells.

Veins transport blood from all parts of the body back to the heart. The blood in most veins carries waste products and very little oxygen. Capillaries are tiny vessels that connect arteries to veins.

Blood is a liquid consisting mostly of water with solid cells floating in it. **Plasma** (PLAZ muh) is the liquid part of the blood. It is primarily water.

*What are capillaries?*

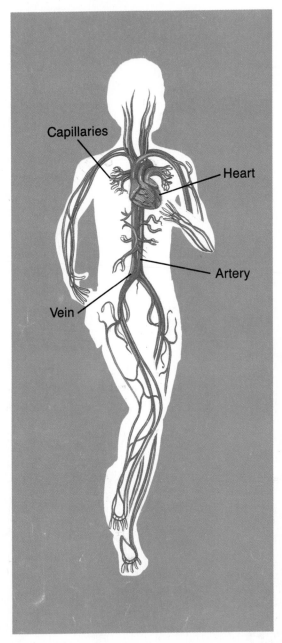

**FIGURE 5–8**. The circulatory system transports oxygen and other gases and nutrients throughout the body.

Capillaries

Heart

Artery

Vein

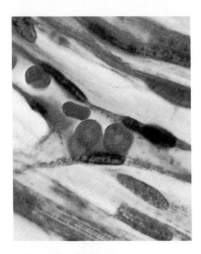

**FIGURE 5–9.** Red blood cells carry oxygen to cells in your body.

*What are platelets?*

Three main kinds of cells are found in plasma. **Red blood cells** are cells that carry oxygen from the air in your lungs to the cells in your body. The cells in your body use the oxygen and, in the process, produce carbon dioxide, a waste product. Red blood cells also carry carbon dioxide away from blood cells. Your blood also contains white blood cells. **White blood cells** are cells that help protect you by fighting pathogens that enter your body.

**Platelets** are cells that help form clots. When you have a cut, platelets in the blood go to the area of the cut. They cause the blood near the cut to become thicker and clot. The clot blocks the blood flow and stops the bleeding.

If your heart does not work well, your body will suffer. Your body cells will not get enough nutrients and oxygen. This can make you feel weak. When you have a healthy heart, the rest of your body functions better.

A healthful diet and exercise will help keep your circulatory system healthy. Avoid eating fried foods. The fat in these foods may clog blood vessels. Clogged blood vessels increase your risk of heart disease as you grow older. Exercises such as running, walking, and biking help keep your heart muscle strong.

## 5:8 The Respiratory System

The respiratory system brings air that contains oxygen into the body. It also removes waste carbon dioxide from the body. The **respiratory system** is the body system that helps you use the air you breathe.

When you inhale and exhale, changes take place in your chest cavity. As you inhale your ribs pull up and out. At the same time, your diaphragm (DI uh fram) contracts and moves downward. The **diaphragm** is a muscle that separates the chest cavity from the abdomen. Your chest expands as your lungs fill with air. As you exhale, the opposite happens. Your ribs move down and in. The diaphragm relaxes and moves upward. Your chest contracts as the air leaves your lungs. Figure 5–10 shows the parts of this body system and how they work.

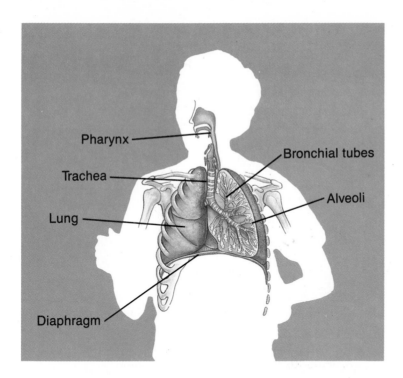

**FIGURE 5–10.** The respiratory system helps you use the air you breathe.

Labels on figure:
Pharynx
Trachea
Lung
Diaphragm
Bronchial tubes
Alveoli

All body cells need a constant supply of oxygen. As oxygen is used, waste carbon dioxide is formed. The respiratory system rids the body of this waste so cells can continue to function. The air that is exhaled is composed mostly of nitrogen, oxygen, and carbon dioxide.

The quality of the air you breathe is very important in keeping the respiratory system healthy. When you breathe air that is polluted, you harm lung tissue. A person who smokes inhales chemicals that will permanently harm lung tissue. Regular exercise is also important in keeping this body system healthy.

*What can happen when polluted air is inhaled?*

# ACTIVITY
## Breathing Rate

When you are at rest, you inhale and exhale about 12 times each minute. Write the number of breaths you take while at rest during a one-minute period. Run in place for 30 seconds. Write the number of breaths you now take during a one-minute period. Why did your rate of breathing increase?

## 5:9  The Urinary System

The **urinary** (YOOR uh ner ee) **system** is the body system that removes liquid wastes from the body. As body cells use nutrients they produce waste. The waste products pass into the blood for removal from the body. As blood circulates through the kidneys liquid wastes are filtered. Healthy kidneys, that are able to filter the wastes, are essential to a healthy body.

*How does the body lose liquid waste?*

The liquid wastes, called urine, collect in the urinary bladder. When the urinary bladder becomes full with urine, nerve signals are sent to the brain. A message from the brain indicates that it is time for the bladder to be emptied. During urination, urine leaves the body through the urethra.

There are ways to help keep the urinary system healthy. The most important way is to replace water lost through urination and other waste production each day. Drinking plenty of water and fruit juices will help keep the urinary system and other body systems working well. If the urinary system does not function properly, liquid wastes will not be removed from the body. This will result in serious health problems.

### Think About It

6. How might a disorder of the salivary glands affect your ability to chew food?
7. Why are white blood cells important to your health?
8. Why is inhaling polluted air dangerous to health?
9. Why does the brain play an important role in the functioning of the urinary system?

## Life Skills

▶ Exercise regularly to keep bones and muscles strong.
▶ Use soap to remove dirt and oil from your skin.
▶ Wear a helmet, if appropriate, when playing sports.
▶ Include fruits and vegetables in your diet.
▶ Drink adequate amounts of water each day.

1. The skeletal system consists of bones and joints that help you move. *5:1*
2. Muscles work in pairs so that when one contracts, the other extends. *5:2*
3. Skin, hair, and nails are part of the integumentary system. *5:3*
4. The nervous system controls all activities in the body including those of the sense organs. *5:4*
5. The endocrine system produces hormones that control body activities. *5:5*
6. The digestive system helps the body use food. *5:6*
7. The heart and blood vessels are a part of the circulatory system. *5:7*
8. The respiratory system helps the body use oxygen that is inhaled and rids the body of the waste gas, carbon dioxide. *5:8*
9. The urinary system helps remove liquid wastes from the body. *5:9*

*Complete each sentence with the correct word.*
*DO NOT WRITE IN THIS BOOK.*

circulatory system
diaphragm
digestive system
endocrine system
hormones
integumentary system
joint
melanin

muscular system
nervous system
ovaries
plasma
respiratory system
testes
urinary system
white blood cells

1. The _____ consists of the brain and the spinal cord.
2. The _____ is involved with the removal of liquid wastes from the body.
3. Two bones meet at a(n) _____.
4. _____ are produced by the endocrine system to regulate body activities.
5. The _____ is composed of both voluntary and involuntary muscles.
6. The lungs belong to the _____.
7. The liquid part of blood is called _____.

8. Skin color is determined by the amount of ____ present.
9. The ____ are endocrine glands that produce egg cells.
10. The ____ helps the body use food.
11. The body system made of parts that cover the body is the ____.
12. ____ help you fight pathogens that enter your body.
13. The ____ is the body system made up of glands that produce hormones.
14. The ____ is a muscle that moves upward and downward as you breathe.
15. ____ are male glands that produce sperm cells.

**Reviewing Health**

1. What are three different kinds of joints in the body?
2. How can you help keep your skeletal system healthy?
3. What are the three kinds of muscles that make up the muscular system?
4. Why is regular exercise important for your muscles?
5. What is one function of skin?
6. How is melanin helpful to the body?
7. How are sense organs important to your health?
8. How can adrenaline help you in an emergency situation?
9. What is the function of the ovaries?
10. What can you do to help keep your digestive system healthy?
11. What is the function of red blood cells?
12. Why are blood platelets important?
13. How can you keep your respiratory system healthy?
14. What happens when the urinary bladder becomes full?

**Using Life Skills**

*Use the life skills from this chapter to respond to the following questions.*

*Situation:* Suppose a person were very fair skinned. During the first warm and sunny day of the season, this person wants to lie in the sun for an hour or two.

1. Why would this not be a healthful thing to do?
2. What should this person do to avoid the harmful rays of the sun?

*Situation:* You are in a restaurant with your parents. You have narrowed your choices of a main course to either broiled fish with a baked potato or fried fish with french fried potatoes.

1. Which is the more healthful selection?
2. What other foods would you select?
3. What are the reasons for your choice?

*Situation:* You are going to compete in a bicycle race. You are given a list of safety rules that you, and every other participant, must follow. One of the rules states that everyone must wear a helmet.

1. What is the purpose of wearing a helmet?
2. What body systems will a helmet protect?
3. What other equipment might you wear as protection?
4. Aside from using protective equipment, how might you prepare for a safe race?

## Extending Health

1. Select a body system. On a large sheet of poster paper, draw and color this system. Label the parts of this system and describe what these parts do. Under your poster, list three ways to keep this body system healthy.
2. There are many different kinds of physicians who focus on specific body systems. For example, a urologist treats problems of the urinary system and a neurologist treats problems of the nervous system. Select any kind of physician who focuses on a body system. Write a report about this physician's work. Describe the responsibilities and the training needed to be this type of physician.
3. Find a current events article about a particular health problem or issue. Identify the body system to which this problem or issue relates. For example, an article about air pollution relates to the respiratory system. Describe how a person's body system would be affected by the health issue or problem.
4. Select one organ of a body system. Draw a picture of this organ and identify its different parts. Explain how the organ works within the body system.

# How You Grow

Birthdays, graduations, and other special family events give family members an opportunity to celebrate growth and development. Family members can help one another understand changes that occur as a person goes through the life cycle.

- describe the unique characteristics of the life cycle from infancy through adolescence.
- describe the physical, mental, and social characteristics of the adult years.

These people have gathered for a special family event. The family members are of all ages. They represent different parts of the life cycle. The life cycle is the different stages of growth and development. Each stage of the life cycle has many unique characteristics. The life cycle ends when an organism dies.

## From Infancy Through Adolescence

Babies receive special attention and care, especially during their first few days of life. Babies grow and develop quickly. They go through many physical, emotional, and social changes.

## 6:1 Infancy

**Infancy** is the period of development from birth to one year. During infancy many physical changes take place. Teeth break through the gums and the muscular and nervous systems continue to develop. During this period, infants begin to recall sights, sounds, color, and people. They also begin to play. Infants will start to crawl as they grow during their first year of life.

Some infants may begin to stand alone and even walk before the age of one. As tasks are performed, self-concept develops.

*How might infants show distress?*

Infants have feelings. In the first six months of life, infants may show distress by crying. As infants approach the age of one year, crying often lessens and they communicate in other ways.

Infants also show feelings of being content. They enjoy being held or rocked. Infants begin to smile soon after birth. Toward the end of infancy, they can begin to recognize situations. For example, infants may become happy as the bathtub fills with water. They know they will be able to play in the water. Infants begin to recognize people, especially family members.

## 6:2 Childhood

As children grow, they become more aware of their environment. They learn new words. They begin to learn that they are special. When playing with others, they learn that helping each other is important.

**Childhood** is the time of life from age one until about age twelve. The first few years of childhood are a period of great change. Each child develops at a different rate. By age three, most children are about 38 inches tall and weigh about 42 pounds.

*How do body proportions change during the early years of life?*

Body proportions begin to change during the early years of life. As bones and muscles grow, the body lengthens. By age four, most children lose the chubby appearance they had as a baby.

**FIGURE 6–1.** During infancy, many physical changes occur.

**FIGURE 6–2.** The first few years of life are a period of great change.

As children near the age of six, muscle control is increased. They discover they can throw balls and run more easily. Skills like using forks, spoons, and knives, and tying shoes develop. Repeating skills becomes important. Children benefit from repeating newly learned tasks. They get satisfaction from seeing that they are able to do tasks well.

By age six, children have a high energy level. If you were to observe six year olds in school, you would notice they have trouble sitting still for long periods of time. You also might notice that their muscle control is not as good as yours. They may be clumsy. As children get older, muscle control improves and attention span increases.

By age six or seven, a child's preference for hand use becomes apparent. A child prefers to use either the right or the left hand.

The physical changes that occur between the ages of seven and twelve are not as rapid as those from age one to age six. Some children will grow two or three inches per year. By the time children are ten or twelve, girls are usually taller than boys.

From ages seven to twelve, friends begin to take on greater importance. Children become sensitive to comments friends may make. They feel hurt when friends make cruel remarks or talk behind their backs.

FIGURE 6-3. Making friends
is an important part of
childhood.

From ages ten through twelve, school becomes an important focus. Social activities and friends take up more time. Secrets become important and the values of the peer group also have meaning. Boys and girls want to dress like their friends. They like to talk with certain friends and may exclude others from their discussions. They become involved in more organized activities. Being in clubs or on teams becomes important.

It is important for parents to be good role models. A **role model** is a person whose behavior sets an example for others to follow. Parents who show their children love and understanding will most likely raise children who will show love and understanding.

*What is a role model?*

## 6:3 Adolescence

**Adolescence** (ad ul ES unts) is the period of time between childhood and adulthood. It usually occurs between the ages of 12 and 19 and is identified with puberty (PYEW burt ee). **Puberty** is the stage of development during which body changes occur that make males and females physically able to reproduce. The visible signs of puberty are physical changes that occur. **Secondary sex characteristics** are the physical changes that occur during puberty in both males and females.

*What is puberty?*

Secondary sex characteristics in the female include the growth of hair in the armpits and on the arms and legs. Hips grow wider and breasts develop.

Between the ages of 11 and 15 an increased production of certain hormones produces a growth spurt. The growth spurt usually occurs over a six- to twelve-month span. During this time, a girl may grow several inches. She may be taller than boys her age.

Normal growth in a girl is accompanied by development of the reproductive organs. The changes in these organs are a sign that a girl is approaching womanhood. One signal is the start of the menstrual (MEN strul) cycle. The **menstrual cycle** is a monthly series of changes that occur in a female's body. These changes begin at puberty. However, a girl is not mentally ready to assume the tasks of being a parent until adulthood.

During the menstrual cycle, one ovary releases an egg cell. Hormones cause the lining of the uterus (YEWT uh rus) to prepare for a fertilized egg. The **uterus** is the reproductive organ in which a developing baby grows. If an egg is not fertilized by a sperm from a male, the lining of the uterus breaks down. The **menstrual period** is the shedding of the lining of the uterus. The menstrual period normally occurs every 28 days. It is common for the number of days between menstrual periods to vary. When a girl first starts having menstrual periods she may not have one every month.

*What is the menstrual cycle?*

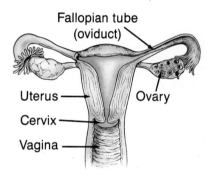

Female Reproductive System

**FIGURE 6-4.** Adolescence is a life cycle stage that is accompanied by puberty and the development of secondary sex characteristics.

*What physical changes occur to boys during puberty?*

Boys usually reach puberty about a year or two later than girls. Boys also experience a growth spurt during puberty. In the six to twelve months in which boys have a growth spurt, they may grow as much as seven inches. Secondary sex characteristics include hair growth on the face, underarms, and on the chest. A deeper voice tone develops. Growth in boys is also accompanied by changes in the reproductive organs. Changes in these organs are a sign that a boy is approaching manhood. As a boy reaches puberty, he is capable of producing sperm. Although a boy may be able to become a father after reaching puberty, he is not mentally ready to assume the tasks of being a parent until adulthood.

Both boys and girls experience social and emotional changes during puberty. Girls may feel awkward if they are taller than boys. Boys may feel awkward if they are shorter than girls. Boys and girls may be more attracted to the opposite sex. However, they may feel uncomfortable talking with members of the opposite sex. These feelings and actions are a normal part of growing up. Adolescence is a time when many changes take place. Most boys and girls adjust to these changes very well and enjoy becoming more mature.

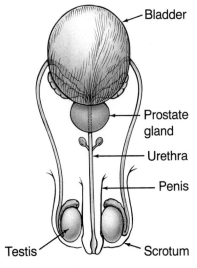

Male Reproductive System

- Bladder
- Prostate gland
- Urethra
- Penis
- Testis
- Scrotum

# ACTIVITY

## Preparing for Adolescence

Imagine that you have been asked to write an article for your local newspaper. The article is titled, "Growing Toward Healthful Adolescence." Write a one page article that would provide tips for healthful ways to approach adolescence.

**Think About It**

1. How do infants show they are hungry?
2. Why is it important for a parent to be a good role model to a child?
3. How might a girl know she is having a growth spurt?
4. How would a boy know if he is going through puberty?

# From Adulthood Through Old Age

Each stage in the life cycle is different and exciting. What changes can you expect as you grow older? How will you change physically, emotionally, and socially?

## 6:4 Adulthood

People between the ages of 20 and 30 are young adults. During this time you may be in college or just have graduated. Perhaps you will have a job. You may live in an apartment. You may be married. Regardless of what you are doing, your life's activities will be different than they are now. You will need to handle the many adjustments that occur. How will you earn a living? If you live on your own, how will you budget your money? How will you take care of your health?

After a person becomes 30 years of age, changes occur. At this age, people often place great importance on a job. They may examine career goals. If they are not happy with their career, they may look for a new job. They may also be busy raising a family.

As people grow older, they may take pride in their accomplishments through the years. They also regard the family as an important part of their life. They feel good knowing they have been successful at many tasks.

*What ages are considered to be young adults?*

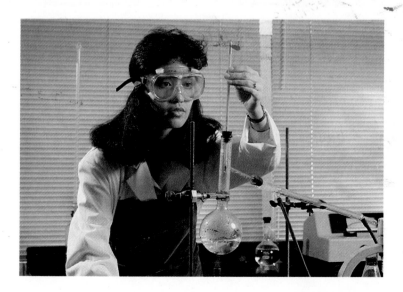

**FIGURE 6–5.** Young adults experience many changes and accept new responsibilities.

## 6:5 The Aging Process

How can you increase your chances of aging healthfully?

Will you age healthfully? The answer depends upon your present health habits. Taking care of your health now increases your chances of aging healthfully. The following behaviors will increase your chances of aging healthfully.

- eating healthful foods
- getting regular exercise
- not smoking
- being able to handle stress
- having a positive attitude
- having goals in life
- having healthful family relationships
- having friendships

Regardless of your health habits, your body will change as you grow older. Aging is a natural process. Suppose you were able to run a marathon when you were in your 20s. The same task will be more difficult in your 60s. However, there are people in their 80s who do run marathons. As people grow older, the risk of illness and injury increases. Yet, many people over the age of 65 are in good health. They are able to do many of the activities they enjoyed when they were younger.

**FIGURE 6-6**. Many adults enjoy good health and participate in a variety of activities.

90

## 6:6 Completing the Life Cycle

Think about how a flower develops. It develops from a seed. It grows and then eventually comes to the end of its life cycle. Throughout this chapter, you have examined the life cycle of people. You have seen how life begins. The changes throughout the different stages of life were described. Aging is normal and natural. It cannot be stopped. Good health habits can help you age healthfully. Eventually the life cycle comes to an end and death occurs. Death occurs because body organs no longer function.

There are healthful ways to handle death. In some societies, people celebrate the contributions a person made when he or she was alive. Other societies have special ceremonies at a grave or other types of services.

People who have died can leave us with many happy and important memories. Think about the people you have studied in your history classes. When these people died, their accomplishments were remembered. However, one does not need to be famous to leave memories. Someone who has died may have been close to you while he or she was alive. The memories of this person may influence you long after the person has died. They may help you grow to become a better person.

*What are some healthful ways some societies handle death?*

5. Why is following healthful habits now important for adulthood?
6. How can having memories of a person be healthful?

**Think About It**

## Life Skills

▶ Realize the changes that occur as you grow so you can adjust to these changes healthfully.
▶ Realize the importance of developing healthful behaviors now so that you will become a healthy adult.

# Health Highlights

## Osteoporosis

Osteoporosis (ahs tee oh puh ROH sus) is a disease in which bones lose calcium and become weak. The inside of the weakened bones looks like sponges with enlarged holes. This disease affects mostly women as they grow older, but men can also be affected. As bones lose calcium, they break easily. A fall, blow, or lifting action can easily break a bone. Fractures of the hip, especially, may lead to other serious complications.

Osteoporosis is a "silent" disease because there are no early warning symptoms. A person may be totally unaware of having the disease until a fracture occurs. Women with osteoporosis will notice their backs becoming curved causing a gradual loss of height. The back will also ache.

Research tells us that this disease may be preventable. Research in regard to osteoporosis focuses on the role of calcium in the diet and exercise.

**Calcium**

Researchers stress the importance of having enough calcium at the beginning of puberty. They state that this may be the best way to prevent getting this disease in later life. Teenage girls need 1200 to 1500 milligrams of calcium every day. Dairy products such as milk, yogurt, and hard cheeses are good sources of calcium. It is best to choose dairy products that are low in fat content. An eight-ounce glass of milk or one cup of yogurt contains 300 milligrams of calcium.

**Exercise**

Lack of activity hastens the thinning of bones in older people. Research shows that exercise helps build strong bones both during growth and old age. Weight-bearing exercises are considered the best type of exercise for building strong bones. These are exercises that force the bones to carry weight. These exercises include walking, playing, tennis, hiking, jumping rope, and doing aerobic dancing. Lifting weights or carrying luggage or groceries are also ways to help bones grow strong.

# Chapter 6 Review

**Summary**

1. During infancy, a person undergoes rapid physical changes such as growing taller. *6:1*
2. During childhood, muscles and bones grow and coordination improves. *6:2*
3. During adolescence, males and females undergo many physical, social, and mental changes. *6:3*
4. Adulthood is a time in which people accept increased responsibility and learn to handle adjustments. *6:4*
5. Following healthful habits now, such as exercising and not smoking, will help you become a healthy adult. *6:5*
6. The end of a person's life cycle can leave many happy memories for others. *6:6*

**Words for Health**

*Complete each sentence with the correct word.*
*DO NOT WRITE IN THIS BOOK.*

adolescence
childhood
infancy
menstrual cycle
menstrual period
puberty
role model
secondary sex characteristics
uterus

1. The period from birth to one year is called ____.
2. The time at which a person becomes physically capable of reproduction is called ____.
3. A baby develops in a woman's ____ before birth.
4. The changes in voice and growth of underarm hair are examples of ____.
5. A person that sets an example is a(n) ____.
6. The stage of growth that is between childhood and adulthood is called ____.
7. The ____ is the time when the shedding of the lining of the uterus takes place.

8. The stage of development that follows infancy is called _____.
9. The _____ is the monthly series of changes that occur in a female's body.

**Reviewing Health**

1. What are some physical changes that take place in infancy?
2. What are some activities enjoyed by infants?
3. Toward the end of infancy, what may infants be able to do?
4. What are some physical changes that take place during childhood?
5. Why is it important for parents to be good role models?
6. Between what ages is a boy or girl in adolescence?
7. What are examples of female and male secondary sex characteristics?
8. What changes occur to the uterus when an egg cell is not fertilized?
9. What happens to the ovaries during the menstrual cycle?
10. What are some social changes that occur during adolescence?
11. What are some characteristics of young adulthood?
12. What are some health behaviors to follow that will increase the chances of aging healthfully?
13. What happens to the risk of injury as a person ages?
14. How is death handled in different societies?

**Using Life Skills**

*Use the life skills from this chapter to respond to the following questions.*

*Situation:* One day one of your friends tells you that she notices physical changes in her body. She cannot understand why she is growing so fast.

1. What can you tell your friend about growth and development?
2. At what ages can these events occur?

*Situation:* You have a friend who has a habit of eating foods that are not healthful. When you make your friend aware of this, you are told, "It doesn't matter. I'm still young."

1. Why are your friend's choices of behaviors important for the future?
2. What helpful hints can you give your friend?

*Situation:* You are at a friend's house watching a movie. In the movie a person dies. This person had a child about your age. Your friend mentions that she would not know what to do if a friend's parent died.

1. How do you suppose a child might act upon losing a parent?
2. Who can help a child whose parent has died?
3. How might you help a friend who has lost a parent?

*Situation:* Your parents asked you to watch your four-year-old brother for the afternoon. You and your friends want to play volleyball in the yard. Your friends think one way for you to play volleyball and watch your brother is to have him sit in a chair and keep score.

1. What do you expect your brother's reaction to be?
2. How long do you think your brother will sit still and help?
3. What other ways can you keep your brother interested so you can play with your friends?

## Extending Health

1. Observe people in the different stages of growth and development discussed in this chapter. Write a report that describes characteristics of each. When possible, use close friends or relatives in different stages. How did your observations match the characteristics identified in this chapter?
2. Design a chart that describes the characteristics of infancy. Use resources in your library to identify many different characteristics. Include the amount of time per day the infant would require close supervision. This task is important in preparing you for parenthood one day. When you know what infants can and cannot do, you are better prepared to become a more responsible parent.
3. Interview adults you consider to be healthy. Ask them to describe their health habits now and when they were younger. You might then ask if there are any habits they would like to have or any habits they would like to change.
4. Use your library to find information about ways people of different cultures respond to death. Describe the different kinds of ceremonies or rituals that take place. Include the length of time the ceremonies or ritual might take, special costumes, food, music, and so on.

# Nutrition

Did you know . . .

▶ following the seven dietary guidelines promotes health?

▶ it is important to have a weight management plan?

# A Healthful Diet

A variety of foods is essential to good health. Food supplies us with nutrients that provide the body with energy and the materials necessary for growth and maintenance of body tissues. Which foods are your favorites? Are they healthful?

# Chapter 7

**STUDENT OBJECTIVES:** *You will be able to*
- *plan a diet that follows the seven dietary guidelines.*
- *read food labels and choose foods that reduce the risk of heart disease and cancer.*

A study done by the Centers for Disease Control examined many elements that influence personal health. These elements included heredity, medical care, the chances that a person might have an accident, and the life skills a person follows. The study concluded that the most important element was the life skills followed. Life skills influence how healthy you will be throughout your life and how long you will live. Choosing a healthful diet is one of the most important life skills you can develop.

## Planning a Healthful Diet

Your diet consists of the foods you eat regularly. To maintain good health, your diet should include the appropriate amount of nutrients found in a variety of foods. You should follow the seven dietary guidelines, and consider disease prevention.

Nutrition is the study of what you eat, your eating habits, and how these affect your health. Think about your eating habits. Do you eat because you are bored, nervous, or upset? Do you eat a healthful breakfast every day? Do you tend to eat too many fast foods? Healthful eating habits are important for good health.

## 7:1 Nutrients and the US RDA

*What is the function of nutrients?*

**Nutrients** are the chemical substances in food that the body uses for growth, repair of cells, and energy. Nutrients provide materials needed to build and maintain body tissues. Nutrients help regulate body processes. There are six main kinds of nutrients in foods that your body needs. They are proteins, carbohydrates, fats, vitamins, minerals, and water.

**Proteins** are nutrients the body uses for the growth and repair of cells. Proteins also help maintain healthy body cells and fight illness. Proteins help keep your muscles, skin, nails, and hair healthy. Some foods that are a good source of protein are fish, chicken, turkey, beef, eggs, milk, peanuts, cheese, and dried beans.

When you do not eat enough protein in your diet, the growth and condition of your hair, nails, and skin are affected. You may lack muscle tone.

*How does your body use fats?*

**Fats** are nutrients the body uses for energy and to help store some vitamins. Fats help build fat tissue needed to protect vital organs and help keep your body warm. Some foods that are a good source of fats are certain cuts of beef, ham, butter, margarine, milk, ice cream, corn oil, and peanut oil.

When you are lacking fats in your diet, you may not have enough tissue to surround and protect your vital organs. Your skin may be dry. Fats provide the oil to keep skin soft. Fat helps the body use vitamins A, D, E, and K.

**Carbohydrates** are nutrients that are the main supply of energy for your body. Sugars and starches are carbohydrates. Some foods that are a good source of carbohydrates include cereal, rice, potatoes, bread, pasta, fruit, popcorn, and jam.

Your body can change carbohydrates to a form it is able to store. If the carbohydrate level is too low, the body can change stored carbohydrates back to be used. When you are lacking carbohydrates in your diet, you might tire quickly.

**Vitamins** are nutrients that help regulate body processes and help fight disease. They help promote the growth and reproduction of cells. Table 7–1 lists some important vitamins, their functions, and sources. It also tells what happens when there is a lack of a vitamin. A **vitamin deficiency** (dih FIHSH un see) is a lack of the amount of one or more vitamins that is needed for good health. For good health, eat the foods that provide these vitamins. This is more healthful than taking vitamin pills.

*What might happen if you eat too few carbohydrates?*

**FIGURE 7–2**. It is better to eat a balanced diet than to rely on vitamin pills for nutrients your body needs.

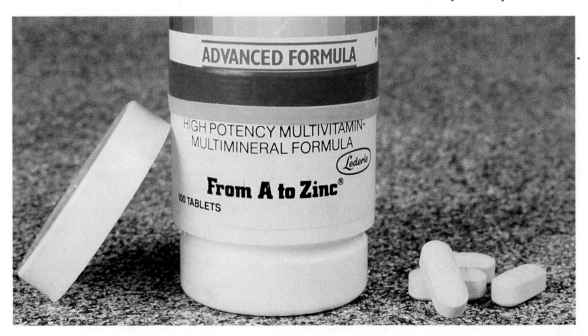

Table 7–1

| Vitamins | | | |
|---|---|---|---|
| **Vitamins** | **Functions** | **Sources** | **Signs of Deficiency** |
| Vitamin A | keeps eyes, skin, and hair healthy | butter, cheese, egg yolk, green leafy vegetables | rough skin, night blindness |
| Vitamin B | necessary for healthful nerves, appetite, digestion | whole grain cereals, poultry, eggs | mental confusion, poor memory, leg cramps, irritability |
| Vitamin $B_{12}$ | necessary for formation of red blood cells | red meats, milk, eggs, cheese | fatigue, anemia, nerve damage |
| Vitamin C | forms a bond that holds cells together, helps resist infection, strengthens blood vessels | citrus fruits, green vegetables | frequent bruising and breaking of blood vessels, loose teeth, gum diseases |
| Vitamin D | necessary for the formation of bones and teeth | dairy products, fish-liver oils | bowed legs, poor teeth, soft bones in adults |
| Vitamin K | necessary for normal blood clotting | green, leafy vegetables, liver | slow healing |

*How does your body use minerals?*

**Minerals** are nutrients that regulate many of the chemical reactions in your body. You need minerals to make your muscles and nerves work. They are also needed to build strong bones and teeth. Table 7–2 lists some minerals and tells their functions and sources. A **mineral deficiency** is a lack of the amount of a certain mineral in the diet that is needed for good health.

There are seven major minerals. These major minerals are calcium, phosphorus, potassium, sulfur, sodium, chlorine, and magnesium. Minerals, such as iron, iodine, and zinc, are found in smaller amounts. Minerals and vitamins work together. For example, vitamin D works with calcium and phosphorus to form strong bones and teeth.

Table 7-2

| Minerals | | | |
|---|---|---|---|
| **Minerals** | **Functions** | **Sources** | **Signs of Deficiency** |
| Calcium | maintains healthy bones and teeth; needed for healthy heart | milk, cheese, clams, oysters | rickets—bowed legs, osteoporosis—thin bones |
| Copper | necessary for the production of hemoglobin in red blood cells | liver, shellfish, whole grains, poultry, nuts | anemia, fatigue |
| Iodine | necessary for the production of the thyroid gland hormone | iodized salt, clams, oysters, lobster | goiter—enlarged thyroid gland |
| Iron | helps use B vitamins; makes up red blood cells; prevents fatigue | liver, lean meats, green leafy vegetables, shellfish | anemia—too few red blood cells, fatigue |
| Phosphorous | makes up bones and teeth; maintains regular heart rate | milk, whole grain cereals, fish, poultry | muscular weakness, irregular heart rate, soft bones |
| Potassium | keeps fluids balanced within cells; regulates body's water balance and heart rate | orange juice, citrus fruits, bananas, green, leafy vegetables | low blood sugar, edema—water collects in legs and ankles, irregular heart rate, muscle cramps |

**Water** is a nutrient that helps with body processes such as digestion and the removal of waste products. Water also helps control body temperature. It is the main element that makes up blood. Water may be obtained from drinking water or juice. Soups and fruits are also good sources of water. **Dehydration** (dee hi DRAY shun) is a deficiency or lack of the amount of water needed for body processes.

*Why is water an important nutrient?*

The **United States Recommended Dietary Allowance** or **US RDA** is a list that suggests daily amounts of nutrients that should be included in a healthful diet. This list is for healthy persons. A physician might suggest a different amount for someone with special health concerns.

## 7:2 The Seven Dietary Guidelines

It is important to use what you have studied about nutrients to plan a healthful diet. A plan for healthful eating will help you maintain high level wellness.

The United States Department of Agriculture and the Department of Health and Human Services have prepared a list of seven dietary guidelines. The **seven dietary guidelines** are suggested guidelines for planning a diet to promote good health. Following the guidelines will help you live longer and more healthfully. You will also reduce your risk of disease.

**FIGURE 7–3.** Choose foods from the four healthful food groups and the combination group when planning a diet for good health.

| MILK | MEAT | FRUIT-VEGETABLE | GRAIN | COMBINATION |
|---|---|---|---|---|
| Supplies these key nutrients:<br>■ calcium<br>■ riboflavin (vitamin B₂)<br>■ protein<br>for strong bones and teeth, healthy skin and good vision | Supplies these key nutrients:<br>■ protein<br>■ niacin<br>■ iron<br>■ thiamin (vitamin B₁)<br>for muscle, bone, and blood cells and healthy skin and nerves | Supplies these key nutrients:<br>■ vitamin A<br>■ vitamin C<br>for night vision and to help resist infections and heal wounds | Supplies these key nutrients:<br>■ carbohydrate<br>■ thiamin (vitamin B₁)<br>■ iron<br>■ niacin<br>for energy and a healthy nervous system | Combination foods contain ingredients from more than one food group, and supply the same nutrients as the foods they contain. |

| A serving is: | A serving is: | A serving is: | A serving is: | A serving is: |
|---|---|---|---|---|
| 1 cup   Milk<br>1 cup   Yogurt<br>1½ oz   Cheese (1½ slices)<br>1 cup   Pudding<br>2 cups   Cottage cheese<br>1¾ cups   Ice cream | 2 oz   Cooked, lean meat, fish, poultry<br>2   Eggs<br>2 oz   Cheese<br>1 cup   Dried peas or beans<br>4 tbsp   Peanut butter | ½ cup   Juice<br>½ cup   Cooked vegetable or fruit<br>1 cup   Raw vegetable or fruit<br>Medium   Apple, banana, or orange<br>½   Grapefruit<br>¼   Cantaloupe | 1 slice   Bread<br>1 cup   Ready-to-eat-cereal<br>½ cup   Cooked cereal<br>½ cup   Pasta<br>½ cup   Rice<br>½ cup   Grits | 1 cup   Soup<br>1 cup   Pasta dish (macaroni and cheese, lasagna)**<br>1 cup   Main course (stew, chili, casseroles)<br>¼ 14"   Pizza (thin crust)<br>1   Taco, sandwich |
| Number of Servings<br>4 | Number of Servings<br>2 | Number of Servings<br>4 | Number of Servings<br>4 | These count as servings (or partial servings) from the food groups from which they are made. |

*Dietary Guideline 1: Eat a variety of foods.* For a healthful diet you need about 50 different nutrients each day. These may be chosen from the four healthful food groups and the combination group. Refer to Figure 7-3 on page 104. The **combination group** is a food group that contains ingredients from more than one of the four healthful food groups and supplies the same nutrients as the foods they contain. Pizza is an example. The crust is a serving in the grain group. The cheese is a serving in the milk group. Toppings might include servings from the meat and vegetable groups. At your age, it is suggested that each day you eat

- four servings from the milk group,
- two servings from the meat group,
- four servings from the fruit and vegetable group, and
- four servings from the grain group.

*Dietary Guideline 2: Be at your best weight.* Your best weight is the weight at which you look best, feel best, and are in the best health. Being overweight increases the risk of high blood pressure, diabetes, heart attack, stroke, and cancer. Persons who are overweight can plan to lose weight by eating fewer Calories, increasing physical activity, eating slowly, and eating fewer fats and sweets.

Being underweight may be a symptom of poor health. Underweight persons may lack energy and be more likely to have infections. Underweight persons can gain weight healthfully by exercising and increasing the number of Calories consumed. Reducing stress may also help these people gain weight.

*Dietary Guideline 3: Eat fewer fatty foods.* There are two kinds of fats. **Unsaturated** (un SACH uh rayt ud) **fats** are fats from foods such as vegetables, nuts, seeds, poultry, and fish. Cooking oils such as corn and peanut oils are unsaturated fats.

**Saturated fats** are fats from dairy products and red meat. Foods such as steak, liver, and ham contain saturated fats. Dairy products such as whole milk, cream, and butter also contain saturated fats.

*What are the daily suggested servings from the food groups that you need?*

**FIGURE 7-4.** Unsaturated fats come from vegetables, nuts, seeds, poultry, and fish.

**FIGURE 7–5**. Fiber is found in foods made from plants.

*Why are foods containing fiber healthful?*

Saturated fats are not as healthful as unsaturated fats. Saturated fats stick to the artery walls, causing a type of heart disease. A diet high in these fats is linked with cancers of the breast and colon. This kind of diet contributes to being overweight.

*Dietary Guideline 4: Eat foods that contain fiber.* Fiber is a natural substance found in foods made from plants. Fruits, raw vegetables, and grains like those found in cereal, contain fiber. Fiber helps you have a daily bowel movement. A high-fiber diet reduces the risks of colon and rectal cancers.

*Dietary Guideline 5: Eat less sugar.* Foods high in sugar are often a poor source of vitamins and minerals. Sugary foods cause weight gain and increase the chances of tooth decay and heart disease. For a healthful diet, try to eat starches, and avoid sugars.

*Dietary Guideline 6: Eat less salt.* Too much salt in the diet is related to headaches and high blood pressure. Less than one teaspoon of salt is needed per day. Many prepared foods contain more than total the amount of salt a person needs per day.

*Dietary Guideline 7: Do not drink alcohol.* Alcohol harms body cells and destroys the liver. Drinking alcohol increases the risk of cancers of the stomach and liver. The best choice for high level wellness is to avoid alcohol at any age.

## ACTIVITY

### Lunch Menus

In groups of four or five, develop lunch menus for one week for your school. Use the seven dietary guidelines to plan the menus. In each lunch menu there should be at least one serving from each of the four healthful food groups.

**Think About It**

1. How might you learn what amount of a particular nutrient is needed each day for good health?
2. How are saturated and unsaturated fats different?

**FIGURE 7-6.** Consumers must make wise choices about buying food.

## Consumer Food Choices

A **consumer** is a person who buys and uses products. You and other family members are consumers when you buy groceries, prepare foods, and plan meals. Knowing how to use information will help you make healthful consumer choices.

### 7:3   Shopping for Groceries

When shopping for groceries, information on food labels can be used to help make choices. In the United States, the following information is required by federal law.

*How can information on food labels be used?*

- *The label must identify the name of the product.* Sometimes there is a description of the variety, style, and method of packing.
- *The net quantity must appear.* The **net quantity** is the amount of the food not including the container. The amount may be measured in pounds and ounces or grams and kilograms. The **unit price** is the price per ounce or gram and can be used to compare the prices of similar products.

- *The name, address, and zip code of the manufacturer, packer, or distributor must be identified.* This allows a person who buys the product to contact someone if the purchase is not satisfactory.
- *The ingredients in the food must be listed.* The ingredients are listed with the one in the largest amount appearing first. The last ingredient listed has the least amount in the product.
- *Special diet foods must be labeled.* A **low-calorie food** contains less than 0.4 Calories per gram. A *reduced-calorie food* is at least one-third lower in Calories than similar foods.
- *Additives and preservatives must be labeled except in ice cream, butter, and cheese.* An **additive** is any chemical added to foods. Additives are used to

  - improve the taste of food.
  - prevent food from discoloring.
  - make food look more appetizing.
  - add or bring out flavor.
  - improve nutritional value.

*Why are additives used in foods?*

*What is the difference between an enriched food and a fortified food?*

An **enriched food** is a food to which vitamins have been added to replace vitamins lost during food processing. A **fortified** (FOR tih fide) **food** is a food to which extra vitamins have been added. A **preservative** (pree ZURV ut ihv) is a chemical added to foods to prevent spoiling. Federal law requires that foods containing certain additives have a warning.

**FIGURE 7-7.** In the United States federal law requires certain information to be on food labels.

## 7:4 Preventing Disease Through Diet Choices ———————

We now know that foods we choose have an effect on our health. Too much of certain foods or chemicals in foods can be harmful.

Reading food labels helps you know what ingredients are in the foods that you purchase. Careful selection and preparation of foods are very important. Healthful diet choices can decrease your risk of both heart disease and cancer.

*How can you decrease your risk of getting heart disease?*

The American Heart Association makes the following suggestions for preventing heart disease.

- Eat margarine rather than butter with a meal.
- Use skim milk rather than whole milk.
- Prepare foods using vegetable oil or margarine rather than butter.
- Trim visible fat off meat or skin off poultry.
- Broil, bake, steam, or poach meat, fish, and poultry rather than cooking in butter or deep frying.
- Limit portion size to four to six ounces of cooked meats, fish, or poultry.
- Leave all butter, gravy, or sauces off foods.
- Eat fresh fruit or fruit in light syrup for dessert.
- Prepare foods without salt or MSG.
- Do not overeat.

The American Cancer Society suggests that the following guidelines might lessen the likelihood of some types of cancer.

- Avoid being overweight. If you are 40 percent overweight, your risk increases for colon, breast, or uterine cancers.
- Cut down on total fat intake. A diet high in fat may increase the chance of breast and colon cancer.
- Eat more high-fiber foods. Studies suggest that diets high in fiber reduce the risk of colon cancer.
- Include foods rich in vitamins A and C in your diet. These foods may help lower the risk for cancers of the larynx, esophagus, or lungs.
- Include cruciferous (krew SIHF uh rus) vegetables in your diet. **Cruciferous vegetables** are vegetables in the cabbage family. Examples include brussel sprouts and cauliflower.
- Limit the intake of salt-cured and smoked foods. These foods increase the likelihood of stomach cancer.
- Avoid alcohol. The use of alcohol increases the likelihood of cancers of the esophagus and stomach.

**Think About It**

3. How should you compare the price of two cans of food?
4. Why should you reduce your intake of fats?

## Life Skills

▶ Eat the correct number of servings from the healthful food groups each day.
▶ Follow the seven dietary guidelines: eat a variety of foods, be at your best weight, eat more fiber, avoid alcohol, and eat less fat, sugar, and salt.
▶ Read food labels when grocery shopping.
▶ Follow the diet suggestions from the American Heart Association and the American Cancer Society.

1. The six main nutrients are proteins, carbohydrates, fats, vitamins, minerals, and water. *7:1*
2. The seven dietary guidelines include: 1) eat a variety of foods, 2) be at your best weight, 3) eat fewer fatty foods, 4) eat foods with fiber, 5) eat less sugar, 6) eat less salt, and 7) do not drink alcohol. *7:2*
3. In the United States, federal law requires that food labels contain specific information to help consumers make choices. *7:3*
4. The American Heart Association and The American Cancer Society have suggested guidelines to reduce the risk of heart disease and cancer. *7:4*

---

*Complete each sentence with the correct word.*
*DO NOT WRITE IN THIS BOOK.*

**Words for Health**

carbohydrates
consumer
combination group
enriched foods
fats
fortified food
nutrients
preservative

proteins
saturated fats
seven dietary guidelines
unit price
unsaturated fats
vitamin deficiency
vitamins
water

1. A(n) _____ is a food to which extra vitamins have been added.
2. _____ are the chemical substances in foods the body uses for growth, repair of cells, and energy.
3. _____ are nutrients that regulate body processes and help fight disease.
4. A(n) _____ is a chemical that is added to foods to prevent spoiling.
5. A(n) _____ is a lack of the amount of a vitamin in the diet that is needed for good health.
6. The _____ are suggestions for eating to help you live longer and more healthfully.

7. The _____ is a food group that contains ingredients from more than one of the four healthful food groups.

8. The _____ is the price per ounce or gram and can be used to compare the prices of similar products.

9. A(n) _____ is a food to which vitamins have been added to replace vitamins lost during food processing.

10. _____ are fats in foods that come from dairy products and the red meat of animals.

11. A nutrient that is the main element in blood and that helps in digestion and the removal of waste products is _____.

12. A(n) _____ is a person who buys and uses products.

13. _____ are nutrients used by the body for energy, to help store some vitamins, and to protect vital organs.

14. Fats in foods that come from vegetables, nuts, seeds, poultry, and fish are _____.

15. _____ are nutrients that are the main supply of energy for your body.

**Reviewing Health**

1. What are the six nutrients in food?
2. How does the body use proteins?
3. How does the body use stored carbohydrates?
4. Why do you need water?
5. What is the US RDA?
6. What are the seven dietary guidelines?
7. Why is it healthful to eat a variety of foods?
8. Why is it healthful to reduce your intake of saturated fats?
9. What are six requirements for food labels?
10. How are ingredients on a food label listed?
11. Why are additives used in foods?
12. Why are vitamins added to enriched food?
13. What are ten suggested guidelines for preventing heart disease proposed by the American Heart Association?
14. What seven suggested guidelines are proposed by the American Cancer Society to reduce cancer?
15. Why should you include high-fiber foods in your diet?

Using Life
Skills

*Use the life skills from this chapter to respond to the following questions.*

*Situation:* Your family is planning a surprise birthday dinner for one of your grandparents. Your grandparent is very concerned about health.

1. What foods would you serve from each of the healthful food groups? Be certain to choose foods that are low in fats, sugar, and salt. Include at least one source of fiber.
2. What dessert might you substitute for a birthday cake?

*Situation:* You and your family are going to eat dinner at a restaurant. You want to follow the dietary suggestions for preventing heart disease that are proposed by the American Heart Association.

1. If you order fish, how would you like to have it prepared?
2. What would you eat with the rolls that are served?
3. What might you order for dessert?

Extending
Health

1. Find two recipes in a cookbook that would be healthful to serve a person who has had heart disease.
2. Read the ingredients on a variety of food labels. Make a list of ten prepared foods that contain sugar.
3. Plan a healthful meal, do the grocery shopping, and prepare the meal for your family.
4. Interview a nutritionist or a dietitian. What training does this person need? Find out about health careers in nutrition education. Learn about nutrition requirements for your age group.
5. Write a research report about salt and discuss:
   a. How much salt do people need?
   b. What health problems may occur from too little salt in a person's diet?
   c. What health problems may occur from too much salt in a diet?
6. Make a list of all the foods you eat in three days.
   a. Did you include the correct number of servings from the healthful food groups?
   b. Did your diet follow the seven diet guidelines?
   c. What changes, if any, should you make?

# Weight Management

Someone once said that we make our habits, and then our habits make us. Daily health behaviors affect your everyday effectiveness and influence your future health. What health behaviors do you perform every day and how might they affect you?

# Chapter 8

- *make and follow a weight management plan.*
- *describe eating disorders.*

A research study in California found that most people might add eleven years to their lives if they followed these life skills.

- Eat three balanced meals a day.
- Avoid snacks between meals.
- Eat breakfast each day.
- Exercise two to three times a week.
- Sleep seven to eight hours each night.
- Do not smoke.
- Do not drink alcohol.
- Maintain desirable weight.

This chapter focuses on what desirable weight is and ways to maintain it.

## The Energy Equation

A plan to maintain your desirable weight is important. You need to follow the plan throughout your life. Maintaining a desirable weight will help you lead a healthier life and form a good self-concept. Basic facts about your body will help you understand weight management. These facts include what your body is made of, how it uses energy from food, and how much food it needs to provide that energy.

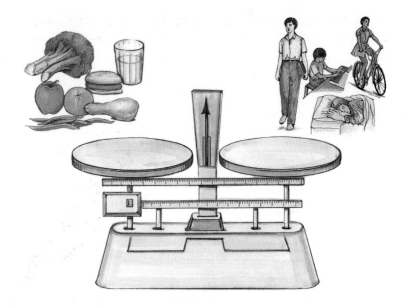

**FIGURE 8–1.** To maintain desirable weight and body composition, a balance between food eaten and energy used is needed.

## 8:1  Weight and Body Composition _____

Your body is made of two kinds of tissue—fat tissue and lean tissue. **Fat tissue** is the tissue that is found just beneath the skin and that surrounds the muscles and internal organs. **Lean tissue** is the tissue that consists of muscles, bones, cartilage, connective tissue, nerves, skin, and internal organs.

Your **body composition** is the percentage of fat tissue and lean tissue in your body. At your age, the amount of body fat needed for good health is about 10 to 15 percent of your total body weight. The amount of body fat that is needed increases as you grow older. During puberty, girls usually begin to have a higher percentage of body fat than boys. One purpose of fat tissue is to surround and protect the female reproductive organs. An adult male should have about 15 percent fat tissue. An adult female should have about 27 percent fat tissue.

Fat tissue is needed for good health. The body uses fat tissue every day. Fat is used as the body stores and uses nutrients. Energy and vitamins A, D, E, and K are stored in fat tissue. Fat tissue protects your internal organs and gives your body shape. It also helps you stay warm in cold weather.

*What are two kinds of body tissue?*

*How does fat tissue keep you healthy?*

When you are lacking a healthful amount of fat tissue, you chill more easily when it is cold. Your body may not be able to store vitamins A, D, E, and K. Because you have less stored energy, you tire more quickly. You may get infections more easily than a person with a healthful amount of fat tissue.

Suppose you have too much fat tissue. Being active is more difficult. Muscles must work harder to carry the extra weight . You will tire more quickly. Excess fat tissue increases the likelihood of developing heart disease, high blood pressure, and diabetes. The heart must work harder to supply blood to the extra fat tissue.

*What might happen if you have too much fat tissue?*

People step on a scale to see how much they weigh. They may think they weigh too much or too little. How can you tell what is a desirable weight for you? Your **desirable weight** is a combination of the weight and body composition recommended for your age, sex, height, and body build. **Weight management** is a plan to maintain your ideal weight. When you are making this plan, you need to consider how much you weigh and what percentage of your body is fat tissue. How much you weigh is one factor that influences health. However, body composition is even more important.

*What are two things to consider in making a plan for weight management?*

One way to check body composition is to use a skinfold measurement. A skinfold measurement is a test used to find a person's percentage of body fat. A tool called a caliper (KAL uh pur) is used to measure the thickness of a fold of skin and fat. The back of the upper arm is the most common place to take this measurement.

# ACTIVITY

## Pinch Test for Body Fat

An easy way to measure percentage of body fat is to use the pinch test. Look at the drawing to the right. Pinch a fold of skin and fat on your upper arm. If you can pinch more than one inch, your percentage of body fat is greater than it should be.

## 8:2   Calories and Metabolic Rate

To maintain your desirable weight, it is important to understand energy input and energy output. The food you eat provides energy for your body. A **Calorie** is a measure of the energy value of food. Look at Table 8–1 to learn how many Calories are in some of the foods you eat. Your energy input is the number of Calories your body needs each day. Most young people your age need 2000 to 3000 Calories per day.

Table 8–1

| Calories in Foods | | |
|---|---|---|
| **Kind of Food** | **Amount** | **Calories** |
| Apple | 3 inches | 75 |
| Banana | 6 inches | 130 |
| Bread, wheat | 1 slice | 60 |
| Broccoli, cooked | 1 cup | 40 |
| Butter | 1 tbsp | 102 |
| Cake, chocolate | 3 inches | 350 |
| Cheese, cheddar | 1 ounce | 112 |
| French fries | 10 | 137 |
| Hamburger on bun | 3 ounces | 330 |
| Ice cream sundae | regular | 400 |
| Milk, whole | 1 cup | 159 |
| Orange | 1 medium | 70 |
| Popcorn, plain | 1 cup | 54 |
| Spaghetti | 1 cup | 260 |
| Steak, T-bone | 1 lb | 1596 |

**FIGURE 8–2**. You use Calories when you are active.

Your energy output is the number of Calories your body uses. **Metabolic** (met uh BAHL ihk) **rate** is the rate at which your body uses Calories. Some basic activities are breathing, digesting food, and the movement of blood. You also use Calories when you play. **Metabolism** (muh TAB uh lihz um) is the way your body uses food. Look at Table 8–2 to learn the number of Calories that your body uses for different activities.

Table 8–2

| Calories Used | |
| --- | --- |
| **Activity** | **Per Fifteen Minutes** |
| Badminton | 87 |
| Basketball | 131 |
| Cycling, 6 mph | 75 |
| Desk work | 33 |
| Horseback riding | 120 |
| Lawn mowing, hand | 115 |
| Roller skating | 100 |
| Running, 6 mph | 150 |
| Sitting and reading | 18 |
| Standing up | 34 |
| Swimming | 75 |

Weight management is based on an energy equation. To maintain your weight, you need to eat the same number of Calories that your body uses. This means your energy input equals your energy output. One pound of body fat is equal to 3500 Calories. To lose one pound, you must use 3500 more Calories than you eat. Your energy input would be less than your energy output. To gain one pound, you must eat 3500 more Calories than you use. Your energy input would be more than your energy output.

*What must you do to lose one pound?*

Table 8–3

| The Energy Equation | |
| --- | --- |
| To maintain weight | Energy input = Energy output |
| To lose weight | Energy input < Energy output |
| To gain weight | Energy input > Energy output |

**FIGURE 8-3**. Exercise helps you maintain your desirable weight.

## 8:3  Overweight and Underweight _____

To be **overweight** is to weigh more than is recommended for a person's age, sex, height, and body build. To be **overfat** is to have too high a percentage of body fat compared to the percentage of lean tissue. An overfat person is not necessarily overweight. Being overweight and overfat affects physical, mental, and social health. Persons who are overweight and overfat also may have shortened lifespans. Such persons are more likely to develop heart disease, high blood pressure, cancer, and diabetes. They also tend to have more accidents than others. Being overweight and overfat also affects physical appearance which may in turn affect a person's self-concept.

What causes a person to be overweight and overfat? When you see such a person, you might think that there is a problem with his or her body. Actually, less than two out of 100 people have a gland problem or a slow metabolic rate that accounts for their being overweight and overfat. Poor eating habits and lack of exercise are two behaviors that most often cause people to be overweight and overfat.

*What two behaviors contribute to being overweight and overfat?*

120

A physician can help make a plan for weight loss. A healthful plan usually includes a weight loss of two pounds per week. When more than two pounds are lost per week, the body might be losing muscle rather than fat tissue. A gradual weight loss is not only more healthful but also more likely to be permanent.

To lose weight, the number of Calories eaten should be reduced and an exercise program maintained. To healthfully reduce caloric input, the amount of saturated fats should be reduced. Also, snacks that contain sugar should be avoided. Smaller portions at meals will help reduce caloric input. An exercise program decreases body fat and increases muscle tissue. During and shortly after exercise, the body's rate of metabolism is increased. While the metabolic rate is higher than usual, the body burns more Calories. This increased metabolic rate after exercise can last up to six hours.

To be **underweight** is to weigh too little for his or her age, sex, height, and body build. To be **underfat** is to have too low a percentage of body fat. Being underweight and underfat may be a sign of poor health. Later in this chapter, you will study about an eating disorder of which being underfat is a symptom.

Being underweight or underfat may affect several areas of a person's health. For example, being underfat after puberty may be a reason for a girl to miss her menstrual periods.

To gain weight and increase body fat, the number of Calories eaten should be increased. Eating larger servings of healthful foods will help add Calories. Healthful snacks will also add weight and body fat. An exercise program is important. It will assure that both body fat and muscle tissue are increased.

*Why should no more than two pounds be lost per week?*

*How can a person gain weight healthfully?*

1. How might having a very low percentage of body fat affect health?
2. What is one way a person might maintain his or her recommended weight?
3. Why should someone who wants to lose weight exercise?

**Think About It**

# Eating Disorders

Our society is very weight conscious. Advertisements often reflect the message that THIN IS IN. This message influences adolescent females more than adolescent males. The result has been an increase in the number of adolescent females who have eating disorders. A disorder is an abnormal function of the body.

## 8:4  Anorexia Nervosa

*What is anorexia nervosa?*

**Anorexia nervosa** (an uh REK see uh · nur VOH suh) is an emotional disorder in which a poor self-concept and an intense fear of being overweight result in starvation. About one in 200 adolescent females has anorexia; rarely do adolescent males have anorexia.

The female with anorexia is usually about five to ten pounds overweight at the beginning of puberty. At puberty she is also experiencing breast and hip development as well as the onset of menstruation. She has a difficult time accepting her weight and the changes in her body. Her self-concept is affected.

The person with anorexia begins to diet as a way to cope with feelings and body changes during puberty. In order to have rapid weight loss, an extreme diet is adopted and very little food is eaten.

**FIGURE 8–4.** Some adolescents view their bodies as overweight when they are not.

**FIGURE 8-5.** Learning to express feelings and accept body changes are important for good health.

To reduce weight further, diuretics (di yuh RET ihks), laxatives, and forced vomiting are frequently used. A **diuretic** is a drug that causes the kidneys to release excess urine. A **laxative** is a medicine that simulates the digestive tract and produces a bowel movement. Persons with anorexia also may exercise too much.

As these behaviors continue, signs of poor physical, mental, and social health begin to show. Self-concept worsens and this person becomes depressed. The person is likely to withdraw from family and friends. Body organs are affected by this condition. A female will have a very low percentage of body fat and her breast and hip development stops. She chills easily, has vitamin deficiencies, and misses menstrual periods. Her heart rate might not be regular and her kidneys may be harmed by the diuretics. If she vomits frequently, there may be tearing and bleeding in the esophagus.

A person with anorexia needs counseling as well as medical help. A counselor can help this person with his or her self-concept. This person must begin to feel good about himself or herself and his or her body. He or she must learn to accept and appreciate the changes that occur to the body. A physician can help with any damage that has been done to the body. The person with anorexia must eat well-balanced meals and develop an effective weight management plan. With proper medical help and diet, the person with anorexia can recover.

*How might a person with anorexia nervosa be helped?*

## 8:5  Bulimia

*What is bulimia?*

**Bulimia** (byew LIHM ee uh) is an emotional disorder in which a person has a poor self-concept and an intense fear of being overweight. The result is secret heavy eating followed by starvation, self-induced vomiting, and the use of laxatives or diuretics.

Bulima is not a way of dieting. Rather, it is a way of controlling weight. A person with bulimia may consume thousands of Calories within a very short period of time. This heavy eating usually is done in private. It often follows some type of stress. Such a person stops eating when he or she feels pain or discomfort. Then this person wants to get rid of the food. He or she may try to vomit or use laxatives and diuretics. There may be abnormal heart rhythm and damage to the kidneys from diuretics. Frequent vomiting causes tearing and bleeding of the gums, stomach, and esophagus. There is an increase in tooth decay. A person with bulimia is more susceptible to urinary tract infections. Muscle spasms, a dry mouth, and brittle hair may result.

*Why is bulimia dangerous?*

**FIGURE 8-6**. A person with bulimia may consume thousands of Calories in a short time.

**FIGURE 8–7.** Psychological and medical help is needed for treatment of bulimia.

The heavy eating followed by getting rid of the food occurs often. In between, there may be periods of normal eating. The person usually feels angry for not being able to control this behavior. He or she may feel very depressed. Drug-related problems and suicide are common in persons with bulimia.

Psychological help focuses on improving self-concept. Lifetime changes in self-acceptance are needed. Treatment for bulimia includes psychological help and medical treatment.

4. How does a person who has anorexia differ from a person who has bulimia?
5. How might frequent vomiting harm the body of a person who has bulimia?

**Think About It**

## Life Skills

▶ Make and follow a plan to maintain your desirable weight.
▶ Maintain a healthful percentage of body fat by exercising regularly.
▶ Feel good about yourself and your body and avoid eating disorders.

## Food Walk

These young people are participating in the Food Walk. The purpose of the Food Walk is to raise money to help put crops in the gardens and food on the tables of those who are not able to do it for themselves.

The Food Walk is a ten kilometer (6.2 miles) walk. People all across the United States can participate in the walk. Each participant has sponsors. The sponsor pledges to donate a certain amount of money for each kilometer that the participant walks on the day of the Food Walk. If the sponsor gives one dollar per kilometer and the participant finishes eight kilometers of the walk, the sponsor gives eight dollars toward the Food Walk fund.

The money collected from all the people who take part in the Food Walk is used in each community that participates. A certain part of the money raised is given to organizations that raise money to buy food for hungry people in other countries.

The climate or weather in some countries may make food production difficult. Also, many countries do not have the agricultural knowledge that we have in the United States. Their farm equipment and methods of farming may be outdated. When food is produced, some countries have problems processing it for use. Poverty and hunger go hand in hand in most countries. The poorer the country, the less likely the country is able to produce the food it needs to feed its people.

Hunger is a leading world health problem. There are many ways in which countries like the United States help with world hunger. Education is an important factor. The United States helps to educate persons in other countries about farming techniques and the food supply. Programs such as the Food Walk that raise money to feed the hungry are another important way.

Young people who participate in the Food Walk are receiving the health benefits of exercise. They are also contributing to the health of others.

126

# Chapter 8 Review

**Summary**

1. When you are making a weight management plan, you need to consider how much you weigh and what percentage of your body is fat tissue. *8:1*
2. Weight management is based upon energy input and energy output. *8:2*
3. Weight gain or weight loss plans should include eating a specific amount of Calories and exercising regularly. *8:3*
4. A person with anorexia nervosa starves as a way of coping with a poor self-concept and puberty. *8:4*
5. A person with bulimia may have periods of heavy eating followed by attempts to quickly rid the body of the food. *8:5*
6. Frequent forced vomiting causes damage to the gums, stomach, kidneys, and esophagus. *8:5*

## Words for Health

*Complete each sentence with the correct word.*
*DO NOT WRITE IN THIS BOOK.*

| | |
|---|---|
| anorexia nervosa | lean tissue |
| body composition | metabolic rate |
| bulimia | metabolism |
| Calorie | overfat |
| desirable weight | overweight |
| diuretic | underfat |
| fat tissue | underweight |
| laxative | weight management |

1. _____ is the body's use of food.
2. To be _____ is to have too low a percentage of body fat.
3. _____ is the percentage of fat tissue and lean tissue in your body.
4. _____ is an emotional disorder in which a poor self-concept and an intense fear of being overweight result in starvation.
5. A(n) _____ is a measure of the energy value of food.
6. _____ is an emotional disorder in which heavy eating is followed by forced vomiting.
7. _____ is a plan to maintain ideal weight.
8. A(n) _____ is a medicine that stimulates the digestive tract so that there is a bowel movement.

9. To be _____ is to have too high a percentage of body fat compared to the percentage of lean tissue.

10. _____ is a combination of the weight and body composition recommended for a person's age, sex, height, and body build.

11. Tissue that is found just beneath the skin and surrounding the muscles and internal organs is _____.

12. A(n) _____ is a drug that causes the kidneys to release excess urine.

13. _____ is the rate at which your body uses Calories for basic actions.

14. To be _____ is to weigh more than is recommended for a person's age, sex, height, and body build.

15. _____consists of muscles, bones, cartilage, connective tissue, nerves, skin, and internal organs.

**Reviewing Health**

1. Why do you need a healthful amount of fat tissue?
2. What is body composition?
3. What are two things to consider when making a plan for weight management?
4. What is a method for measuring body fat?
5. What is the difference between energy input and energy output?
6. Explain the energy equation for 1) maintaining weight, 2) losing one pound, and 3) gaining one pound.
7. What is metabolic rate?
8. How are being overweight and overfat different?
9. How does being overweight affect a person's physical, mental, and social health?
10. How can a person gain weight?
11. How can a person lose weight?
12. When losing weight, why should no more than two pounds be lost per week?
13. What is anorexia nervosa?
14. What are some health problems that result from anorexia nervosa?
15. How can a person with anorexia nervosa be helped?
16. What is bulimia?
17. How does someone with bulimia try to control weight?
18. What kinds of treatment might help a person with bulimia?

*Use the life skills from this chapter to respond to the following questions.*

*Situation:* You and your friends decide to weigh yourselves on a scale. One of your friends is a few inches shorter than you but weighs more. Another friend is also a few inches shorter than you and weighs less. You have all been told by your physicians that you weigh the correct amount.

**1.** How are your body compositions different?
**2.** To maintain your desirable weight, what would you need to know before you made a weight management plan?
**3.** How might your weight management plan change as you get older?

*Situation:* A friend of yours feels very uncomfortable with the bodily changes that are occurring with puberty. Your friend is quite thin but complains about being fat. You have noticed that your friend does not eat lunch or have a snack after school.

**1.** What type of eating disorder might your friend have?
**2.** Besides starvation, what are other ways your friend might try to lose weight?
**3.** How might her eating habits be harmful to her health?

**1.** Locate resources in your community that are available to help persons with eating disorders.
**2.** Write a report that describes the energy equation.
**3.** Learn about the different "fad diets" that persons your age follow to lose weight. Write a report called "The Best Diet."
**4.** Interview a physician. Discuss your desirable weight and use this information to devise a weight management plan.
**5.** Make a list of five or more reasons why you need to examine your eating habits.
**6.** For more information about eating disorders write to:
National Association of Anorexia Nervosa and
Associated Disorders
Box 271
Highland Park, Illinois 60035

# Exercise and Fitness

Did you know . . .

▶ you can participate in lifetime sports when you are older?

▶ you can protect yourself from exercise and sports injuries?

# Unit 5

# Physical Fitness for a Lifetime

Physical activity does more than just get you in shape, it affects all areas of your health. By choosing activities that allow you to stay active throughout your life, you will influence your lifespan and promote quality living. How active are you?

# Chapter 9

**STUDENT OBJECTIVES:** *You will be able to*

- *discuss the areas of physical fitness, different fitness skills, and benefits to health.*
- *choose exercises and lifetime sports to develop a physical fitness plan.*

The boy and his grandfather enjoy a brisk walk through the woods. While they walk, they share both quiet time and conversation. At the same time, the kind of exercise they get helps their physical fitness. Physical fitness is a part of health that is important throughout life. People of all ages and abilities benefit from physical fitness.

## Physical Fitness and Health

In this textbook, you have been studying about habits that improve both the quantity and quality of your life. The quantity of your life is the number of years that you will live. The quality refers to the happiness and good health you enjoy while you are alive. Physical fitness adds to both the quantity and quality of life.

You should begin a physical fitness plan now. Being active and physically fit will help you do your best in all areas of your life. This will help improve your self-concept and lead to good health.

## 9:1 Benefits of Physical Fitness

*What is physical fitness?*

**Physical fitness** is the condition of your body as a result of a regular exercise program. Physical fitness benefits all ten areas of health.

- *Mental Health*  When you are physically fit, you are better able to deal with stress. You are less likely to become tired or ill. Regular exercise helps your body use the sugar released into your bloodstream by your liver during stress. After exercise, you feel more relaxed and are better able to get a good night's sleep.

*How might a regular exercise program improve social skills?*

- *Family and Social Health*  An exercise program can be shared with your family and friends. There are many activities in which you and your family can participate. Social skills, such as fairness and cooperation, can be practiced when you are with others.

- *Growth and Development*  Regular exercise helps strengthen and tone your muscles. Your bones will become stronger. Your circulation will be improved. Your brain and other body parts will function more effectively. A high level of physical fitness will help you enjoy a wide range of activities now and as you get older.

**FIGURE 9-1**. Being physically fit can improve all areas of your health.

FIGURE 9–2. Regular exercise releases beta-endorphins, which create a feeling of well-being.

- *Nutrition*   A regular program of exercise helps you balance your caloric intake and caloric output. Routine exercise affects a part of the brain that controls your appetite. When you are physically fit, your body systems work well and you are less likely to overeat and to become overweight.

- *Exercise and Fitness*   When you are physically fit, you are able to enjoy many exercises and activities. You might enjoy playing on sports teams at school. Regular exercise will strengthen all muscles, including your heart muscle. A strong heart can pump more blood with each beat. Thus, regular exercise lowers your resting heart rate. A lower heart rate means the heart muscle is able to get more rest between beats and its work is less demanding.

- *Drugs*   Regular energetic exercise causes beta-endorphins (BAYT uh • en DOR fihnz) to be released. **Beta-endorphins** are substances produced in the brain that relieve pain and promote feelings of pleasure and well-being. You may have heard of a runner's "high." This refers to the good feelings a person may have while participating in a long-distance run or at the completion of any endurance activity. These good feelings are caused by the release of the beta endorphins.

*What is a runner's "high"?*

What diseases can regular exercise help prevent?

- *Diseases and Disorders*   Regular exercise helps clear fat from the bloodstream. You are less likely to have fat deposits on your artery walls. Regular exercise helps your body use sugar in your bloodstream. This helps prevent conditions such as diabetes. Research also shows that asthma attacks may be reduced with a well planned exercise program. A program of regular exercise is believed to prevent diseases such as high blood pressure and reduce the likelihood of breast cancer in women.

- *Consumer and Personal Health*   Exercises such as walking and running do not cost money. As a consumer, exercise can be a low-priced form of entertainment. Regular exercise improves the condition of all parts of your body. Your body systems are able to function efficiently. Your skin, hair, and nails also will have a healthful look.

- *Safety and First Aid*   Accidents may result from mistakes made when you are tired. When you are physically fit, you are more alert and may have fewer accidents. Should an injury occur, your body might handle it better if you are fit. Your recovery may be quicker if your body is strong.

- *Community and Environmental Health*   Your surroundings can contribute a great deal to the quality of your life. When you are physically fit and participate in many activities, you might better enjoy your community and environment. You might take walks. You might ride a bike through the woods, through parks, and along beaches. You might enjoy swimming in a lake.

## ACTIVITY

### Bulletin Board on Physical Fitness

Make a bulletin board with your classmates. Divide into ten groups. Each group can take one of the ten areas of health to illustrate ways that physical fitness improves health.

## 9:2 The Areas of Physical Fitness

Someone who is physically fit has muscular strength, muscular endurance, and flexibility. He or she has cardiovascular fitness and a low percentage of body fat. These characteristics represent the five areas of physical fitness.

**Muscular strength** is the amount of force your muscles can produce. Strong muscles help you lift, kick, push, and pull. You are able to kick a football with force or carry a heavy bag of groceries.

**Muscular endurance** is the ability to use the same muscles over a long period of time. Suppose you ride your bike up and down hills. You need muscular strength in your legs to pedal. You need muscular endurance to continue to pedal for a long time.

**Flexibility** is the ability to bend and move your body in many directions easily. For instance, you need to be flexible to do a cartwheel or play baseball. If you are flexible, you are less likely to injure your muscles.

**Cardiovascular fitness** is the condition of your heart and blood vessels. When you have this kind of fitness, you can be active for a long period of time without tiring. You might be able to swim many laps in a pool or run a long-distance race without stopping.

**Body composition** is the amount of fat tissue and lean tissue in your body. For good health, you should have a lean body and a low percentage of body fat.

*What are the five areas of physical fitness?*

*Why is cardiovascular fitness important?*

**FIGURE 9–3.** Swimming is an exercise that helps develop all areas of fitness.

Tests have been developed to measure the physical fitness of boys and girls your age. These tests can be given by your teacher at your school. One test is the Physical Best test. This test includes

- body composition
- modified sit-ups
- pull-ups
- sit and reach
- one-mile walk/run

Another test is the President's Challenge. This test includes

- curl-ups
- pull-ups
- v-sit reach
- one-mile walk/run
- shuttle run

See Figure 9–4 a and b. These symbols represent the awards that are given for passing either test.

If your school participates in a physical fitness test, you might want to have a physical checkup at the same time. It is recommended that you have your blood pressure taken and your posture checked. **Posture** is the way you hold your body as you sit, stand, and move. Correct posture allows your body parts room to work as they should. Circulation may improve when your posture is correct.

**FIGURE 9–4**. Two tests given for physical fitness have awards such as (a) Physical Best award and (b) President's Challenge award.

a

b

**FIGURE 9–5.**                                                    **PHYSICAL FITNESS TEST**

**Pull-ups** are exercises that measure arm and shoulder muscular strength and endurance.

**Curl-ups or modified sit-ups** are exercises that measure abdominal muscular strength and endurance.

**The v-sit reach or sit and reach** measures the flexibility of your lower back and thighs.

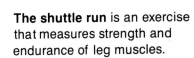

**The shuttle run** is an exercise that measures strength and endurance of leg muscles.

**The one-mile walk/run** is an exercise that measures cardiovascular fitness.

**Body composition** uses skinfold measurements to determine percentage of body fat.

**FIGURE 9–6**. You can practice to better develop fitness skills.

## 9:3 Fitness Skills

**Fitness skills** are skills that can be used when participating in a variety of sports and games. You can develop your fitness skills with practice. As your fitness skills reach a higher level, your overall physical fitness also improves.

**Agility** is the ability to move with ease and speed. When playing soccer, you use agility to change direction, and run and kick the ball.

**Balance** is the ability to keep from falling. You first used balance when you learned to sit up without falling over. Now you use balance to roller skate, ride a skateboard, or ride a bike.

**Reaction time** is the length of time you use to move after you see, hear, feel, or taste a signal. When running a race, the more quickly you respond to the signal to start the race, the faster your reaction time.

**Coordination** is the ability to use body parts and senses together for movement. For example, when you play kickball, your eyes watch the ball as you move your leg and foot to kick it.

**Power** is the ability to combine strength with speed. You use power to hit a baseball with a bat or kick a soccer ball. As your power increases, you can hit or kick the ball farther and faster.

**Speed** is the ability to move rapidly. You need speed to swim quickly across the pool in a race or run bases in a baseball game.

**Think About It**

1. How might physical fitness help with growth and development throughout your life?
2. What is the difference between muscular strength and muscular endurance?
3. What is the difference between balance and coordination?

## Your Plan for Physical Fitness

Many factors are used to develop a personal plan for physical fitness. Your health status, body build, and the activities you enjoy should be considered. It is also important to understand the benefits you can get from different kinds of exercises, lifetime sports, or other activities. Understanding these factors will help you in making your personal physical fitness plan.

### 9:4 Types of Exercises

There are five types of exercises from which you can obtain benefits for physical fitness. They are isometric (i suh MET rihk), isotonic (i suh TAHN ihk), isokinetic (i suh kuh NET ihk), aerobic (er ROH bihk), and anaerobic (an uh ROH bihk) exercises.

An **isometric exercise** is an exercise in which muscles are tightened for five to ten seconds without any movement of body parts. Pushing against a wall is an example of an isometric exercise. Isometric exercises develop muscular strength. They make your muscles larger and stronger. They do not help endurance or flexibility.

An **isotonic exercise** is an exercise in which there is a muscle contraction that causes movement. Lifting weights, doing curl-ups, and doing push-ups are examples. Isotonic exercises build muscular strength and improve flexibility. They are usually done for short periods of time. They do not strengthen the heart muscle or improve cardiovascular fitness.

An **isokinetic exercise** is an exercise in which a weight is moved through an entire range of motion. Exercise machines with weight plates or air pressure are used often. Because it is easy to become injured when using these machines, it is wise to have an instructor help you. The instructor will tell you how much weight to lift. He or she also will tell you when to add more weight, and how many times to repeat the exercise. Isokinetic exercises develop flexibility and muscular strength and endurance.

**FIGURE 9–7.** Isometric exercise will develop muscular strength.

*How do isokinetic exercises help the body?*

**FIGURE 9–8.** Performing anaerobic exercise may help muscular strength and endurance.

An **aerobic exercise** is a form of exercise that requires a continuous use of oxygen over an extended period of time. You breathe in the same amount of oxygen that your body uses. The American College of Sports Medicine recommends that aerobic exercises be performed at your target heart rate. **Target heart rate** is a heart rate of 75 percent of the difference between your resting heart rate and your maximum heart rate plus your resting heart rate. **Maximum heart rate** is 220 minus your age. An average resting heart rate is about 70.

*How should aerobic exercises be performed?*

Suppose you are 12 years old. Your maximum heart rate would be 220 minus 12, or 208. Your resting heart rate is 70. Target heart rate is 75 percent of the difference between your resting heart rate and your maximum heart rate plus your resting heart rate.

208 (maximum heart rate) − 70 (resting heart rate) = 138
.75 × 138 = 103.5 + 70 = 173.5 target heart rate

Aerobic exercises help develop cardiovascular fitness. They also help decrease your percentage of body fat.

Anaerobic means without air. An **anaerobic exercise** is a form of exercise in which the body's demand for oxygen is greater than the supply. Anaerobic exercises are done in short bursts of energy. For example, running the 100-meter dash as fast as possible leaves you out of breath. These exercises may help with flexibility or muscular strength and endurance.

*How do anaerobic exercises improve physical fitness?*

## 9:5 Lifetime Sports

**Lifetime sports** are activities in which you can participate for the rest of your life provided you stay in good health. Some lifetime sports have many benefits. Walking, swimming, bowling, and tennis are lifetime sports. Although you may enjoy team sports and other activities, you should begin to participate in lifetime sports at your age. Research shows that adults who participate in lifetime sports developed their interest and skills during their childhood.

*What are lifetime sports?*

## 9:6 A Complete Workout

It is important for you to plan a complete physical fitness workout to meet your needs. Begin by warming up. **Warming up** is three to five minutes of exercise to get muscles ready to do more work. When you take time for warming up, you help prevent injury and soreness to muscles. Your individual physical fitness workout should include exercises to develop each of the five areas of physical fitness. After these exercises, you should have a time for cooling down. **Cooling down** is a three to five minute period of reduced exercise. This gives your heart a chance to slow down and lowers the body temperature. Examine the Complete Physical Fitness Workout in Table 9–1. When making your individual plan, choose exercises that you enjoy.

*What is cooling down?*

**FIGURE 9–9.** Participating in lifetime sports will help keep you in good health.

Table 9-1

| A Complete Physical Fitness Workout | |
| --- | --- |
| **Exercises for** | **Types of Exercises** |
| 1. Warming up | Plan three to five minutes of each exercise to prepare your muscles and joints for harder exercises. Choose an aerobic exercise to gradually raise the heart rate. Choose some stretching exercises. |
| 2. Flexibility | Include stretching exercises to keep your range of motion for muscles and joints. |
| 3. Cardiovascular Fitness and Body Composition | Include aerobic exercises. The American Academy of Sports Medicine recommends 15 to 60 minutes of aerobic exercise at least three times per week at your target heart rate. |
| 4. Muscular Strength and Endurance | Include isometric, isokinetic, and isotonic exercises to tone your muscles. Include exercises for all major muscle groups and joints. |
| 5. Cooling Down | Include three to five minutes of reduced exercise. During this time, the heart rate will return to normal and the blood in the lower part of the body will return to the heart and brain. Stretching exercises prevent soreness. |

**Think About It**

4. How are isometric and isokinetic exercises different?
5. What are the advantages of lifetime sports?
6. Why is it important to cool down after exercise?

# Life Skills

▶ Make and follow a complete fitness plan that promotes all areas of physical fitness.
▶ Complete and pass a physical fitness test.
▶ Sit, stand, and move with correct posture.
▶ Practice fitness skills to develop agility, balance, coordination, reaction time, power, and speed.
▶ Select enjoyable isometric, isotonic, isokinetic, aerobic, and anaerobic exercises.
▶ Participate in lifetime sports.

# Chapter 9 Review

**Summary**

1. A routine program for physical fitness contributes to all ten areas of health. *9:1*
2. A person who is physically fit has muscular strength, muscular endurance, flexibility, cardiovascular fitness, and a low percentage of body fat. *9:2*
3. Six fitness skills are agility, balance, coordination, reaction time, power, and speed. *9:3*
4. Five types of exercises to improve fitness are isometric, isotonic, isokinetic, aerobic, and anaerobic. *9:4*
5. Walking, bowling, and swimming are lifetime sports because you can participate in them for the rest of your life. *9:5*
6. A complete physical fitness workout includes warming up, exercises for the five areas of fitness, and cooling down. *9:6*

**Words for Health**

*Complete each sentence with the correct word.*
*DO NOT WRITE IN THIS BOOK.*

| | |
|---|---|
| aerobic exercise | isotonic exercise |
| anaerobic exercise | lifetime sports |
| beta-endorphins | muscular strength |
| body composition | one-mile walk/run |
| cardiovascular fitness | physical fitness |
| curl-ups | reaction time |
| fitness skills | target heart rate |
| flexibility | warming up |

1. _____ is three to five minutes of exercise to get muscles ready to work more.
2. _____ are substances produced in the brain that relieve pain and create a feeling of well-being.
3. A(n) _____ is an exercise in which there is a muscle contraction that causes movement.
4. _____ is the condition of your heart and blood vessels.
5. _____ are skills that can be used when participating in a variety of sports and games.
6. _____ are activities in which you can participate for the rest of your life provided you stay in good health.

7. _____ is the length of time you use to move after you see, hear, feel, or taste a signal.
8. _____ is the condition of your body as a result of a regular exercise program.
9. _____ are exercises that measure abdominal muscular strength and endurance.
10. _____ is the amount of force that your muscles can produce.
11. The amount of fat tissue compared to the amount of lean tissue in your body is _____.
12. _____ is a form of exercise that requires a continuous use of oxygen over an extended period of time.
13. An exercise to measure your level of cardiovascular fitness is the _____.
14. A(n) _____ is a form of exercise in which the body's demand for oxygen is greater than the supply.
15. _____ is the ability to bend and move your body in many directions easily.

**Reviewing Health**

1. What are ten health areas that can be benefitted by your participation in a regular exercise program?
2. What are the five areas of physical fitness?
3. How is physical fitness tested using the President's Challenge or Physical Best tests?
4. What are six kinds of fitness skills?
5. What is coordination?
6. What are five types of exercise from which you can obtain benefits for physical fitness?
7. How is maximum heart rate determined?
8. What is the target heart rate?
9. Why is it important to begin to participate in lifetime sports at your age?
10. What might you do when you are warming up?
11. Why is cooling down important?
12. What five types of exercises should be included in a complete physical fitness workout?

*Use the life skills from this chapter to respond to the following questions.*

*Situation:* You want to develop a complete physical fitness workout to develop each area of physical fitness. You decide to make a health behavior contract to follow.

**1.** How would you begin your workout?
**2.** What kinds of exercises would you include in your workout?
**3.** How would you end your workout?

*Situation:* Your class has decided to participate in the President's Council on Physical Fitness and Sports test in three weeks. Your teacher suggests that each of you practice.

**1.** What five tests will you practice for?
**2.** What might be included in a physical checkup that you have before the test?
**3.** How could you prepare for a physical fitness test?

*Situation:* You have never participated in a school sport before. However, you are planning to go out for your school's track team next month.

**1.** In which events would you be most interested in participating?
**2.** Which fitness skills would be needed for the events in which you would prefer to participate?
**3.** What exercises could you do to develop these skills?

**1.** Select a lifetime sport of interest to you. Write a one page report on this sport to share with the class. Include a discussion on the benefits of this sport, the equipment needed, and the fitness skills that are developed.
**2.** Design a pamphlet that describes physical fitness and explains how it benefits the ten areas of health.
**3.** Write a report on one of the following careers: sports psychologist, athletic trainer, athletic director, physical education teacher, or coach.
**4.** Make a list of the exercises you are presently doing. Tell how each exercise is making you physically fit.

# Exercise and Sports Injuries

Participation in sports and exercise puts you at greater risk to injury. This risk, however, can be reduced by your taking several safety measures. When injury does occur, proper care can help you recover and get active more quickly.

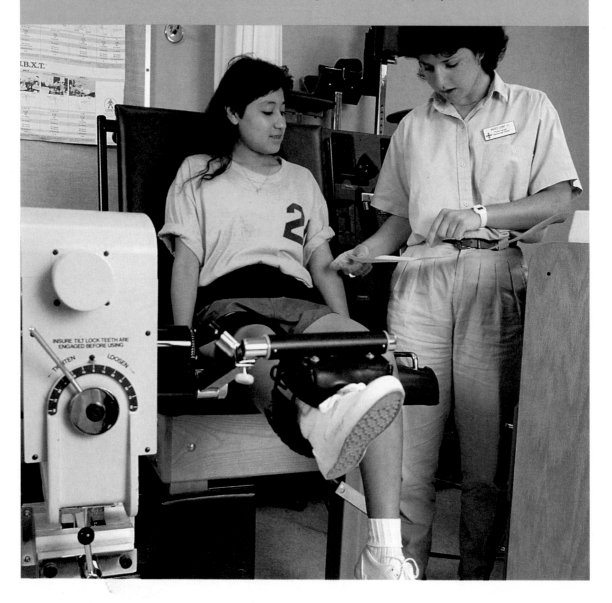

# Chapter 10

**STUDENT OBJECTIVES:** *You will be able to*

- *identify and follow safety rules for team and individual sports.*
- *discuss what to do for common sports injuries.*

Each year there are more than ten million injuries to young people involved in individual and team sports. Injuries also occur when people are exercising. Many of these injuries might have been prevented. Following safety rules, knowing the rules of the game or sport, and using proper equipment are some ways to help reduce the risk of injury.

## Safety Rules

Before you begin to play a card game or a board game, you read the directions. When you know the rules of the game, it is more enjoyable. Before you participate in exercises or in sports, it is also important to know the rules. Rules are made to help you and others enjoy exercises and sports. More importantly, rules help protect you and others from injury.

## 10:1  Safety in Team Sports ————

In a team sport, many people play at the same time and the chances of injury increase. However, there are ways you can help reduce the chances of becoming injured in a team sport.

*What are three ways to help reduce the chances of becoming injured in a team sport?*

- *Wear the proper equipment*  Many team sports involve physical contact. Most physical contact sports require special equipment. Using or wearing the proper equipment is an important factor in reducing the risk of injury. The equipment should be in place before the start of play, and it should fit well. Poorly fitting equipment might also cause injuries.
- *Know the rules of the game*  Injuries may occur when players do not know or follow the rules of the game. When you know the rules, you know what you can and cannot do. Doing something unexpected may confuse fellow team members and cause accidents or injuries. Penalties for fouls in sports are necessary to encourage all players to follow the rules to have a safe and enjoyable game.
- *Know your teammates' abilities*  If you know how your teammates play, you will know how to react. Suppose a person on your basketball team throws a quick pass. You need to be alert. If you do not expect a quick pass and the ball is thrown, it might hit you in the face and cause an injury.

**FIGURE 10-1**. It is important for all participants to follow the rules to insure safety.

**FIGURE 10-2.** It is important to follow safety rules while biking.

## 10:2 Individual Exercise and Sport Safety

When you participate in individual exercises and sports, it is important to know and follow safety rules. Following are lists of safety rules for biking, walking, running, swimming, and diving. These rules are for your protection.

### Safety While Biking

- Check your bike to see that it works properly.
- Carry identification and change for an emergency phone call.
- Know your route and where you plan to end the trip.
- Wear a safety helmet.
- Ride in the same direction as the traffic is moving.
- Obey all traffic signs. Use hand signals when turning.
- Allow pedestrians to have the right of way.
- Use lights on your bike at night.
- Wear clothing that reflects or can be seen at dusk, dawn, or night. Use reflective tape on your bike.
- Avoid biking on narrow, winding roads whenever possible.
- Never ride double.

**FIGURE 10–3.** Wearing reflective clothing helps drivers see you.

## Safety While Walking or Running

- Carry identification and change for an emergency call.
- Know your route and where you plan to end the trip.
- Walk or run in the opposite direction of traffic.
- Use paths and sidewalks when possible.
- Avoid narrow, bending roads and highways.
- Wear reflective clothing.
- Obey all traffic signs.
- Be defensive. Watch for and try to predict what the drivers of cars will do.
- Avoid walking in places that may be slippery.

## Safety While Swimming and Diving

- Learn to swim well.
- Swim close to the shore.
- Always swim with another person.
- Know the depth of the water.
- Do not dive into shallow water.
- Swim only in supervised areas.
- Walk, do not run, around a pool.
- Never swim during an electrical storm.

**Think About It**

1. How can you be safe when playing sports?
2. Why should you carry change with you when you are biking, walking, or running?

# Common Injuries

Suppose you become injured while exercising or playing with a friend. Knowing what to do in this situation will help you and your friend remain calm. You will be able to care for your injury. Knowing what to do can also prevent further injury. Some injuries happen often and can be cared for easily.

## 10:3  Scrapes

A **scrape** is a wearing away of the outer layers of the skin due to rubbing against a hard surface. A scrape usually results from a fall. The parts of the body most often scraped are the hands, elbows, and knees. These areas usually hit the ground first when you fall.

When a part of your skin is scraped, nerve cells are irritated, causing pain. Usually, there is only a small amount of bleeding. Though typically not serious, scrapes need to be treated to prevent infection.

The treatment for scrapes is simple to follow. Wash the injured area with soap and warm water. Soap and water clean and remove pathogens from the scrape. After cleaning, a bandage should be used if the scrape continues to bleed. A bandage will help prevent pathogens from entering the scrape.

*What is the treatment for scrapes?*

A scab will form shortly after a scrape occurs. A **scab** is dried blood that forms over a cut or injury to protect the opening to the body. Platelets in your blood cause red blood cells to clot and dry over the injury.

Suppose you do not clean a scrape. An infection can result when pathogens remain in the opening from the scrape. An **infection** is a condition in which pathogens cause swelling and redness in an injured area. There may also be pus in the scrape. Infections should always be treated by a physician.

Often scrapes can be prevented. Many people who roller skate wear knee and elbow pads. Wearing long sleeved shirts and long pants can also help protect the knees and elbows. What other ways might you protect yourself from scrapes?

**FIGURE 10-4.** Proper treatment for scrapes can help prevent infection.

## 10:4 Cuts

Another common injury that may occur while playing a sport or exercising is a cut. Because cuts are deeper than scrapes, dirt is more likely to remain in a cut. Like scrapes, cuts should be cleansed thoroughly to prevent infection. Shallow cuts can be cleaned with soap and water to remove dirt and pathogens.

Most cuts bleed. To stop bleeding from minor cuts, apply pressure with a bandage. If a cut appears deep and continues to bleed, try to stop bleeding by placing pressure on the cut. Get medical treatment for deep cuts. A physician may need to clean the cut and close the area with stitches.

Many cuts can be prevented. Follow safety rules. Before playing, make sure the play area is free from hazards such as broken glass. If schoolyards, playgrounds, or parks are not safe, report the problems to the proper persons.

*How do you stop cuts from bleeding?*

**FIGURE 10–5**. The playground shown is (a) safe and (b) unsafe.

a

b

**FIGURE 10-6.** Stretching exercises help muscles get ready for hard work.

## 10:5 Muscle Soreness

People sometimes overuse their muscles by starting exercises or sports before their muscles are ready. For example, you may not be used to running a long distance. Instead of slowly building up to it, you try to run the longer distance right away. Later, you have muscle soreness. Or, you may not be used to throwing a baseball. You begin by throwing the baseball as hard as you can. You do not gradually stretch your arm and shoulder muscles before throwing harder. Later, you have muscle soreness.

**Muscle soreness** is the pain that results when you overuse muscles. Although muscle soreness is not a serious injury, it is usually painful.

Muscle soreness can be prevented by doing warm-up and cool-down exercises. The same easy, stretching exercises can be used for both the warm-up and cool-down. Warm-up exercises help the muscles get ready for harder work. Cool-down exercises help keep the muscles from getting tight.

Muscle soreness can be relieved by applying ice on the area for half an hour, removing it for fifteen minutes, then reapplying it. You can continue this treatment for three hours. Do not apply heat until 48 hours after the injury. Always rest sore muscles. When you begin to exercise again, begin gradually.

*How can muscle soreness be prevented?*

**FIGURE 10–7**. Dislocations should always be treated by a physician.

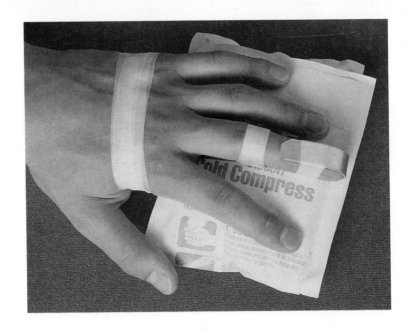

## 10:6  Dislocations

*What is a dislocation?*

A **dislocation** is the movement of a bone away from its joint. Dislocations of fingers are common when playing basketball and volleyball. If a ball strikes the top of an extended finger, the force may cause a dislocation. Pain and swelling usually follow. The pain will increase if there is movement of the joint. The joint will usually appear misshapen.

A physician should always treat dislocations. A physician can sometimes treat a dislocated finger by pulling the finger beyond the joint. Cold packs can then be applied to stop swelling. A dislocated thumb should never be pulled because there may be a broken bone.

# ACTIVITY

### Pamphlet for Exercise and Sports Injuries

Make a pamphlet in which you describe first aid procedures for common exercise and sports injuries. Inside the pamphlet, write a summary of first aid procedures for scrapes, cuts, muscle soreness, and dislocations. On the cover of your pamphlet, draw a picture of your favorite sport.

## 10:7  Sprains

A **sprain** is an injury to the tissue that connects bones at a joint. A sprain can occur when you suddenly twist a joint. As a result, the tissue stretches or tears. A sprain is followed by sharp pain, soreness, and swelling. The injured part usually turns black and blue. A sprain most often occurs at the ankle or wrist. Besides tissue, sprains may also damage blood vessels, tendons, nerves, and muscles.

To treat the pain, elevate the injured joint and apply cold packs to stop the swelling. Cold packs may be applied for half an hour, removed for fifteen minutes, then applied for another half hour. Repeat this twice a day until the swelling goes down. Elastic bandages may also be used.

If the swelling and soreness increase or continue, you should see a physician. The physician can determine whether any bones are broken or dislocated.

*What is a sprain?*

3. Why does a scab form over scrapes?
4. Why should a physician examine a deep cut?
5. How might you prevent having muscle soreness from a bike trip?
6. Why are cold packs applied to dislocations?
7. How should you treat a sprain?

**Think About It**

## Life Skills

▶  Wear the proper equipment for sports.
▶  Follow safety rules for biking, walking, running, swimming, and diving.
▶  Wash scrapes with soap and warm water and cover with a bandage.
▶  Apply pressure to cuts to stop bleeding.
▶  Always rest sore muscles to prevent injury.
▶  See a physician for all dislocations.

# Health Highlights

## Mouth Protectors

What do acrobatics, basketball, field hockey, gymnastics, ice hockey, martial arts, skiing, soccer, volleyball, and wrestling have in common? The American Dental Association recommends wearing a mouth protector for each of these sports.

A mouth protector is a device that helps prevent injury to the mouth area, including the teeth, lips, cheeks, and tongue. There are three types of mouth protectors. These include the ready-made or stock mouth protector, the mouth-formed protector, and the custom-made protector. Each type helps protect a person from injury. They are, however, different in comfort, fit, and cost.

*The stock mouth protector* The stock mouth protector is a ready-made mouth protector. It can be purchased at a sporting goods store or a drugstore. It comes in many shapes and sizes and is made of rubber or a polyvinyl material. This mouth protector is the most uncomfortable type because it cannot be adjusted. The jaws must be closed to keep it in place.

*The mouth-formed protector* The mouth-formed protector is usually shaped to an athlete's teeth by a dentist. There are two kinds. One kind is called a shell-liner, mouth-formed protector. An acrylic gel is put into a premade outer lining. It forms a lining that is then shaped to the athlete's teeth. Another kind is softened by placing it in hot water. Then it is shaped to the teeth by using finger, tongue, and biting pressure.

*The custom-made mouth protector* The best mouth protector is constructed over a model made from a dentist's impression of the athlete's teeth. A material is placed over the model to make the mouth protector fit the mouth exactly. This is the most expensive and the most comfortable mouth protector. It does not interfere with speaking.

There are ways to care for a mouth protector. Rinse it with cold water or a mouth rinse before wearing. After wearing a mouth protector, rinse it in cool water, occasionally adding soap. Check the mouth protector for tears and loose linings.

# Chapter 10 Review

**Summary**

1. To prevent injuries during team sports, wear proper equipment, know the rules of the game, and know your teammates' abilities. *10:1*
2. Safety rules for biking, walking, running, swimming, and diving protect you from injury. *10:2*
3. Scrapes should be washed with soap and warm water and covered with a bandage. *10:3*
4. Infections result when a scrape is not cleaned well. *10:3*
5. Pressure can be applied to a cut to stop the bleeding. *10:4*
6. Report any safety problems in a schoolyard, playground, or park. *10:4*
7. Muscle soreness can be prevented by doing warm-up and cool-down exercises. *10:5*
8. Muscle soreness can be relieved by applying ice for half an hour, removing it for 15 minutes, and repeating this procedure for three hours. *10:5*
9. When dislocations force a bone away from a joint, a physician should be consulted. *10:6*
10. A sprain is an injury to the tissue that connects bones at a joint and can be treated with rest, elevation, cold packs, and an elastic bandage. *10:7*

## Words for Health

*Complete each sentence with the correct word.*
*DO NOT WRITE IN THIS BOOK.*

dislocation          scab
infection            scrape
muscle soreness      sprain

1. A(n) _____ is dried blood that forms over a cut or injury to protect the opening to the body.
2. A(n) _____ is the movement of a bone away from its joint.
3. A(n) _____ is the wearing away of the outer layers of the skin against a hard surface.
4. _____ is the pain that results when you overuse muscles.
5. A(n) _____ is a condition in which pathogens cause swelling and redness in an injured area.
6. A(n) _____ is an injury in which tissue is torn or stretched.

# Chapter 10 Review

**Reviewing Health**

1. What are three ways to reduce the chances of becoming injured in a team sport?
2. What are eight safety rules for biking?
3. What are seven safety rules to follow while walking or running?
4. What are six safety rules for swimming and diving?
5. Why are the hands, elbows, and knees most often scraped?
6. What should you do if you receive a scrape if you fall while playing?
7. What might happen if a scrape is not cleaned and an infection develops?
8. How might scrapes be prevented?
9. How do you stop bleeding from a cut?
10. How can you prevent muscle soreness?
11. What can you do to relieve muscle soreness?
12. What happens when you dislocate your finger?
13. Describe how a dislocation may look and tell how it should be treated.
14. What is a sprain?
15. How do you know if you have a sprain?

**Using Life Skills**

*Use the life skills from this chapter to respond to the following questions.*

*Situation:* You and your family are planning a bike trip. You will be traveling 60 miles in two days. You want to plan to be safe, especially in the late afternoon and early morning.

1. What will you and your family do to prepare for your trip to prevent muscle soreness?
2. What safety equipment will you need to bring along on this trip?
3. What clothing will you wear to insure safety?
4. What other safety rules will you follow?

*Situation:* Recently you began a running program. You have been running one mile every evening with a friend. Your leg muscles are very sore tonight.

1. What may have been the cause of the muscle soreness?

2. How might you relieve the muscle soreness?

3. What will you do to prevent muscle soreness the next time you get to run?

*Situation:* While playing basketball, your friend jams her thumb. She says that the joint at the thumb hurts. The thumb looks swollen. Your friend keeps playing in the game. She tells you that she will pull her thumb to make it feel better.

1. What may your friend have done to her thumb?

2. What first aid would you give to your friend?

3. What should your friend do to help treat her thumb?

*Situation:* You are playing in a soccer tournament. The score is tied, and the game is in the second half. One of your teammates falls after being tripped by a player on the other team. Your teammate is hurt and is holding his leg.

1. Why are rules important in sports?

2. What might you do to help your teammate?

---

**Extending Health**

1. Interview a referee for one of your favorite sports. What type of training did this person receive in order to be a referee? How does this person keep current with rule changes in his or her particular sport. Why does this person enjoy being a referee?

2. Plan a two mile walking course for your community. Explain why you have selected the area for the course. Write a pamphlet showing a map of the course. You may include half-mile markers. Include safety suggestions for walking your course.

3. Visit an athletic trainer. Ask the trainer how he or she helps prevent others from becoming injured. Find out what types of injuries occur most frequently and how the trainer treats these injuries. Find out what type of instruction this person received in order to become an athletic trainer.

4. Visit a sporting goods store. Choose two sports that interest you, and make a list of all available safety equipment for each sport. On your list, include the prices of the safety equipment for both sports. Tell how each piece of equipment protects the athlete. Compare the prices of the equipment.

# Drugs

Did you know . . .

▶ prescription drugs must be taken as directed to ensure the desired effect?

▶ help is available for the families of an abusive drinker?

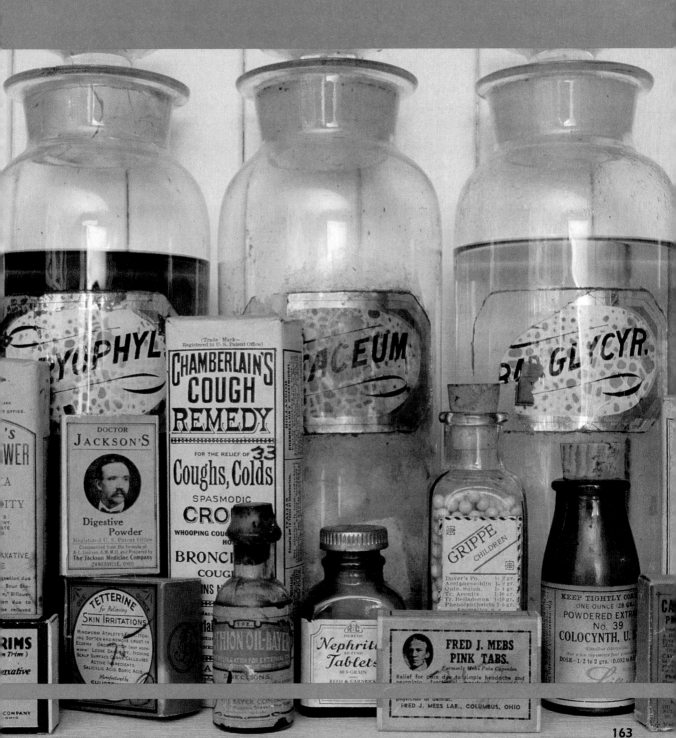

# Drugs: What You Should Know

Just as you attempt to balance the mental, physical, and social aspects of your life, your body systems work to maintain a particular chemical balance. Because drugs upset this balance, there are many facts about drugs you need to know.

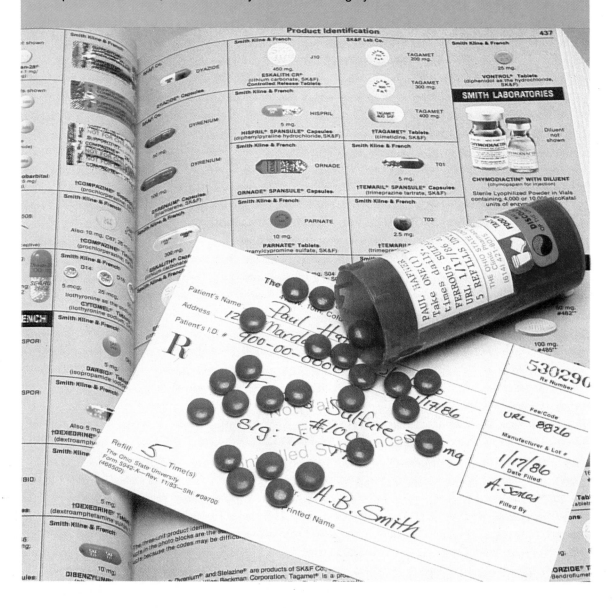

# Chapter 11

**STUDENT OBJECTIVES:** *You will be able to*

- *identify the effects of drugs on the body and describe how to be drug-free.*
- *describe the different classes of drugs and their unique characteristics.*

You are beginning to understand the importance of working toward the goal of good health. You have studied how responsible decision making helps you work toward this goal. An important area of responsible decision making is related to drugs. Studies show that more and more people are choosing to be drug-free. They know the dangers of illegal drugs. What facts should you know about drugs? How can you and others be drug-free? How can you make responsible decisions about drugs?

## Facts About Drugs

Millions of people have been helped by drugs. Drugs have been used to cure, treat, and prevent diseases. Drugs have been used to treat many different physical conditions. However, drugs have created problems when they have not been used responsibly. There are many facts you need to know about drugs. Understanding and using these facts can help you have a healthful life.

## 11:1  Drugs and the Body _____

To understand drugs, it is important to know what a drug is. A **drug** is any substance other than food that changes the way the body works. **Drug misuse** is using a drug improperly in the hopes of feeling better. For example, taking someone else's medicine is drug misuse even though one may think the medicine may be helpful. **Drug abuse** is using a drug improperly and for no medical reason. Using an illegal drug to change one's thinking is an example of drug abuse. A person who misuses or abuses drugs cannot make his or her best effort for physical, social, or mental health.

*What is drug misuse?*

For any drug to have an effect, it must get inside the body systems. There are three main ways drugs get into the body. When swallowed, drugs dissolve in stomach fluids and pass into the bloodstream from the small intestine. Drugs can be injected into a vein or directly below the skin where they are absorbed into the bloodstream. Drugs can be inhaled through the mouth or sniffed through the nose. Taken in either of these ways, drugs pass quickly from the lungs into the bloodstream. In fact, it only takes seconds for drugs that are inhaled to get to the brain and produce effects.

## 11:2 Drug Effects

Once a drug is introduced into the body, many factors determine the effects of the drug. It is important to be aware of these factors or combination of factors that may change the effects a drug may produce.

- *Dose*  The dose is the amount of the drug that is taken at any given time. A physician determines the dose of any medicine prescribed for a patient. Usually the greater the dose, the greater the effect of the drug. It is important to take the correct dose of a drug. Taking too much is dangerous.

- *Weight*  Sometimes a person's weight will determine the effect of a drug. The more a person weighs, the greater the dose needed for an effect.

- *Physical Health*  Drugs can more easily affect people in poor health than they can affect people who are in good health.

- *Expectation*  Often a drug will seem to have a greater effect because a person expects a greater effect. It is possible for people to imagine they are feeling the effects of a drug. This might happen if they swallow a substance they are told is a drug when, in fact, it is not.

*What effect does dose have on the use of a drug?*

**FIGURE 11–2.** A pharmacist will explain the directions for the use of a prescription or an over-the-counter drug.

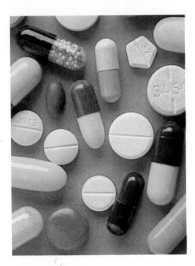

**FIGURE 11–3.** The development of some form of dependence is a hazard connected with the use of many drugs.

*What is drug tolerance?*

## 11:3 Drug Dependence

Any person who takes drugs can become dependent on them. **Drug dependence** is a mental or physical need for a drug. Chemical dependence is another name that is used for drug dependence. There are different characteristics of drug dependence. Among these are psychological (si kuh LAHJ ih kul) dependence, physical dependence, tolerance, and withdrawal.

When people take certain types of drugs again and again, they may think they need that drug. The desire to repeat the use of a drug for mental reasons is called psychological dependence. **Psychological dependence** is the mental desire for a drug. People who are psychologically dependent on a drug think the drug helps them get through the day. They believe they must have the drug to carry on certain activities. They may also think they can control their use of the drug and are not harming themselves. This conclusion is false. They harm themselves each time they take the drug.

Physical dependence on the drug may develop. **Physical dependence** is a bodily need for a drug. The drug must be present in the body for the person to feel he or she can function normally and not feel sick. This is often thought to be the most dangerous part of drug dependency because it changes the normal functioning of the body. Physical dependence makes it difficult for the drug user to stop taking the drug. Yet, each time the person takes the drug, the body and mind continue to be harmed.

**Drug tolerance** is the change in the body's response to a drug so that larger and larger doses are needed for a desired effect. Suppose a person were dependent on the drug heroin. Perhaps the person takes this drug once each day. Over a period of time, this person's body may get used to the presence of heroin once each day and show no effect. It may become necessary to take heroin twice a day to feel the desired effect. The dose would have to continue to increase over time for the person to get the same desired effect. Soon, getting heroin would be the focus of this person's life. If the person did not get heroin, withdrawal would take place.

**Withdrawal** is a condition that develops when a drug that causes physical dependence is suddenly not available. Signs and symptoms of withdrawal may be vomiting, becoming restless, losing sleep, and depression. The seriousness of the signs and symptoms depends on the type of drug used. The extent of withdrawal symptoms also depends on the length of time the drug was used. Withdrawal can be dangerous. All people withdrawing from drugs should receive medical treatment.

*What is withdrawal?*

## 11:4 Choosing to be Drug-free _____

When you choose to be drug-free, you make a choice not to misuse or abuse drugs. The choice to be drug-free depends on many factors. One factor is knowledge about drugs. By knowing facts about drugs, you understand the dangers of drug misuse and abuse. Then you are prepared to make responsible decisions.

There is another way to remain drug-free. You can choose friends who are drug-free. Studies show peer pressure is an important factor in a person's choice to not use drugs. If you choose friends who do not use drugs, most likely you will not use them. Choosing drug-free activities will also help you remain drug-free.

**FIGURE 11–4.** Just say NO to illegal drugs.

Fortunately, most of the things you do with your friends probably are healthful. However, you may experience a time when friends try to talk you into doing something you do not feel comfortable doing. If someone you know offers you drugs, use refusal skills to say NO. You can say, "I do not use drugs." You might suggest another activity, such as playing a game or riding bikes. If the person continues to pressure you to take the drugs, just walk away. Do not let anyone push you into doing something you know is wrong.

*Why are there laws against drugs?*

The laws in a country determine what drugs are legal. In some countries, penalties for the possession of even small amounts of drugs may be very severe. In the United States, there are many laws to control illegal drugs. Old laws are updated to prevent illegal drugs from being available to users. It is against the law to make, sell, possess, or grow many kinds of drugs. These laws exist to protect people from harming themselves and others. You will study about some kinds of illegal drugs later in this chapter.

# ACTIVITY

## The Drug-free Record

Imagine that you have been hired as a writer for a big record company. This company wants to produce a recording that will promote a drug-free lifestyle. You have been asked to write the song. Form a small group with three other classmates. Think of a popular song. Make up your own words to the tune of this song. Your words should describe a healthful, drug-free lifestyle. Write the words for your song onto a "record" made from a colored piece of construction paper. Sing your song for your classmates. Display your "records" in the classroom.

**Think About It**

1. Why is inhaling drugs very dangerous?
2. Why might certain drugs affect thin persons more quickly than overweight persons?
3. Why can psychological dependence be harmful to the body?
4. Why should you choose friends who are drug-free?

# Types of Drugs

Drugs can be classified as either legal or illegal. Drugs sold in stores are legal drugs. They are used to treat illnesses and diseases. Illegal drugs often have no medical use. It is against the law to purchase, sell, or use these kinds of drugs. They are harmful to health. This section describes the different types of drugs and their characteristics. It is important to remember that any drug, even medicine, can be misused or abused.

## 11:5 Drugs That Promote Health

At some time when you have been ill, you may have taken a drug to help you get well. This type of drug is a medicine. There are two types of medicines. One is called a prescription drug; the other is called an over-the-counter drug.

**Prescription drugs** are drugs that are ordered by a physician for a specific person. The prescription is prepared by a pharmacist according to what the physician ordered. The dosage prescribed is according to the person's age, weight, and general health in addition to the particular illness. Therefore, it would be dangerous for one person to take someone else's prescription drug.

*What are prescription drugs?*

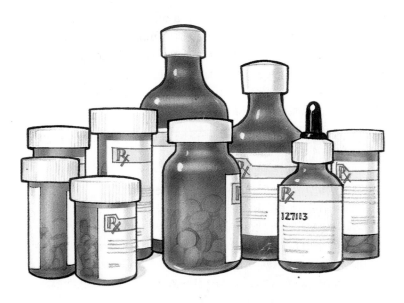

**FIGURE 11–5.** It is important that you become familiar with drugs that have been prescribed for you.

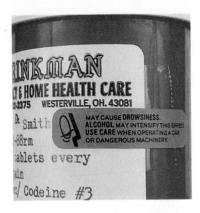

**FIGURE 11-6.** Prescription drugs are labeled to provide clear directions for their proper usage and to warn of their potential side effects.

Sometimes a prescription drug may cause a side effect. A **side effect** is an unwanted result from a drug. Examples of side effects include dizziness, rashes, and nausea. Tell your parents if you get a side effect. They will tell the physician. The physician may prescribe another drug or tell you to stop taking the drug. Table 11-1 tells what you should know about prescription drugs.

Table 11-1

| Safe Use of Prescription Drugs |
| --- |
| • Know the name of the drug. |
| • Know when and how often the drug should be taken. |
| • Know if the drug can be taken with other medicines. |
| • Know what the possible side effects are. |
| • Know if you should finish the entire medication even if you feel better. |
| • Read the label on the drug container each time to make sure you are taking the right drug. |
| • Do not take a drug prescribed for someone else. |
| • Only your parent or a health professional should give you prescription drugs. |
| • Call your physician if you get a side effect from a prescription drug. |

**Over-the-counter (OTC) drugs** are drugs that can be bought without a physician's prescription. They are sold in drugstores and other stores. These drugs are used to treat headaches and minor aches and pains. Aspirin and cough medicine are common OTC drugs.

It is important to read the label on all drugs, especially OTC drugs. The label should give the following information.

*What will the label of an OTC drug tell you?*

- the symptoms treated by the drug
- how often the drug should be taken
- the amount of the drug to be taken
- the number of days the drug should be taken
- possible side effects that might occur from taking the drug and procedures to follow if they should occur

If an OTC drug does not relieve the symptoms, the person should see a physician. This should be done to prevent a serious illness from going untreated. All OTC drugs should be taken only with the supervision of a parent or guardian. If a side effect occurs, the person should stop taking the drug. A physician should be informed if an OTC drug and a prescription drug are taken at the same time. Taking both types of drugs at the same time could cause serious problems.

## 11:6 Opiates, Depressants, and Stimulants

**Opiates** are drugs made from the opium poppy plant. Morphine and codeine are examples of opiates. Morphine is used to relieve pain. Codeine is sometimes found in cough medicine and helps control coughing. Heroin is an illegal opiate that has no medical value. Use of opiates can easily produce psychological and physical dependence as well as tolerance. Their use can also slow down body functions to the point where the heart can stop beating.

**Depressants** are a group of drugs that slow down the functions of the body so they become slower than normal. Depressants are dangerous drugs and their use can develop into physical and psychological dependence. They produce tolerance. Withdrawal from these drugs can cause serious effects. Without medical treatment, a person withdrawing from depressants may have serious health problems. Table 11–2 on page 174 gives important facts about three kinds of depressants.

**Stimulants** are drugs that speed up the functions of the body so they become faster than normal. There are many different kinds of stimulants. Some of them are described in Table 11–2. **Cocaine** is a stimulant obtained from the leaves of coca shrubs. Cocaine enters the bloodstream when it is sniffed or taken into the body by injection. Cocaine is very dangerous and easily produces physical dependence. Its effects on the body cannot be predicted. It causes the beating of the heart to become abnormal. As a result, a person using cocaine for the first time can die.

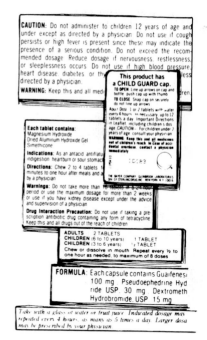

**FIGURE 11–7.** Information is provided on the packaging of over-the-counter drugs to safeguard their use.

*What are stimulants?*

The American College of Emergency Physicians issued a warning concerning the use of cocaine. The warning stated that cocaine is a highly dangerous drug that, in pure form, can kill in minutes.

**Crack** is an illegal drug made with cocaine and other unknown substances. Crack causes the same effects as cocaine but is even more dangerous. The substances added to crack are often impure and can cause a person to have convulsions. Crack can also cause death after just one use.

*Why is crack dangerous?*

Table 11–2

| Depressant Drugs | | | |
|---|---|---|---|
| **Name of Drug** | **Legal/Illegal** | **Possible Effects** | **Dependence** |
| Barbiturates (sopor) | illegal except when prescribed by a physician | slurred speech; confusion, slow breathing and heart rate; drowsiness; sleepiness; death | physical; psychological |
| Tranquilizers (Valium, Librium) | illegal except when prescribed by a physician | slurred speech; drowsiness, headaches, death | physical; psychological |
| Alcohol | legal | impaired coordination, nausea, death | physical; psychological |
| **Stimulant Drugs** | | | |
| Amphetamines (Benzedrine, Methedrine) | illegal except when prescribed by a physician | increased breathing rate, heart rate, and blood pressure; heart damage; death | psychological |
| Cocaine (Crack) | illegal | damage to nasal lining, restlessness; increased breathing rate, heart rate, and blood pressure; excitability | physical; psychological |
| Caffeine | legal | increased heart rate; restlessness; irritability | physical; psychological |
| Nicotine | legal | increased heart rate and blood pressure | physical; psychological |

## 11:7　Hallucinogens

A **hallucinogen** (huh LEWS un uh jun) is an illegal drug that changes how a person's brain works. A person may have the experience of seeing, hearing, smelling, or feeling things that do not exist. Although hallucinogens do not produce physical dependence, they may cause psychological dependence and produce tolerance. Some of the common drugs of this type are LSD, PCP, and mescaline.

Hallucinogens may have different effects on people. Three people may use the same dose of a hallucinogen and they each would have a different reaction. Some may experience hearing sounds that do not exist. Others may think they are touching something when they are not. Later, they may get flashbacks. This means that they may see things that do not exist months or years after they have taken the drug. Hallucinogens are extremely dangerous drugs. Their use can result in violent behavior. People who use hallucinogens can harm themselves and others.

## 11:8　Marijuana

**Marijuana** (mer uh WAHN uh) is a drug made from the crushed leaves, flowers, seeds, and stems of the hemp plant. Except in some cases where marijuana can be used in medicine, this drug is illegal. Its effect on the body depends on the amount of THC present. THC is a harmful ingredient in marijuana that causes many of the effects. The effects of short-term marijuana use vary. Some of these include shaky hands, clumsiness, and memory loss. The harmful effects of this drug can last for eight hours.

The effects of long-term marijuana use are more dangerous. Marijuana is fat-soluble and can stay in the body cells for weeks. It also can produce dependence as well as tolerance. Long-term use can result in personality changes. A person who has repeatedly used marijuana will lack a willingness to perform tasks. This person may show a lack of concern for the future and have no goals. Marijuana also affects the ability to remember even simple things.

*What is a hallucinogen?*

---

**Effects of Marijuana Use**
- damages lung tissue; reduces breathing capacity
- increases heart rate
- reduces oxygen supply to the heart
- interferes with thinking and learning
- slows reaction time
- causes loss of coordination
- causes confusion, anxiety and fear
- causes lack of ambition
- possibly harms a pregnant woman's developing baby

**FIGURE 11–8.** Marijuana is a dangerous and illegal drug.

Marijuana can also harm the lungs. Studies show that marijuana smoke contains more harmful products than cigarette smoke. Because marijuana smoke is held deep in the lungs for long periods of time, lung tissue can be destroyed.

## 11:9 Designer Drugs

**Designer drugs** are drugs that imitate the effects of other drugs. These drugs are produced in homemade labs. These drugs might be much more powerful than the drugs they imitate. The results of using these drugs are unpredictable. Permanent damage to the brain and even death may result.

Unlike legal drugs, designer drugs are not tested on animals in a lab. People who use designer drugs are somewhat like the lab animals. They are the ones upon whom experimentation takes place. When these drugs are used, the results are not known in many cases until it is too late.

**Think About It**

5. Why can taking any illegal drug be harmful?
6. Why are opiates depressant drugs?
7. Why is cocaine, used even once, very dangerous?
8. Why might a person who uses a hallucinogen do something foolish?
9. Why should a person never smoke marijuana?
10. Why might designer drugs be even more dangerous than the drugs they imitate?

## Life Skills

▶ Use your knowledge about drugs to be drug-free.
▶ Choose drug-free friends.
▶ Never misuse or abuse any kind of drug.
▶ Know how to read drug labels on prescription and OTC drugs.
▶ Tell your parents if you have a side effect from a medicine.

# Chapter 11 Review

**Summary**

1. Drugs are harmful when they are misused or abused. *11:1*
2. Dose, weight, physical health, and expectation are factors that influence drug effects. *11:2*
3. Drug misuse and abuse can lead to psychological and physical dependence and can result in tolerance. *11:3*
4. Knowing about drugs and choosing friends who are drug-free will help you be drug-free. *11:4*
5. Prescription and OTC drugs can be both helpful and harmful. *11:5*
6. Morphine, codeine, and heroin are opiates. *11:6*
7. Depressant drugs include barbiturates and tranquilizers; stimulant drugs include crack and cocaine. *11:6*
8. Hallucinogens are harmful drugs that can produce psychological dependence and tolerance. *11:7*
9. Marijuana is a dangerous and illegal drug. *11:8*
10. Designer drugs can cause harmful and unknown effects. *11:9*

*Complete each sentence with the correct word.*
*DO NOT WRITE IN THIS BOOK.*

**Words for Health**

crack
depressants
designer drugs
drug
drug abuse
drug dependence
drug tolerance
hallucinogen

marijuana
opiates
over-the-counter drugs
physical dependence
prescription drugs
side effect
stimulants
withdrawal

1. Drugs that increase body activities are called ____.
2. PCP is an example of a(n) ____.
3. Morphine and heroin are examples of ____.
4. The effects the ____ will produce often cannot be predicted.
5. A(n) ____ is the general name given for any substance that changes the way a person thinks or feels.
6. ____ is a drug that comes from the hemp plant.
7. Restlessness and an inability to sleep are signs of ____.

8. Legal drugs for which a prescription is not needed are ____.
9. ____ are drugs that slow down body activities.
10. A person who has developed ____ will need increased doses to get an effect.
11. A person with a mental or physical need for a drug is experiencing ____.
12. ____ are drugs that are ordered by a physician for a specific person.
13. Using a drug improperly for no medical reason is an example of ____.
14. A rash is an example of a(n) ____, or an unwanted result after taking a drug.
15. ____ is an illegal drug made from cocaine and other unknown substances.

**Reviewing Health**

1. How do drug misuse and abuse differ?
2. What are the three main ways drugs get into the body?
3. What are four factors that determine the effects drugs will have on the body?
4. Why is it important to take the correct dose of a drug as prescribed by a physician?
5. What are the different characteristics that describe drug dependence?
6. Why is medical treatment necessary for people who are withdrawing from drugs?
7. What is one way to remain drug-free?
8. Why is it dangerous for you to take someone else's prescription drug?
9. What are some examples of side effects?
10. What are three examples of opiates?
11. What effect do depressants have on the body?
12. Why is crack a dangerous drug?
13. What are the three common types of hallucinogens and the dangers of using them?
14. How does marijuana use affect memory?
15. How is long-term marijuana use dangerous?
16. Why are designer drugs dangerous?

*Use the life skills from this chapter to respond to the following questions.*

*Situation:* Your friend calls you to get together and watch a video. You tell your friend that you want to study for a test about drugs. Your friends says, "There's no need to study for a test about drugs. Drug information is not important anyway."

1. Why is it important to know information about drugs?
2. What can you do to convince your friend that the information about drugs is important?

*Situation:* You have an infection and the physician has prescribed a drug for you. You notice that, after taking the drug, you begin to feel dizzy. You think the dizziness is due to your illness.

1. What might be the cause of your dizziness?
2. Should you continue to take the drug? Explain.
3. What might your physician do about the drug that was prescribed for you?

1. States have different laws about drugs. Research information about drug laws in your state and write the main points about the laws you should know.
2. There are many careers in the drug field such as drug counselor, drug educator, and pharmacist. Select one of these careers and describe what the responsibilities are. Describe the career training that is needed.
3. Make a list of the different drug commercials you see on TV during one week. Which types of drugs are advertised most often? Why do you think they are advertised so often? Which of these drugs do you have in your home? What anti-drug commercials did you see during the same week? Which anti-drug commercials, if any, have had an effect on you?
4. All drugs must be tested and meet certain government standards before they are sold. Write a drug company for information about standards and testing.

# Alcohol

Fruits, vegetables, and grains can be used to make alcoholic products. Alcohol is produced by yeast cells that use the sugar in fruits, vegetables, and grains for food.

# Chapter 12

Think about the many different movies you have seen at school, in a theater, or at home. Perhaps you have seen movies that showed life during the times of the Roman Empire. Perhaps you have seen movies that showed life during the Civil War or when pioneers were settling in the American West. Regardless of the period in history, you might have noticed a common element in the different lifestyles. You may have seen people drinking alcohol. Alcohol has been used throughout history. Alcohol has also caused problems throughout history.

## Alcohol and Health

There are many false ideas about alcohol. The following are some of these ideas.

- Alcohol is not a dangerous drug.
- A person cannot become dependent on alcohol.
- Anyone can easily stop drinking if he or she so chooses.

You will study many facts about alcohol in this chapter. These facts will help you tell the difference between true and false ideas concerning alcohol.

**FIGURE 12–1.** Ethyl alcohol is formed when yeast cells act upon grains, fruits, and vegetables.

## 12:1   What Is Alcohol?

**Alcohol** is a depressant drug found in beer, wine, whiskey, wine coolers, and some other kinds of beverages. It may be the most abused drug in our country today. Alcohol is illegal for those who are under a certain age. This age is determined by state laws. However, in every state it is against the law for someone your age to drink alcohol.

*What products contain alcohol?*

There are many kinds of alcohol. Two familiar kinds are ethyl (ETH ul) alcohol or grain alcohol and methyl (METH ul) alcohol. **Ethyl alcohol** is a beverage made from the action of yeast cells on grains, fruits, and vegetables. **Methyl alcohol** is made from wood products and other substances. This poisonous kind of alcohol is found in paint thinner and shellac. A person who drinks methyl alcohol will die.

Different kinds of beverages that contain alcohol have varying amounts of alcohol. **Proof** is a word used to represent the amount of alcohol in a beverage. The proof of a beverage is double the percent of its alcohol content. For example, if a drink is 80 proof, it contains 40 percent alcohol. The higher the proof, the greater the amount of alcohol in a drink.

Beer and wine coolers contain from three to six percent alcohol. Wine contains about 12 percent alcohol. Brandy, gin, vodka, and rum may contain as much as 50 percent alcohol. The greater the amount of alcohol in a drink, the faster the effects of alcohol will be noticed. Any amount of alcohol is harmful for someone your age.

## 12:2   Determining the Effects of Alcohol

Suppose two people drank the same amount of alcohol. Each may be affected differently. There are factors that determine the effects alcohol will have on a person.

*Amount consumed*   The more a person drinks, the greater the effect.

*Rate consumed*   The faster a person finishes a drink, the quicker the effect.

*Rate absorbed in the bloodstream*   Most of the alcohol a person drinks is absorbed into the bloodstream from the stomach and small intestine. **Blood alcohol level** is the amount of alcohol in a person's blood. Alcohol will enter the bloodstream more quickly if there is no food in the stomach. If a person has eaten before drinking, food in the stomach will absorb some of the alcohol.

*Body weight*   The more a person weighs, the slower the effect of alcohol. Suppose persons who weigh 100 pounds and 200 pounds each have a drink that contains the same amount of alcohol. The lighter-weight person will be more affected because he or she will have a higher blood alcohol level sooner.

*Expectations*   Some people expect a certain feeling from alcohol. These people think, for example, that alcohol will make them act silly and have a good time. They may then act silly regardless of how much alcohol they consume. Some people may even act silly if they think they have been given alcohol when they have not.

*Tolerance*   People who drink alcohol may build a tolerance to this drug. They may need to increase the amount of alcohol they drink to have the same effects. The development of tolerance can be rapid or gradual.

*What is blood alcohol level?*

**FIGURE 12-2.** The breathalyzer measures the amount of alcohol in a person's blood.

## 12:3 Mental and Social Effects

Alcohol is harmful to persons of any age. It prevents them from reaching optimum mental and social health. There are different ways in which alcohol affects mental and social health.

*Solving Problems* As you grow older, you learn to accept more responsibilities. For example, you are expected to achieve more in school or you may be asked to help with more difficult tasks at home. You will be developing skills that challenge your thinking. Drinking interferes with your ability to think clearly and act responsibly.

*Relationships with Friends* Often, people drink because of peer pressure. They may be among friends who are drinking who say, "Why don't you drink and have fun like us?" Perhaps some people feel they may not be included in a group if they do not drink with the people in it. Friends may try to convince others that drinking is a social thing to do. But the fact remains that drinking is not a responsible social activity. Drinking provides a false sense of security. It prevents people from learning to get along with others in a social situation. Drinking interferes with a person's ability to learn social skills.

*How can drinking interfere with friendship?*

**FIGURE 12–3.** Responsible social skills are learned without using alcohol.

*Achieving Goals*   Most people think about and plan for their future. Some may think about the grades they will be getting this year. Others may consider the type of work they would like to do as an adult. People have the ability to achieve their present goals and future goals. However, the use of alcohol will interfere with or prevent people from reaching their goals.

*Crime*   Crime has become a major health problem. People become injured due to violent actions. Many of these violent actions involve alcohol. There is a saying, "Alcohol brings out the worst in people." Violent actions are examples of the worst in people.

## 12:4   Physical Effects of Alcohol

Suppose you had just eaten. Your digestive system would change the food so it can be used by your body. It would take about eight hours for the food to be thoroughly digested. Alcohol does not go through the digestive process. It begins to enter the bloodstream soon after a person drinks it. It takes only several minutes before alcohol travels to the brain and affects body activities. There is an interference of messages from the brain to the muscles. Simple tasks such as walking and running become more difficult. The risk of becoming injured increases.

*How does alcohol affect muscles?*

**FIGURE 12–4**. When people use alcohol, it interferes with messages from the brain to the muscles.

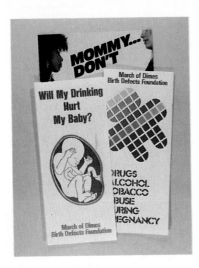

**FIGURE 12–5**. Women who are pregnant are advised not to drink alcohol.

*What is fetal alcohol syndrome?*

Alcohol also gives a false sense of feeling warm. Alcohol causes blood vessels near the surface of the skin to expand. A person drinking alcohol may feel warmer, however, body heat is being lost. Lowered body temperature in cold weather may threaten health if the person is not aware of conditions that cause frostbite.

Alcohol may harm some body organs. Alcohol increases acid production in the stomach that can harm the stomach linings. Long-term drinking also harms the liver. It is a main cause of cirrhosis (suh ROH sus). **Cirrhosis** is a disease in which liver cells are destroyed due to the use of alcohol.

Alcohol use is also related to cancer of the mouth and throat. Risk of these types of cancers increases when alcohol use is combined with tobacco use. This includes both the use of cigarettes and smokeless tobacco.

Alcohol use has become a major concern among pregnant women. Studies show that there is a danger when a pregnant woman drinks alcohol. She increases her risk of having a baby born with fetal alcohol syndrome. **Fetal alcohol syndrome (FAS)** is a condition in which a baby is born with birth defects caused by the mother's drinking during pregnancy. Women are advised not to drink alcohol when they are pregnant.

There are important facts to know about using alcohol and other drugs at the same time.

- A person taking over-the-counter drugs should not drink alcohol.
- Alcohol should not be used with prescription drugs.
- The effects of alcohol are increased when it is combined with another drug.

**Think About It**

1. What is the relationship between the proof of liquor and its effects on the body?
2. Why would a heavier person not feel the effects of alcohol as quickly as a person of lower weight?
3. Why should a pregnant woman not drink alcohol?
4. Why is it important to choose friends who do not drink?

## Alcohol and Behavior

Will drinking alcohol ever become a problem for you? This is a question that people must ask themselves before they choose to drink. People cannot forecast whether or not they are at great risk of having problems related to drinking. Drinking alcohol is a major health concern for all persons. The use of alcohol affects body chemistry and the ability to enjoy many activities. Drinking is against parental rules and most likely will result in feeling a lack of respect. You will not have self-respect and others will not respect you.

## 12:5 Progression of Abusive Drinking ___

**Abusive drinking** is drinking alcohol in a manner that is not responsible. If you were to drink just once, you would abuse alcohol. This is because it is illegal for someone your age to drink. A person who drinks and drives abuses alcohol. A person who gets drunk abuses alcohol. Abusive drinking may occur just once or it may occur repeatedly for months or even years. Abusive drinking can also lead to dependency on alcohol. Dependency on alcohol develops through different stages.

*What is abusive drinking?*

**FIGURE 12–6.** A person who drinks and drives abuses alcohol.

**FIGURE 12–7.** For good health, choose a lifestyle without alcohol.

*What is alcoholism?*

*Experimentation*   A person will not have a drinking problem if he or she never takes a drink. Today there is an increase in the number of teenagers who decide not to try alcohol. However, some young people are curious about alcohol. They may be influenced by ads or by peers and they will try alcohol. Experimenting is the first step in alcohol dependency.

*Mood Change*   When a person drinks, he or she feels the effects of this depressant drug. At first, a pleasant mood may result. This is because the part of the brain that thinks seriously becomes relaxed. A person may then drink greater amounts hoping to experience even more of a relaxed feeling. This is the beginning of a drinking problem.

*Intoxication*   **Intoxication** is the state of being drunk. The amount of alcohol needed to become drunk varies with each individual. Being drunk causes more physical and mental changes. Again, the changes vary among people. One person may be very depressed and withdrawn. Another may be angry and loud. Most persons who are drunk do not feel well. Later, they may have a hangover. A **hangover** is the sick feeling a person has the day after drinking too much. A person may have symptoms such as a headache and nausea. A **blackout** is a period in which a person cannot remember what he or she has said or done. Anyone who has had one blackout has a drinking problem.

*Chemical Dependence*   A person who becomes chemically dependent on alcohol can no longer function without this harmful drug. He or she will have some physical symptoms such as illusions, shaking, and nausea. Medical help is always needed when a person has a dependency on alcohol. **Alcoholism** is a disease in which a person is chemically dependent on alcohol. It can be treated and controlled but not cured. A person treated for alcoholism should *never* drink alcohol again.

Alcohol is a harmful and dangerous drug. Remember, you are responsible for your own actions. The best choice for health is to say NO to drinking alcohol. Choosing a lifestyle without alcohol is a rewarding and responsible decision.

## 12:6 How Drinking Affects Families

It is often said that alcoholism is a family disease. One family member's abusive drinking can affect all other family members. It can cause feelings of anxiety, anger, violence, guilt, isolation, and embarrassment or shame.

*Anxiety* Family members become anxious over an abusive drinker's behavior. They may not be able to perform daily tasks easily because they worry about the person's drinking. They may be confused because they do not know how to cope with the person's drinking problem.

*Anger* Family members may become angry over an abusive drinker's behavior. Young people may become angry at a parent who has a drinking problem. They may express their anger to other family members, friends, or to people at school. Parents may express their anger to each other or to other people when a son or daughter is an abusive drinker.

*Violence* Sometimes the anger caused in a family by an abusive drinker's behavior is expressed in violence. The violence can come from the abusive drinker. It can be directed toward members of the person's family. Sometimes the abusive drinker's behavior can cause violence in other members of the family. This violence can result in harmful behaviors.

*Why is alcoholism often called a family disease?*

**FIGURE 12–8.** Drinking problems can affect people who live in any neighborhood.

189

*Guilt*   Often family members feel they are the cause of abusive drinking. They may also feel guilty because they cannot help the person stop the abusive drinking. One or more family members may play the role of an enabler. An **enabler** is a person who takes actions that help someone continue a destructive behavior. The enabler for an abusive drinker makes excuses for the abusive drinker's actions. Being an enabler is not helpful to an abusive drinker or to the enabler.

*Isolation*   Family members may feel alone or neglected. If the abusive drinker is a parent, it is difficult for him or her to care for the child's needs and the child will feel neglected. The other parent may feel alone because the abusive drinker also may neglect his or her needs. If the child is the abusive drinker, the parents may feel isolated from other parents or friends whose children do not have a drinking problem.

*Embarrassment or Shame*   Family members may feel ashamed of the abusive drinker. Children may not feel comfortable bringing friends home because a parent drinks. Family members may lie or make excuses to other people to hide the abusive drinker's problem.

*How can a person who abuses alcohol affect a child?*

## 12:7   Help for the Abusive Drinker ──────

When there is an abusive drinker in the family, help is needed. Alcoholism is a disease that will not go away by the actions of family members. Families can seek help from different sources.

*Health Professionals*   A physician or a religious leader can give or recommend counseling. Community health agencies also have skilled people who can provide counseling for both the abusive drinker and the family.

*People at School*   The principal, school nurse, guidance counselor, and health teacher can give suggestions for ways to get help.

*Alcohol Programs*   **Alcoholics Anonymous (AA)** is an organization for abusive drinkers. The members recognize their drinking problems and discuss them at the meetings. They give each other support so they will not drink.

**FIGURE 12–9**. Activities are enjoyed more when alcohol is not used.

**Alateen** is a treatment organization for teenage children of abusive drinkers. **Al-Anon** is an organization that helps family members of abusive drinkers. Members of Alateen and Al-Anon learn how they can help the abusive drinker. They also learn how to handle their own lives when affected by another person's drinking.

## 12:8  Choosing to be Alcohol-free

According to the responsible decision-making model, you have learned the following about alcohol.

- It is not safe.
- It is not healthful.
- It is illegal to drink at your age.
- Choosing to drink will go against your parents' rules.
- Choosing to drink shows a lack of self-respect.

You can control your actions. You never need to have a problem with abusive drinking.

- Avoid being in places with friends where alcohol is used.
- Use refusal skills to say NO to using alcohol.
- Communicate your thoughts with parents to encourage family support.
- Get involved in healthful activities in school and at home.

**FIGURE 12–10.** You can choose to say NO to alcohol.

Saying NO to alcohol influences your peers in healthful ways. When your friends know that you do not drink and that others cannot influence you, it makes it easier for your friends to say NO.

Remember, alcohol brings out the worst in you by hiding the best in you. Choose an alcohol-free lifestyle. Say NO to alcohol.

## ACTIVITY

### Being Alcohol-free

Imagine that you have taken a job at a publishing company as a designer of book covers. The company will be publishing a book about the joys of being alcohol-free. This book will be used in schools across the country. Use a sheet of paper that would be large enough to wrap around this textbook. Design a cover for this book that will match the theme of being alcohol-free. Develop a catchy title. Give some information that will attract people to read the book. Draw pictures. Use the front and back parts of the cover. Display your book cover in class.

**Think About It**

**5.** Why should people your age not experiment with alcohol?

**6.** Why does drinking harm family relationships?

**7.** Why is the community a good source of help for a person who is an abusive drinker and for the family of an abusive drinker?

**8.** What can you do to avoid ever having a problem with alcohol?

## — Life Skills —

► Do not experiment with alcohol.

► Be aware of the dangers that result when alcohol is used with medications.

► Be able to identify community resources that can be used to get help for a person who has problems related to alcohol.

# Chapter 12 Review

1. Two kinds of alcohol are ethyl and methyl alcohol. *12:1*
2. Among the factors that determine the effects of alcohol are amount consumed, rate consumed, rate absorbed in the bloodstream, body weight, expectations, and tolerance. *12:2*
3. Alcohol interferes with the ability to learn social skills. *12:3*
4. Alcohol use can result in cirrhosis, fetal alcohol syndrome, and many other harmful effects. *12:4*
5. Experimenting with alcohol, even once, can lead to alcoholism. *12:5*
6. A family member who has a drinking problem will affect other family members. *12:6*
7. Community resources such as Alcoholics Anonymous can be useful in helping people who abuse alcohol. *12:7*
8. The most responsible decision a person your age can make about alcohol is *not* to drink. *12:8*

**Summary**

---

*Complete each sentence with the correct word.*
*DO NOT WRITE IN THIS BOOK.*

**Words for Health**

abusive drinking
Al-Anon
Alateen
alcohol
Alcoholics Anonymous (AA)
alcoholism
blackout
blood alcohol level

cirrhosis
enabler
ethyl alcohol
fetal alcohol syndrome (FAS)
hangover
intoxication
methyl alcohol
proof

1. An example of _____ is getting drunk.
2. The amount of alcohol in a drink is measured by its _____.
3. A pregnant woman who drinks may have a baby born with _____.
4. _____ is a kind of alcohol that can easily cause death.
5. Another term for the state of being drunk is _____.
6. A person who abuses alcohol and who feels sick afterward is said to have a(n) _____.
7. _____ is an organization that can help a person who abuses alcohol.

8. The amount of alcohol in a person's body is measured by _____.

9. A disease of the liver caused by alcohol is _____.

10. The kind of alcohol that is found in certain beverages is _____.

11. A depressant drug found in beer, wine, and whiskey is _____.

12. A(n) _____ is a period in which a person cannot remember what he or she has said or done.

13. Teenage children of abusive drinkers may receive treatment through _____.

14. A(n) _____ is a person who takes actions that help someone continue a destructive behavior.

15. _____ is an organization that helps family members of abusive drinkers.

---

**Reviewing Health**

1. What are two different kinds of alcohol?
2. What is the meaning of 40 proof?
3. What are six factors that determine the effects of alcohol on a person's body?
4. How does a person's weight help determine how he or she will be affected by alcohol?
5. In what areas does alcohol affect mental and social health?
6. How might drinking alcohol affect relationships with friends?
7. What is the relationship between alcohol and crime?
8. How might a person drinking alcohol in cold weather threaten his or her health?
9. How does alcohol affect the liver?
10. Why should pregnant women avoid drinking alcohol?
11. What are the stages in the development of alcohol dependency?
12. Why is it important for someone your age to not experiment with alcohol?
13. Why might an abusive drinker cause a family member's school grades to drop?
14. Why are the actions of an enabler not helpful?
15. What community resources are available to help an abusive drinker?
16. What is the way to be alcohol-free?

*Use the life skills from this chapter to respond to the following questions.*

*Situation:* An adult you know has to take medication daily for a health problem. He has been told not to drink alcohol when taking this medication. One night at a dinner, this person is offered alcohol.

1. What other beverage could he choose to drink?
2. Why is it important for this person to know that the effects of alcohol will be increased when it is combined with another drug?

*Situation:* Your friend tells you that there is a problem in her family. A family member is an abusive drinker.

1. Why is it important for your friend to ask for help?
2. What are some resources in the community that can help your friend and your friend's family?

*Situation:* You and a friend are at a party. Some of the people are drinking beer. They are trying to talk you and your friend into having one also. Your friend says, "Let's try it. One bottle of beer won't hurt us."

1. What response would you give your friend?
2. What choices of other responsible actions would you give your friend?

1. Write to agencies in your community that are concerned about alcohol abuse. You can find the addresses of these agencies in your telephone book. Ask for free materials such as brochures. Collect your materials and share them in class.
2. Design an advertisement that emphasizes the dangers of drinking. Use this advertisement to encourage people your age not to drink. Use artwork and exciting comments.
3. Read the newspaper or listen to the news to find stories about crimes or accidents that are related to alcohol abuse. Discuss these incidents in class.
4. Research diseases that are a result of alcohol abuse, such as cirrhosis or fetal alcohol syndrome. Find out the signs, symptoms, and the effects on the body. Make a chart to organize your information.

# Tobacco

Smoking cigarettes is a behavior that can prove to be deadly, or disabling at the very least. How can the cigarette smoke from others affect you? What precautions can you take to avoid the dangers of cigarette smoke?

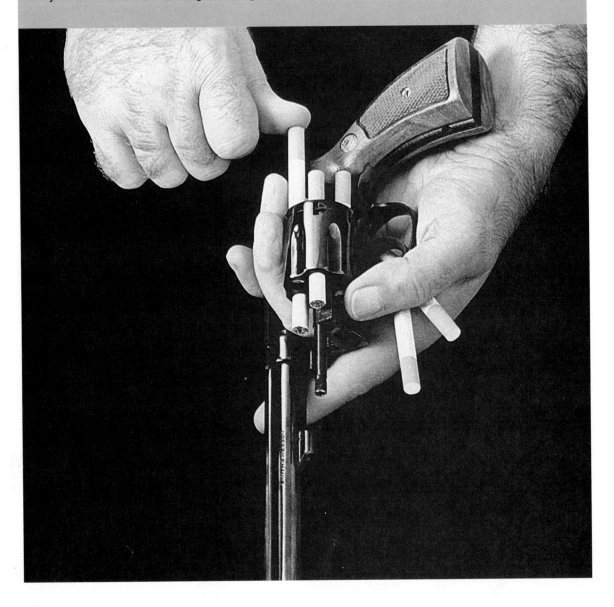

# Chapter 13

- *describe the harmful effects of tobacco on health.*
- *discuss the actions being taken to help people avoid the harmful effects of tobacco products.*

Suppose a friend asks you to try something that would do the following.

- cause you to cough
- cause your eyes to tear
- cause your breath, clothes, and hair to smell bad
- most likely shorten your life

What your friend asked you to do was smoke a cigarette. If you are like most people, you would say NO to avoid these unpleasant effects. Most people have chosen not to use tobacco. The number of people who are choosing to be tobacco-free is increasing every day. They are saying NO to tobacco and YES to good health.

## Tobacco and Health

Thousands of people are alive today who might otherwise be dead. These people are alive because they quit smoking. Cigarette smoking is the number one cause of preventable death. The facts are clear. Do not begin to smoke.

## 13:1 Tobacco: A Drug ————————

Cigarette smoke has over 1000 substances that are harmful to the body. These substances can cause physical and mental dependence. Tolerance may also develop from the effects of the substances.

*What is nicotine?*

One harmful substance in tobacco that causes mental and physical dependence is nicotine. **Nicotine** is a colorless, oily stimulant in tobacco. This drug enters the bloodstream from the lungs after smoke is inhaled. Throughout this chapter, you will study how nicotine affects health.

Like other stimulant drugs, nicotine causes physical changes and dependence because the body gets used to its effects. When the body does not have enough nicotine, withdrawal occurs. A person may become irritated easily and find it hard to sleep. To temporarily reduce the effects of withdrawal from nicotine, a person will begin to smoke again. It is very difficult for a person to stop smoking once he or she starts. It may feel easier to postpone the effort to stop smoking.

As with other drugs, some people will continue to smoke because they think smoking has benefits. Perhaps they feel smoking makes them look important. They may think smoking reduces boredom by giving them something to do with their hands. These are poor excuses for smoking. There are healthful substitutes for smoking.

## ACTIVITY

### Health Pack

Make a box that is shaped like a cigarette pack. Draw a label to place over your pack. Develop a creative name for your cigarettes that shows good health. For example, you may name your "cigarette pack" Healthful Tips. Take five sheets of paper, each about two or three inches long and the length of a cigarette. Write one healthful thing to do instead of smoking on each sheet. Roll each sheet into the shape of a cigarette and place it in your pack. Use tape to hold your "cigarette" together. Share your "Healthful Tips" with the class.

## 13:2 Smoking and the Circulatory System ⎯⎯⎯⎯⎯⎯⎯⎯⎯⎯⎯⎯

Suppose a person's resting heart rate is 65 beats per minute. If that person smoked a cigarette, his or her heart rate would increase to between 80 and 85 beats per minute. The increase is primarily due to nicotine. This means smoking a cigarette would cause his or her heart to work harder than it would at rest. Smoking puts an added stress on the heart. This added stress increases the risk of developing heart disease. Heart disease is a leading cause of death in the United States.

Nicotine also raises blood pressure. High blood pressure increases the risk of harm to the blood vessels. High blood pressure increases the risk of heart attack.

Cigarette smoke also contains carbon monoxide. **Carbon monoxide** is a colorless and odorless gas that acts as a poison in the body. The increased carbon monoxide is carried through the bloodstream. Carbon monoxide replaces oxygen in the body when a person smokes. Thus, the heart begins to beat faster so the body cells can get enough oxygen. Many researchers believe that carbon monoxide from cigarette smoke also causes harm to the arteries.

*How does nicotine affect blood pressure?*

**FIGURE 13-1**. A healthy heart (a) can be damaged by smoking (b).

a

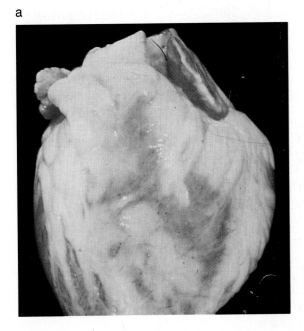

b

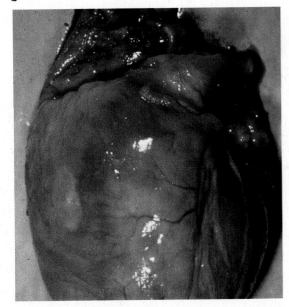

## 13:3 Smoking and the Respiratory System

The next time you go to a restaurant, observe what happens in the smoking section. Most likely, you will hear people coughing. You will not hear as many people coughing in the nonsmoking section. Coughing is a result of smoking. There is a reason people who smoke often cough. Cilia (SIHL ee uh) in the throat help keep the respiratory system clean. **Cilia** are hair-like structures that trap dust and other particles that get into the air passage. Smoke inhaled from a cigarette causes the cilia to work poorly or become paralyzed. The cilia cannot trap these substances and move them from the air passage. A person must cough to force them out of the body. However, coughing is not as effective as the function of cilia. If harmful substances reach the lungs, a respiratory infection may result. Research shows that people who smoke get more respiratory infections than those who don't.

Another harmful substance in cigarette smoke is tar. **Tar** is a thick, sticky substance that is produced from burning tobacco. When a smoker inhales tobacco smoke, tar remains in the lungs. The tar irritates the lining of the lungs. This irritation can result in lung cancer. The longer a person smokes, the greater the amount of tar that will build up in the lungs. This increases the risks of getting lung cancer.

*How do cilia help protect you?*

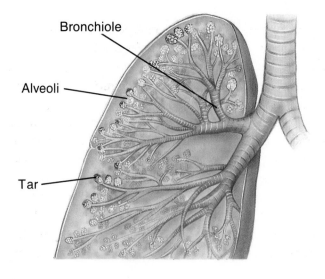

Bronchiole

Alveoli

Tar

**FIGURE 13-2.** Tar produced from burning tobacco sticks to the lungs of a person who smokes.

There are two other lung diseases that are common in smokers. **Pulmonary** (PUL muh ner ee) **emphysema** (em fuh SEE muh) is a disease in which the alveoli in the lungs lose their ability to work. Oxygen does not pass into the bloodstream easily. A person who has this disease gets out of breath from doing simple tasks like walking. His or her heart has to work very hard to supply oxygen throughout the body. **Chronic** (KRAHN ihk) **bronchitis** (brahn KITE us) is an inflammation of the bronchial tubes. The tubes become filled with mucus. The smoker must cough to remove the mucus. Coughing interferes with normal breathing. The more a person coughs, the more the cilia and bronchial tubes are harmed. People with pulmonary emphysema and chronic bronchitis are more likely to develop other respiratory diseases.

It is important to understand that smokers can increase their chances of good health whenever they quit smoking. When they quit, they lower their risks of developing lung and heart disease.

**FIGURE 13–3.** Mucus is magnified by an electron microscope.

*What is pulmonary emphysema?*

## 13:4 Other Aspects of Smoking and Health

Negative effects start the first time people smoke cigarettes no matter what age they are. Damage to the heart and lungs begins immediately. Nicotine reaches the brain in about seven seconds after being inhaled. There is no safe age to start to smoke.

Smoking is not socially accepted today. Smoking causes the breath to smell and the teeth to become yellow. A smoker's clothing and hair hold the odor of smoke even when he or she is not smoking. The smell of smoke is offensive to many people.

Studies show that a pregnant woman who smokes may harm her developing baby. Some of the harmful products in cigarette smoke such as carbon monoxide and nicotine can enter the bloodstream of the developing baby. Babies born to mothers who smoke weigh less than babies born to mothers who do not smoke. The less a baby weighs, the greater the risk to the baby's health. For this reason, pregnant women are warned not to smoke.

## 13:5 Smokeless Tobacco

*What is smokeless tobacco?*

**Smokeless tobacco** is tobacco that is placed inside the mouth and is not smoked. There are different kinds of smokeless tobacco. Chewing tobacco is made up of chopped tobacco leaves that are placed between the gum and cheek. Snuff is a powdered tobacco that is also placed between the gum and cheek. Some people believe that smokeless tobacco is safe to use because it is not smoked. These people think that since no harmful products are inhaled, the body will not be harmed. But the truth is that smokeless tobacco is dangerous.

*What are some harmful substances in smokeless tobacco?*

Like the tobacco in cigarettes, smokeless tobacco contains nicotine. Nicotine can enter the bloodstream through the lining of the mouth. Nicotine from smokeless tobacco affects the body in the same ways when chewed as when smoked. A person can easily become dependent upon smokeless tobacco. People who use it have a difficult time giving up this habit.

Smokeless tobacco contains many other harmful products. For example, it has small bits of sand in it. This causes the enamel on teeth to wear away. Smokeless tobacco also contains sugar. When the tobacco is kept between the gum and cheek, the sugar stays on the teeth. The sugar causes tooth decay. Leaving smokeless tobacco in one place in the mouth causes the gums to pull away from the teeth. If the gums pull away, the roots of the teeth will not be protected. This causes the teeth to fall out.

**FIGURE 13–4.** Smokeless tobacco is made from tobacco leaves.

**FIGURE 13–5.** Smokeless tobacco is dangerous to oral health.

People do not always like to be around others who use smokeless tobacco. It causes the teeth to become yellow and the breath to smell. Also, people who use smokeless tobacco need to spit often. The tobacco causes an increase in the saliva in the mouth. This saliva contains harmful tobacco products. If the saliva is swallowed, these products get into the body and can cause damage.

Studies show that there is a strong relationship between the use of smokeless tobacco and the development of cancer of the mouth and throat. The tobacco irritates the mouth linings. These linings will become hard and rough. This is similar to the formation of a callus. If you were digging dirt or shoveling snow, you might see a callus or rough area on the inside of your hand. However, a rough area in the mouth differs. It can develop into cancer.

Smokeless tobacco is dangerous. It is not a safe substitute for cigarettes.

*How does smokeless tobacco affect the lining of the mouth?*

1. In what way is nicotine like other harmful drugs?
2. Why is smoking particularly dangerous to people who have high blood pressure?
3. Why do smokers cough more often than nonsmokers?
4. Why is it socially unacceptable to smoke?
5. Why is the use of chewing tobacco considered dangerous?

**Think About It**

**FIGURE 13–6.** A person who gives up smoking gains health benefits.

## Smoking and Behavior

People have a right to breathe fresh air and to protect their health. People can use their rights to avoid the harmful effects of cigarettes. Everyone should follow laws that will keep the air around them clean. People can avoid being in places where the air is filled with smoke. Most importantly people also have a right to never begin to smoke cigarettes.

### 13:6 Mainstream and Sidestream Smoke

*What is sidestream smoke?*

Studies show that a nonsmoker can be harmed by the smoke from a smoker's cigarette. Suppose you were in a room where others were smoking. The air you would inhale would be filled with smoke. The smoke a person inhales from someone else's cigarettes is called **sidestream smoke.** Sidestream smoke includes the smoke in the air that is exhaled by a smoker or the smoke from a cigarette lying in an ashtray. People who smoke breathe mainstream smoke. **Mainstream smoke** is the smoke a person inhales and exhales from his or her cigarette.

Perhaps you live in a home where people smoke. It may be difficult for you to convince a smoker to quit. Studies show that children in a home where people smoke have an increased risk of infections of the respiratory system. Perhaps agreements can be made with a smoker. The smoker may agree to avoid smoking in the home during times when others are around. Perhaps a certain room in the home can be set aside for a smoking area. This can help reduce the amount of smoke in the air.

Many nonsmokers find cigarette smoke annoying. Their eyes may tear and they may cough. They may even get headaches. Cigarette smoke is a problem for the nonsmoker. Try to avoid being in places where there are smokers. Sit in nonsmoking areas of restaurants. Stay in places where the air can circulate if you are around smokers. Perhaps going into another room can help you feel more comfortable.

*How can cigarette smoke affect nonsmokers?*

Nonsmokers should use assertive behavior when dealing with smokers. For example, a nonsmoker should be honest when asked if it is alright to smoke by someone visiting in his or her home. The nonsmoker should feel comfortable replying that the family does not want smoking in their home.

**FIGURE 13–7.** The former Surgeon General of the United States has determined that smoking is hazardous to health.

**FIGURE 13-8.** Smoking is not allowed on airplanes during short flights.

*What laws have been passed to protect nonsmokers?*

## 13:7 Smoking and the Law

There are many debates taking place about smoking. Cigarette companies believe that smokers have a right to smoke. Antismoking groups believe there should be strict laws passed to protect the rights of nonsmokers. Laws have been passed to help protect nonsmokers from cigarette smoke. In many public buildings there are rules prohibiting smoking. Smoking has become illegal in some kinds of transportation. Smoking is not allowed on buses or on airplanes during short flights. Many companies will not allow their workers to smoke during working hours. It is believed that people who do not smoke are more productive than smokers. Nonsmokers are absent from work less often than smokers because they do not become ill as often. Nonsmokers are not as likely to have accidents or cause fires.

New laws in regard to smoking are being passed to protect everyone. Cigarette companies cannot give out free samples of cigarettes to young people. Cigarette and smokeless tobacco ads are not allowed on TV.

The Surgeon General of the United States has determined that smoking is hazardous to your health. As required by law, warnings must be posted on *all* cigarette packages. There are four warnings that are rotated every three months on cigarette packages.

1. "Smoking causes lung cancer, heart disease, emphysema, and may complicate pregnancy."
2. "Quitting smoking now greatly reduces serious risks to your health."
3. "Smoking by pregnant women may result in fetal injury, premature birth, and low birth weight."
4. "Cigarette smoke contains carbon monoxide."

Laws and information about cigarette smoking are having an effect. Today, only slightly more than 26 percent of the adults in the United States smoke. The number of people who are choosing not to smoke is rising. Choosing not to smoke is the choice of the greatest number of people—both young and old. Choose to be smoke-free. Protect your health. Help protect the health of others.

## 13:8 The Advantages of Being Tobacco-free

Not using tobacco products has many advantages. When you do not use tobacco, you do not harm your senses of taste and smell. Foods taste and smell better. You do not harm your respiratory and circulatory systems. You increase your chances of growing up healthy. You also increase your chances of doing everyday tasks easier. Suppose you smoked. You would tire easily. If you wanted to play on a sports team, a coach may not allow you to do so unless you quit smoking.

*What are the benefits of not smoking?*

It is important to choose friends who do not smoke. Tobacco is often considered a drug whose use leads to other dangerous drugs. Studies show that people who choose friends who do not smoke lower their chances of smoking or using harmful drugs later in life. By not smoking, you create an advantage for good health. You develop other healthful behaviors as you grow.

Saying NO to using tobacco products helps you feel good about yourself. You know that you have made a healthful decision. People feel good about themselves when they take actions to improve their health. They have a positive self-concept. Others enjoy being with those who choose healthful behaviors.

6. Why are many people choosing to live in smoke-free environments?
7. Why do companies now prefer to hire nonsmokers?
8. Why should athletes choose not to smoke?

**Think About It**

## Life Skills

▶ Follow the law and encourage others to do the same to protect your health.
▶ Do not use any form of tobacco including cigarettes and smokeless tobacco.
▶ If possible, avoid places in which there are smokers.
▶ Choose friends who do not use tobacco.

# Health Highlights

## Are There Safe Cigarettes?

Research concerning cigarette smoking has increased over the past years. All the research studies show that smoking is harmful to health. To try to find a way to "smoke safely," many different kinds of cigarettes have been produced. Companies call these cigarettes lower-yield cigarettes. Lower-yield cigarettes are cigarettes that have reduced amounts of tar and nicotine. Companies that make these cigarettes say that they are safe to smoke. They say that the reduced tar and nicotine will lower the harmful effects produced by smoking regular cigarettes.

Are lower-yield cigarettes safe? The answer is no! They do have reduced tar and nicotine, but smokers are still dependent on nicotine. When people switch to these kinds of cigarettes, they smoke more cigarettes more often. They do this to get the nicotine they desire. It appears that lower-yield cigarettes increase the smoking habit rather than reduce it.

There are other problems connected with lower-yield cigarettes. To get an effect, smokers take longer puffs. The smoke from these cigarettes is inhaled deeper into the lungs. In addition, lower-yield cigarettes have certain substances added for flavor. The added substances can be harmful to lung tissue.

Clove cigarettes, made from tobacco, ground cloves, and clove oil have also been found to be dangerous. Eugenol, the major chemical of clove, when placed in the lungs of rats caused them to die. Other studies relating clove cigarettes and lung damage have convinced several states to ban the sale of clove cigarettes.

Is there such a thing as a safe cigarette? The answer is no! Any cigarette is a harmful cigarette.

# Chapter 13 Review

1. Tobacco is a dangerous drug that affects physical health. *13:1*
2. Nicotine and carbon monoxide in cigarette smoke cause the heart to work harder than it should. *13:2*
3. Smoking can cause pulmonary emphysema and chronic bronchitis. *13:3*
4. Smoking can harm a pregnant woman and her baby. *13:4*
5. Smokeless tobacco causes cancer of the mouth and throat. *13:5*
6. Mainstream and sidestream smoke are harmful. *13:6*
7. There are laws to protect the nonsmoker from cigarette smoke. *13:7*
8. Being tobacco-free lowers the risk of developing health problems. *13:8*

**Summary**

---

*Complete each sentence with the correct word.*
*DO NOT WRITE IN THIS BOOK.*

**Words for Health**

carbon monoxide
chronic bronchitis
cilia
mainstream smoke
nicotine

pulmonary emphysema
sidestream smoke
smokeless tobacco
tar

1. The substance in tobacco that remains in the lungs and irritates the lining of the lungs is _____.
2. The smoke someone inhales from a smoker's cigarette is called _____.
3. A person who has _____ has inflamed bronchial tubes filled with mucus.
4. _____ is a colorless, odorless, and dangerous gas.
5. Smoke that a smoker inhales from his or her cigarette is called _____.
6. _____ is a dangerous stimulant found in tobacco.
7. Tobacco that is chewed is called _____.
8. When a person has _____, the alveoli cannot work as they should.
9. _____ help keep the respiratory system clean.

---

1. How does nicotine act like a stimulant drug in a person's body?
2. What mental effects or emotional attitudes that result from cigarette smoking make it difficult for smokers to quit?

**Reviewing Health**

3. What are two specific responses of the circulatory system to nicotine?
4. How does carbon monoxide affect the delivery of oxygen by the circulatory system?
5. Why might people who smoke develop a cough?
6. What lung diseases are caused by cigarette smoking?
7. Why is smoking considered socially unacceptable?
8. How might smoking by a pregnant woman harm her developing baby?
9. What are the effects of smokeless tobacco on teeth and gums?
10. How can the use of smokeless tobacco lead to cancer of the mouth or throat?
11. What can a nonsmoker do to avoid sidestream smoke?
12. How is cigarette smoke a problem for a nonsmoker?
13. What are the opinions of the groups debating about smoking?
14. What are some examples of laws that have been passed to protect young people from tobacco products?
15. Why is it important to choose friends who do not smoke?

| Using Life Skills | *Use the life skills from this chapter to respond to the following questions.* |

*Situation:* You and your friends are watching a baseball game. You notice that one of the baseball players is using smokeless tobacco. One of your friends says that it's OK to use smokeless tobacco. Your friend says, "At least you don't inhale smoke."

1. Why is your friend's statement considered poor reasoning?
2. How can you use refusal skills to avoid ever trying smokeless tobacco?

*Situation:* You have been invited to two parties on the same evening. One party is attended by friends who do not smoke. Friends who do smoke are at the other party.

1. Which party might be the best one for you to attend?
2. How would you respond if you were being encouraged to attend the party where people will smoke?

*Situation:* You and your friend are at the mall. Your friend tries to convince you to go to the drugstore and buy a pack of cigarettes for her. She says you look older and can get away with buying cigarettes. She says the cashier at the drugstore never checks ages anyway.

1. What is wrong with your friend's attitude?
2. How would you respond to your friend?

## Extending Health

1. Heart disease is the number one killer in our society. Certain behaviors and conditions, called risk factors, increase your chances of having heart disease. Three major risk factors for heart disease are cigarette smoking, high blood pressure, and high cholesterol (elevated levels of fat in your blood). There are other factors that influence your chances of disease. Contact your local Heart Association to get copies of their risk tests.
2. Assume a pack of cigarettes costs $1.25. Estimate what a pack-a-day smoker would save by not smoking over a one-year period. Do the same for a two- and a five-year period. What might be done with the money saved?
3. The Office of Smoking and Health is concerned with the problems of tobacco, smoking, and their effects on health. It is an agency in the Department of Health and Human Services. Write to the following address to request information on smoking and health.
   Public Inquiries Office of Smoking and Health
   Park Bldg., Room 1−58
   5600 Fishers Lane
   Rockville, MO 20857
4. Research the methods of treatment for cigarette smoking. Several methods include hypnosis, nicotine chewing gum, and analysis of reasons for smoking. Find out the success rate for each method of treatment.
5. Study further the effects of smoking on a pregnant woman, the developing baby, and the infant. Some ideas to research may be how smoking might be a factor in hyperactivity in children or oxygen starvation (hypoxia).

# Diseases and Disorders

Did you know . . .

▶ taking care of your body reduces the risk of getting both communicable and noncommunicable diseases?

▶ many people with chronic diseases can lead full and productive lives?

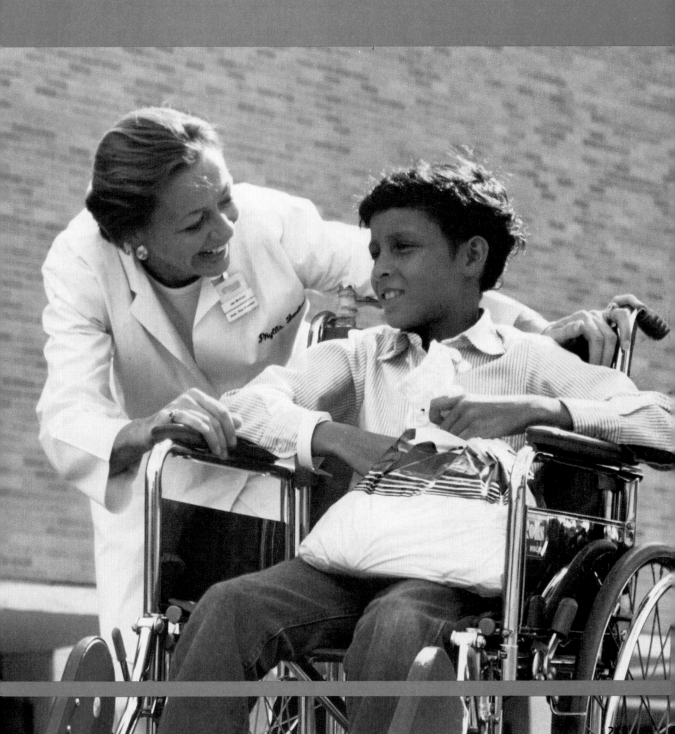

# Understanding Disease

There are two types of diseases, those that can be passed from one person to another and those that cannot. You can practice health behaviors to reduce your risk of acquiring either type. Steps may also be taken to lessen their effects.

# Chapter 14

STUDENT OBJECTIVES: *You will be able to*

- *tell how certain communicable diseases are spread and the stages through which they progress.*
- *describe how heart disease and cancer can be treated and prevented.*

Of the major health problems throughout the world, diseases are at the top of the scale. There are many different kinds of diseases. There are many different causes of diseases. Yet many diseases can be prevented. If they cannot be prevented, their effects on health often can be controlled. The prevention and control of diseases begins with knowledge about them.

## Understanding Communicable Diseases

Imagine that you are playing ball with your friends. One friend passes a ball to you. You catch the ball. You pass the ball to another friend. Communicable diseases are spread in a similar way to playing ball. You can get communicable diseases from others. You also can pass them along to others. What are some ways communicable diseases might be passed among people? How can you stop such a disease from being passed to you?

## 14:1  How Diseases Are Spread ⎯⎯⎯⎯

*What are pathogens?*

A **communicable disease** is a disease that a person gets from contact with an infected person. **Pathogens** are harmful living organisms that cause communicable diseases.

Communicable diseases can be spread through direct or indirect contact. In direct contact, an infected person can spread disease through touch. Suppose a person who has a cold touches his or her mouth. Pathogens from this person's mouth get on the hand. You shake hands with this person. The pathogens are now on your hand. If you touch your eyes, nose, or mouth with your hand the pathogens may enter your body. You may now become ill. In indirect contact, an infected person does not have to touch anything. Suppose you are next to a person with a cold who sneezes. Mist from the sneeze is in the air and you inhale the mist containing the pathogens. The pathogens may cause an illness.

*How can pathogens be spread through water?*

There are other ways communicable diseases are spread. One example is water. Pathogens can be found in water. Suppose you swim where the water is dirty. Pathogens can enter your mouth as you swim in the water. To avoid infection, do not swim in water where there are signs that warn you of pollution.

**FIGURE 14–1**. We are often unaware of the passing of pathogens from one person to another.

Pathogens also can be spread by eating spoiled food. Meat that has not been refrigerated may have pathogens growing on it. If you eat the unrefrigerated meat, the pathogens would enter your body. To avoid becoming ill in this way, keep meat refrigerated before and after cooking. The cold temperature helps prevent pathogens from growing on meat. Never eat food if it looks, tastes, or smells spoiled.

Communicable diseases also can be spread by insects. Suppose an insect lands on a substance that has pathogens on it. The insect might then land on food that you plan to eat and pathogens are transferred. You may become infected. Keeping food covered will help prevent the transfer of pathogens in this manner.

**FIGURE 14–2.** To prevent the growth of pathogens, meat products should be kept refrigerated.

## 14:2  Defenses Against Diseases

Your body has natural defenses that help protect you from pathogens. For example, skin is the first line of defense. As long as it is not broken, skin will keep many kinds of pathogens from entering your body.

Openings in your body also protect you from pathogens. Your body openings are lined with membranes. **Mucous** (MYEW kus) **membranes** are the linings of body openings. They protect you by producing mucus (MYEW kus), a sticky fluid that traps harmful products. For example, the membranes inside your nose produce mucus that traps any dirt you might inhale.

The body openings through which you breathe also have cilia to protect you from pathogens. Cilia are the little hairs in your nose and throat that trap pathogens. When you cough or sneeze, cilia help force out any trapped pathogens.

*What are mucous membranes?*

Inside your body are special defenses that protect you from communicable diseases. Suppose a pathogen such as a virus were to enter a person's body. Let us call this virus, Virux X. Special cells in the bloodstream called T cells detect Virus X. The T cells signal B cells. B cells produce antibodies. **Antibodies** are protein substances in blood that destroy pathogens.

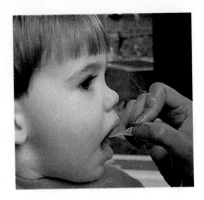

Certain antibodies are produced for each type of virus. B cells produce Virus X antibodies to kill Virus X. Even though Virus X is killed, the Virus X antibody remains in the person's body, often for a lifetime. If Virus X enters the body again, it would be killed by the Virus X antibody. This is the reason you usually get some diseases, such as chicken pox, only once. The chicken pox antibody gives you immunity from chicken pox. **Immunity** is the body's protection from, or resistance to, disease. Immunity provides long-lasting or permanent protection from a disease.

Vaccines (vak SEENZ) also give immunity from some communicable diseases. A **vaccine** is a substance that contains weakened or dead pathogens that cause your body to produce antibodies. You were given certain vaccines before you were allowed to attend school. These vaccines were either injected or swallowed. They caused your body to produce antibodies to protect you from certain diseases.

## 14:3 Stages of Diseases

Think about the last time you had a cold. Perhaps, you remember how your cold developed. At first, you may have had mild signs and symptoms, such as a runny nose and low fever. As the cold progressed, your nose may have become more stuffed and your fever may have gone higher. The cold may have been very annoying. With proper care, in time, the signs and symptoms became milder and the cold went away.

Most communicable diseases progress through stages. The first stage of infection is the incubation (ihn kyuh BAY shun) stage. The **incubation stage** is the period of time between a pathogen's first entry into the body and the first signs and symptoms. This period varies with the type of disease. The second stage is the prodromal (proh DROH mul) stage. The **prodromal stage** is the period of time when a person first begins to feel ill. However, the exact illness may not be known. The **peak stage** is the time during which signs and symptoms of a specific disease are present and may be identified.

*At what stage during an infection can a specific disease be identified?*

The last, or **convalescent** (kahn vuh LES unt) **stage,** is the period of time immediately following an illness when a person's body is still not as strong as before the illness. It is easy for a person to become too active during the convalescent stage. If a person does not get enough rest and sleep, he or she may become ill again. During this time, a person is weak and more likely to get another communicable disease.

## 14:4 The Common Cold and Flu _____

Did you know that most people get one or two colds each year? This is why a cold is often called the common cold. A cold can be caused by any of hundreds of different viruses. Yet these viruses produce similar symptoms. Among these are coughing, runny nose, sneezing, watery eyes, and headache.

*What can cause a cold?*

You can get a cold through direct or indirect contact with an infected person. Because so many viruses can cause a cold, you cannot get immunity. However, you can reduce your risk of getting a cold by not coming in close contact with an infected person. If you do get a cold, rest and drink fluids, such as juices. A cold that is not cared for can develop into a more serious illness such as pneumonia (noo MOH nyuh). **Pneumonia** is a lung infection with symptoms including a high fever, shortness of breath, chest pain, and coughing. A physician can detect pneumonia by listening to your breathing. He or she may take a chest X ray to further check the lungs for infection.

**FIGURE 14–4.** A cold that is not cared for can develop into a more serious illness.

**Influenza** or **flu** is a disease that affects the respiratory system and produces fever, chills, and muscle pain. Headache, coughing, and sore throat are also present. Many kinds of flu can be controlled by vaccines. Often, older people are given flu shots to protect them. They may not be strong enough to fight a specific flu virus.

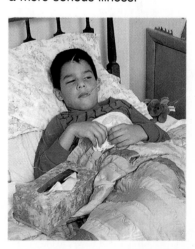

The signs and symptoms of flu are frequently similar to those of a cold. For this reason, some people take aspirin to treat flu. However, this practice is not recommended.

**FIGURE 14-5.** Use of aspirin to treat a cold or flu can increase children's and teenager's risk of getting Reye syndrome.

**WARNINGS:** Children and teenagers should not use this medicine for chicken pox or flu symptoms before a doctor is consulted about Reye syndrome, a rare but serious illness. Keep this and all drugs out of the reach of children. In case of accidental overdose, seek professional assistance or contact a poison control center immediately. As with any drug, if you are pregnant or nursing a baby, seek the advice of a health professional before using this product. See important directions in leaflet, including use for arthritis and rheumatism.

It is believed that the risk of getting Reye (RI) syndrome is increased if a person takes aspirin to relieve symptoms of the flu or chicken pox. **Reye syndrome** is a serious disease that may damage the liver and brain. This disease develops most often in young people. Symptoms of Reye syndrome are vomiting followed by drowsiness, difficult breathing, and stiffness.

## 14:5 Sexually Transmitted Diseases ⎯⎯

**Sexually transmitted diseases (STDs)** are communicable diseases that are spread through sexual contact. Sometimes STDs are called venereal (vuh NIHR ee ul) diseases. STDs are spread when pathogens from an infected person enter the bloodstream of a partner. If a person has an STD, pathogens will be found in body fluids. The pathogens also may be present on the skin or in mucous membranes. Suppose Person A has an STD and has sexual contact with Person B. Person B may have a small break in the skin. If this part of the skin comes in contact with the pathogens of Person A, the pathogens will infect Person B.

Specific STDs produce different signs and symptoms. Some STDs are more dangerous than others. Some can be treated and cured, others cannot. Some can last a lifetime or even result in death. Symptoms and treatments of STDs are shown in Table 14-1. There is one thing that is common to all STDs. They can be prevented by avoiding sexual contact.

*Where may pathogens be found in a person infected with an STD?*

Table 14-1

## Sexually Transmitted Diseases

These diseases can be prevented by using responsible decision-making skills and refusal skills to say NO to intimate sexual contact.

| Name of Disease | Signs and Symptoms | | Treatment | Health Problem That Can Result |
|---|---|---|---|---|
| | Male | Female | | |
| Gonorrhea | Painful urination | Burning during urination | Penicillin or other medicine | Inability to reproduce; inflammation of the reproductive organs |
| Syphilis | Rashes on body; heart disease; harm to the nervous system | Rashes on body; heart disease; harm to the nervous system | Penicillin or other medicine | Heart disease, brain damage, and death can result; harm to the newborn |
| Genital herpes | Rash and blisters in genital area; swollen glands; fever | Rash and blisters in genital area; swollen glands; fever | No cure. Certain drugs and taking warm baths can relieve signs and symptoms | Harm to newborn |
| Genital warts | Warts in genital area | Warts in genital area | Special treatments | Infections Cancer |
| Chlamydia | Similar to gonorrhea | Similar to gonorrhea | Antibiotics | Inflammation of reproductive organs |
| AIDS | Fatigue; fever; chills; nausea; late stages include pneumonia and cancer | Same as male | No cure. Use of certain drugs may extend life | Weakens or destroys the immune system |

1. Why should you avoid close contact with a person who has a cold?

**Think About It**

2. Why is mucus important in preventing disease?
3. Why is getting plenty of rest important in preventing disease?
4. How can STDs be completely prevented?

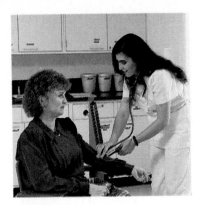

**FIGURE 14–6.** Checking blood pressure regularly is important in keeping hypertension under control.

*What is atherosclerosis?*

*Why is hypertension dangerous?*

# Understanding Noncommunicable Diseases

Some diseases are not spread through direct or indirect contact. Two of the most serious diseases of this type are cardiovascular disease and cancer.

## 14:6 Cardiovascular Disease

A cardiovascular disease is a disease of the heart and blood vessels. It is also a noncommunicable disease. A **noncommunicable disease** is a disease that is not caused by direct or indirect contact with a pathogen. Among the conditions that affect the cardiovascular system are atherosclerosis (ath uh roh skluh ROH sus) and high blood pressure. **Atherosclerosis** is a disease in which fat deposits inside artery walls block blood flow. These fatty deposits also may cause arteries to lose their ability to expand and contract. A deposit in the artery can break away from the wall and travel to other parts of the body. Blocked blood vessels in these areas may result. If the flow of blood is blocked in the brain, a person will have a stroke. With the reduced blood flow, the brain will not receive oxygen. The person will lose function of part of the brain and may become paralyzed or even die.

If a fatty deposit blocks an artery in the heart, the person will have a heart attack. If blood flow in the heart completely stops or is reduced greatly, death can occur.

Atherosclerosis is often associated with hypertension. **Hypertension** is high blood pressure. Hypertension can cause the heart to work harder and beat faster. This may cause fatty deposits to build up more quickly in the arteries.

In most cases, the causes of hypertension are not known. There are, however, some risk factors about which you need to be aware.

- *Heredity*  The risk increases when high blood pressure is present in family members.
- *Age*  Young people may be affected, but the older a person gets, the greater the risk.

- *Race*  About twice as many black Americans have hypertension as do white Americans.
- *Sex*  Men are at greater risk than women until the age of 50.

Many people who have hypertension are not aware they have a problem. They do not know they need treatment to relieve the condition. Most hypertension can be controlled. Some people require medication. Other ways to not only control hypertension but to also reduce the risk of developing it are

- remain at a healthful weight.
- exercise regularly.
- reduce salt intake.
- do not smoke.

# ACTIVITY

## Blocked Blood Vessels

Work in groups of three. Each group member is to bring a cardboard tube from an empty toilet tissue or paper towel roll. Line the inside of one tube lightly with clay. Line the inside of another tube with even more clay. Do not line the third tube. (See illustration.) Bring a package of marbles to class. See how many marbles you can roll through each tube in 15 seconds. Each tube should be lying flat on a table. Imagine that each tube represents a blood vessel. The inside of each tube differs. Assume that each marble represents a red blood cell. What conclusions can you draw after observing how many marbles passed through each tube? How can you relate this to arteries that have fat deposits in them?

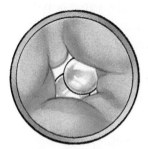

Most blockage

Less blockage

No blockage

## 14:7 Types and Causes of Cancer _____

**Cancer** is a disease in which abnormal cells grow and multiply. There are many different kinds of cancers. Some cancers attack bones. Other types may attack the skin or different body organs.

Cancer is dangerous because the abnormal cells can spread from one body part to another. When these cells spread, they destroy other body tissues and organs.

The exact causes of many types of cancer are not known. However, some risk factors increase the chances of getting certain cancers.

*Smoking* Smoking is the main cause of lung cancer. Tobacco contains carcinogens (kar SIHN uh junz). A **carcinogen** is any substance that causes cancer.

*What is a carcinogen?*

*Heredity* Certain kinds of cancer appear to be more common in some families. This is true in regard to breast cancer. Breast cancer is more likely to occur in a woman if her mother or sister had breast cancer.

*Diet* The development of some cancers seems to be related to the kinds of foods eaten. Research shows that fatty foods increase the risk of cancer. Foods with fiber may reduce the risk of cancer of the colon.

*Radiation* Exposure to the sun increases the risk of skin cancer. Exposure to radiation in tanning booths also increases the risk of skin cancer.

**FIGURE 14–7.** Blocking the sun's rays is the best way to reduce the risk of skin cancer.

## 14:8 Treatment and Prevention of Cancer

Many kinds of cancer can be detected early during regular physical checkups. Early detection is important to the success of certain treatments. Be aware of the warning signals of cancer. These signals are listed in material put out by the American Cancer Society.

There are different ways to treat cancer. Through surgery, some cancer cells can be removed. Through radiation, cancer cells can be destroyed. Cancer cells can also be destroyed through chemotherapy (kee moh THER uh pee). **Chemotherapy** is the use of chemicals to kill cancer cells.

The risks of developing certain kinds of cancer can be reduced. Avoiding exposure to the sun for long periods of time can reduce the risk of skin cancer. Not smoking will lower the risk of lung cancer. Eating fruits and vegetables each day and reducing the intake of fatty foods will lower the risks of cancers of the digestive tract. It also is important to have regular physical checkups. A physician can detect many kinds of cancer that can be treated in the early stages.

*How can the risk of cancer be reduced?*

6. Why is it important to have blood pressure checked?
7. Why should you avoid overexposure to the sun?
8. How can you avoid risks of developing certain kinds of cancer?

**Think About It**

## Life Skills

▶ To avoid the risk of Reye syndrome do not take aspirin if you have signs of flu or chicken pox.
▶ Be aware of the risk factors of developing hypertension.
▶ Eat foods with fiber to lower the risk of cancer of the colon.
▶ Have regular physical checkups.

# Health Highlights

## "What Do We Know About AIDS?"

No disease in recent times has caused more concern than Acquired Immune Deficiency Syndrome or AIDS. Many people have questions about this disease. Here are some facts you should know.

**What is AIDS?** AIDS is a disease caused by a virus called HIV. It affects a person's immune system. When people have AIDS, they are not protected from diseases that normally would not affect them.

**How do you get AIDS?** There are three main ways AIDS is transmitted. It is transmitted through infected blood, through other body fluids, and by being born to a mother who has AIDS. Suppose a person who has AIDS uses a needle to inject a drug and then gives it to someone else to use. The infected blood can enter the bloodstream of the uninfected person through the needle. AIDS also is spread when infected body fluids enter the bloodstream of an uninfected partner during close sexual contact. The AIDS virus enters the bloodstream when there is a break in the skin or a membrane. Finally, a pregnant woman infected with the AIDS virus can pass it to her developing baby from her bloodstream.

**How can you know if you have AIDS?** People can be infected with the AIDS virus and yet not have the disease. Even though they have no signs and symptoms, they can transmit the AIDS virus to others. A blood test can show if a person is infected with the AIDS virus. It may be several years before the person will have signs and symptoms. Among these are weakness, diarrhea, swollen glands, and the presence of certain diseases.

**Is there a cure for AIDS?** There is no cure for AIDS. Certain drugs can help a person who has AIDS live longer than if no treatment is given. A person infected with AIDS will be infected for life.

**How can AIDS be prevented?** AIDS can be prevented. Say NO to drugs, especially those taken through needles. Say NO to being sexually active. You will not get AIDS if you follow these actions.

# Chapter 15

*STUDENT OBJECTIVES:* *You will be able to*

- *describe the different kinds of nervous system disorders.*
- *describe the characteristics of muscular dystrophy, diabetes, asthma, sickle-cell anemia, and allergies.*

There are many kinds of chronic (KRAHN ihk) disorders that affect young people in many different ways. Chronic means long-lasting or occurring often. Some of these are inherited, such as muscular dystrophy (DIHS truh fee) and sickle-cell anemia. Researchers continue to look for the causes and cures for these disorders. Other chronic disorders occur for no known reason. This chapter describes some of these conditions, their causes, signs and symptoms, and treatments.

## Nervous System Disorders

Some chronic conditions affect certain body systems. The person in Figure 15–1 has a chronic condition that affects the nervous system. In this lesson you will study chronic disorders that affect the nervous system. These include multiple sclerosis (skluh ROH sus), epilepsy, and cerebral (SER uh brul) palsy.

## 15:1 Multiple Sclerosis

*What is multiple sclerosis?*

**Multiple sclerosis (MS)** is a condition in which the covering of nerve fibers in the brain and spinal cord breaks down. When this happens, scar tissue forms.

The scar tissue slows or blocks messages being sent along the neurons. This may result in different symptoms. A **symptom** is a change in body function that cannot be seen. The first symptom for multiple sclerosis may be numbness or tingling in a part of the body. Vision may be blurred. Symptoms may continue and get worse quickly. As the symptoms worsen, muscular control may be affected. Simple tasks like walking and standing may become difficult.

In some cases, symptoms may disappear. However, certain conditions may cause the symptoms to return. For instance, stress, injury, or an illness may cause the symptoms to reappear.

Much research about MS is taking place. The cause of this condition and a cure are not known. A person with MS might get help through physical therapy. In physical therapy, body parts are exercised to keep as much muscle strength as possible. A balanced diet is recommended along with plenty of rest. These help keep the body strong.

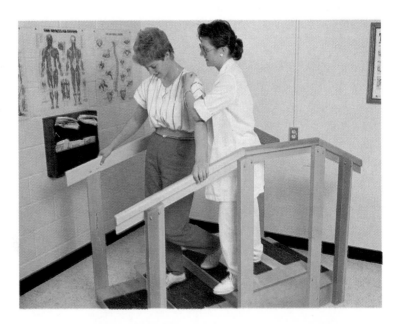

**FIGURE 15-1**. Physical therapy may provide help for a person with multiple sclerosis.

## 15:2 Epilepsy

**Epilepsy** is a condition in which nerve messages in the brain are disturbed for a brief time. This brief involuntary brain activity causes the person to lose mental and physical control. A **seizure** is the period during which there is a loss of mental and physical control.

In a petit mal (PET ee mahl) seizure the effects are mild. There may only be twitches on one side of the body. A person having a petit mal seizure may appear to be daydreaming. More severe reactions occur in a grand mal seizure. A person having a grand mal seizure may shake and fall to the ground.

If you have ever seen a person during a seizure, you may have been frightened or worried. However, most seizures are not dangerous. They may last only a minute. There are actions you can take if you see a person having a seizure.

- Do not try to stop the person from moving.
- Move objects out of the way so that the person does not bump into them.
- Be calm.
- When the seizure has ended, help the person feel comfortable.
- Let the person rest.

In many cases, the cause of epilepsy is not known. It may be caused by an injury to the head. Or, it may be caused by a lack of oxygen to the brain.

With special medication, some epilepsy can be controlled. If the medication is not taken correctly, the seizures can worsen. The earlier epilepsy is diagnosed, the more effective the treatment will be.

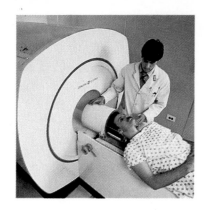

**FIGURE 15-2.** An injury to the brain can be detected with a CAT scan.

## 15:3 Cerebral Palsy

**Cerebral palsy** is a nervous system disorder resulting in a loss of control of nerve and muscle movement. Sometimes cerebral palsy is caused by injury to the brain. In many cases, however, the causes of this disorder are not known.

*What is cerebral palsy?*

Cerebral palsy has many different signs as well as symptoms. A **sign** is a visible change in the body. For example, a rash may be a sign of poison ivy. Signs and symptoms of cerebral palsy include

*What are some of the signs and symptoms of cerebral palsy?*

- poor muscle movement.
- awkward leg movement while walking.
- difficulty standing or walking.
- poor balance.
- slurred speech, poor vision, and poor hearing.

The physical signs and symptoms of cerebral palsy remain throughout a person's lifetime. People who have this disorder can think clearly. They can be as intelligent as anyone else. As a result, they can do very well in school.

There is no cure for cerebral palsy. Treatment focuses on special therapy to help the person lead as normal a life as possible. A person with cerebral palsy may need help with speech or hearing. Physical therapy may help muscle coordination. Some persons who have this disorder may wear leg braces to help them move more easily. Sometimes these persons may take special medicines.

# ACTIVITY

## Having Cerebral Palsy

Take the arm you use most and bend it as far as you can at the elbow. At the same time, keep your hand bent as far as possible at the wrist and do the following: write your name, turn to a certain page in your book, and tie your shoelace. What was it like to do these things? This is what it may feel like for a person who has cerebral palsy.

## Think About It

1. Why should a person who has MS try to avoid stressful situations?
2. How does medication help a person who has epilepsy?
3. Why is cerebral palsy considered a nervous system disorder?

# Other Disorders

Many disorders affect body systems other than the nervous system. The effects can vary. Some signs and symptoms may be severe; others may be mild. The disorders described in this lesson usually last for a lifetime.

## 15:4 Muscular Dystrophy

**Muscular dystrophy** is an inherited disease in which the muscles lose their ability to function. There are different forms of this disease. The most common form usually affects young boys.

Muscular dystrophy is often noticed when a child first begins to walk. The child may seem clumsy or have trouble standing. As the child gets older, the disease continues to weaken the muscles. By the age of 10 to 15, the person with this disease may no longer be able to walk.

In many cases of muscular dystrophy, the arm and leg muscles are the first to lose full function. Physical therapy may help the person get back some muscle function.

There is no cure for muscular dystrophy. A person who has a minor form of this disease may have a normal life span. However, this disease may shorten life. Research continues to be done to find its cure.

*What is muscular dystrophy?*

**FIGURE 15-3**. Muscular dystrophy weakens the muscles.

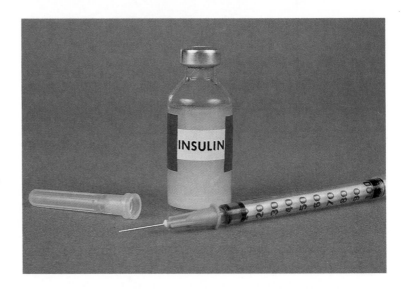

## 15:5 Hemophilia

*What is hemophilia?*

**Hemophilia** (hee muh FIHL ee uh) is a disease in which a substance necessary for clotting is missing from the blood. Hemophilia can be detected during the first two years of life. Signs and symptoms include bruising easily, excess bleeding from small cuts, and bleeding in the joints.

A person who has this disease must be careful during physical activities. A small cut can result in a great loss of blood. While there is no cure for hemophilia, certain medicines can be given to help the blood to clot. People with this disease can lead full lives with a normal life span.

## 15:6 Diabetes

**Diabetes** (di uh BEET us) is a disease in which the body cannot use sugar in foods in normal ways. Diabetes is a result of the pancreas (PAN kree us) not functioning properly. The **pancreas** is a large gland that produces insulin. Insulin helps the body use sugar to produce energy. When a person has diabetes, the pancreas produces too little or no insulin.

There are two types of diabetes. In one type that affects young people, very little, if any, insulin is produced. This means that the person must take insulin.

In another type of diabetes, the pancreas produces some insulin, but the body still cannot use sugar the way it should. This type often affects people who are over 40. They may take insulin. In many cases, however, this type of diabetes can be controlled by diet and exercise. When controlled in this way a person is said not to be dependent on insulin.

During a physical checkup, the physician checks the patient's urine. This is one way to check for diabetes. The urine would contain much sugar. This would happen because there was not enough insulin in the body to use the sugar. There are other signs and symptoms of diabetes. Among these are frequent urination, thirst, weakness, and tiredness. Other signs are blurred vision, a tingling and numbness in the hands and toes, and cuts that heal slowly. In some cases, only some of these symptoms may appear.

*What are some signs and symptoms of diabetes?*

People can have diabetes, yet not know it. Undetected diabetes may damage the body. This is one reason that regular physical checkups are recommended. There is no cure for diabetes, but it can be treated. For both types of this disease, a strict diet is recommended. Only certain amounts of sugar can be eaten. People with diabetes must eat at regular times and watch their sugar intake. With proper diet, exercise, and insulin, people with this disease can lead healthful, active lives.

**FIGURE 15–5.** Diabetes may be detected during a regular physical checkup.

## 15:7 Allergies

An **allergy** is a condition in which the body reacts to a food or substance in the environment. Allergic reactions might include itchy eyes, runny nose, coughing, difficulty in breathing, and skin rashes. An **allergen** is a substance that causes an allergic reaction. Some allergens such as pollen and dust are in the air. Dog hairs are allergens to some people. Allergens are in some foods, such as milk, eggs, and tomatoes.

Most of the time, allergies cannot be cured. However, they can be treated by a pediatrician or by an allergist. An allergist is a physician who treats people who have allergies. Suppose you had unexplained rashes. You might see an allergist. The allergist may test you with different allergens. The allergens are placed in the body through small scratches on the skin. If a reaction results, the allergist may give you treatments. The treatments will help reduce your reaction to the allergens. In some cases the treatments will cause the reaction to the allergens to disappear.

Some allergies can be treated with shots. For example, people who have hay fever may be given a series of shots of a certain medicine. This treatment will reduce the signs and symptoms of hay fever.

*What are examples of allergens?*

**FIGURE 15–6.** An inhaler helps open the air passages to give an asthma victim temporary relief.

## 15:8 Asthma

**Asthma** (AZ muh) is a condition that involves the closing or blocking of tubes in the respiratory system. Air has difficulty flowing through the lungs. This causes a person to gasp for breath. A person may wheeze. There may be a tightness around the chest area.

Asthma tends to run in families. The exact causes of this condition are not known. An asthma attack may be brought on by different factors. For people your age, some common reasons include a cold, cold air, stress, or smoke in the air. Sometimes exercise may produce an asthma attack. In many cases, allergic reactions to allergens in the air or to certain foods can trigger an asthma attack.

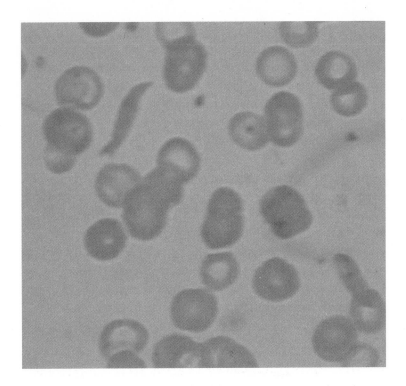

**FIGURE 15–7.** Sickle-shaped cells do not carry oxygen as normal round, red cells do.

Asthma cannot be cured, but it can be treated. A person can spray a special medicine into the throat. This helps open the air passages. In severe asthma attacks, an injection of a certain medicine can be given. It is important that the cause of an asthma attack be determined. For instance, if caused by a food, the food can be removed from the diet. If caused by stress, the cause of stress can be relieved.

## 15:9 Sickle-Cell Anemia

**Sickle-cell anemia** is an inherited disease in which many red blood cells are curved instead of round. These long sickle-shaped cells do not carry oxygen as normal red cells do. The cells are very stiff. For this reason, these cells have trouble passing through small blood vessels in the body.

There are many problems related to having this disease. Tissue in the body is damaged. A person may have pain in certain body parts. This can cause a person to reduce physical activity. His or her life may be shortened.

*What is sickle-cell anemia?*

A condition known as sickle-cell trait is different from sickle-cell anemia. A person with sickle-cell trait is a carrier of the sickle-cell gene. A gene is a part of a body cell that carries traits. This person does not have sickle-cell anemia. However, he or she has the ability to pass the gene to his or her child.

*Who is affected by sickle-cell anemia?*

Some people think that sickle-cell anemia affects only black people. It is true that this disease is most common in people of African descent. But it also affects people of Asian descent.

Sickle-cell anemia cannot be cured. New treatments are being discovered. One treatment helps the red blood cells carry more oxygen. When carrying a lot of oxygen, many sickle-cells will return to their normal shape.

People who are concerned they may have sickle-cell trait should be tested. After they are tested, they can receive medical care and counseling. Counseling can help a person be at his or her best.

## Think About It

4. Why would a person who has muscular dystrophy have difficulty lifting heavy objects?
5. Why is a person who has hemophilia in danger from a small cut?
6. Why is insulin important to the body?
7. What signs and symptoms might cause a person to suspect he or she has an allergy?
8. Why should a person who has asthma avoid being under stress?
9. Why might a person who has sickle-cell anemia have trouble with hard physical activity?

## Life Skills

▶ If you see a person have an epileptic seizure, move objects away so that the risk of injury is reduced.
▶ Any unexplained conditions that may indicate an allergy exists should be checked by a physician.

# Chapter 15 Review

**Summary**

1. Blurred vision and tingling in some body parts may indicate that a person has multiple sclerosis. *15:1*
2. A person who has epilepsy may have different types of seizures. *15:2*
3. A person who has cerebral palsy will probably be able to think very clearly and probably do very well in school. *15:3*
4. Muscles lose their ability to function in a person who has muscular dystrophy. *15:4*
5. A person who has hemophilia can bleed heavily from a small cut. *15:5*
6. Diabetes is a disease in which the pancreas produces little or no insulin. *15:6*
7. There are many different kinds of allergens that can cause physical reactions. *15:7*
8. Asthma cannot be cured but it can be treated successfully. *15:8*
9. Sickle-cell anemia is an inherited disease affecting red blood cells and resulting in many related problems. *15:9*

**Words for Health**

*Complete each sentence with the correct word.*
*DO NOT WRITE IN THIS BOOK.*

| | |
|---|---|
| allergen | hemophilia |
| allergy | multiple sclerosis (MS) |
| asthma | muscular dystrophy |
| cerebral palsy | pancreas |
| diabetes | seizure |
| epilepsy | sickle-cell anemia |

1. _____ is a condition characterized by seizures.
2. _____ may first be noticed when a child begins to walk.
3. A reaction to something eaten may indicate a person has a(n) _____.
4. Scar tissue on nerve fibers is associated with _____.
5. A person who has _____ has a lack of insulin in the body.
6. _____ is a disease in which the red blood cells are curved.
7. A person who has _____ should avoid activities in which bleeding can easily occur.
8. Poor balance and slurred speech are signs of _____.
9. A substance that causes an allergic reaction is a(n) _____.

10. A large gland that produces insulin is the ____.
11. ____ is a condition that results in the closing or blocking of tubes in the respiratory system.
12. A(n) ____ is the period during which a person loses mental and physical control.

**Reviewing Health**

1. How does multiple sclerosis affect the nervous system?
2. What are the first signs of multiple sclerosis?
3. What are the signs that a person with epilepsy may be having a seizure?
4. What can you do to help a person who has a seizure?
5. What is one possible cause of cerebral palsy?
6. Describe the treatment of cerebral palsy?
7. What effect does muscular dystrophy have on the body?
8. What are the signs of muscular dystrophy?
9. Why should a person who has hemophila be careful during certain kinds of physical activity?
10. Can a person with hemophilia have a normal life span? Explain.
11. Why does a physician check a patient's urine for diabetes?
12. What are the differences in treatment between the two types of diabetes?
13. What are some examples of allergens?
14. What are the signs of asthma?
15. What conditions may trigger an asthma attack?
16. How does sickle-cell trait differ from sickle-cell anemia?

**Using Life Skills**

*Use the life skills from this chapter to respond to the following questions.*

*Situation:* While in your classroom, the person next to you has an epileptic seizure. The other boys and girls around you begin to panic. You are concerned about the person having the seizure.

1. What should you do if this person falls to the ground and is having convulsions.
2. Why is it important for you to take the actions in number one?

*Situation:* You notice that every time you eat a certain food, you get a rash. This concerns you.

1. What condition might exist that is causing the rash?
2. What action should you take? Why?
3. How might your condition be treated?

1. There are many other chronic health concerns that have not been addressed in this chapter. Select a chronic health concern. Make a visual aid about it. Then write a one page report that describes the causes, signs and symptoms, and treatment of this chronic health condition. Give a presentation to the class.

## Extending Health

1. There are many other chronic health concerns that have not been addressed in this chapter. Select a chronic health concern. Make a visual aid about it. Then write a one page report that describes the causes, signs and symptoms, and treatment of this chronic health condition. Give a presentation to the class.
2. There are organizations and community health agencies that focus on specific health problems. For example, the Muscular Dystrophy Association is concerned with providing funds for research that will lead to a cure for muscular dystrophy. Identify an agency that is concerned about a specific chronic health problem. You may find the name of an agency in your local phone directory. Call or write to this agency for information about the health problem for which it is concerned. Ask for brochures and pamphlets. Bring your materials to class and help prepare a bulletin board about chronic health conditions.
3. Interview someone who is active in the field of medical research. Find out about the research that is being done on one of the chronic health concerns mentioned in the chapter. How is the research carried out? What new discoveries have been made? Is a cure for the disease a possibility?
4. Visit a facility that provides physical therapy for people with chronic health disorders, such as muscular dystrophy, cerebral palsy, and multiple sclerosis. The facility may be located in a hospital or it may be a separate facility. Observe the various activities and methods of therapy used.
5. Research the career of a physical therapist. Find out about the different areas in physical therapy and the training that is necessary. Also, find out about the different ways a physical therapist treats those people with chronic health disorders.

# Consumer and Personal Health

Did you know . . .

▶ you can assist your dentist and physician by following a plan for health care?

▶ the movies, videotapes, and TV programs that you watch may affect your health?

# A Responsible Health Consumer

Health services help you improve your health. They influence your physical health, mental health, and social health. What health service have you recently received that affected at least one of these areas for you?

# Chapter 16

**STUDENT OBJECTIVES:** *You will be able to*

- *discuss the responsible choices of products for physical, mental, and social health.*
- *explain services for physical, mental, and social health, to include an explanation of health quackery.*

A group of young people, ages 12 to 18, were asked what they enjoyed doing most during their free time. Over 90 percent of the teenagers questioned said they enjoyed shopping. Advertisers are aware of your interest in shopping. They try to influence your decisions about what you buy. What factors do you use to decide which products to buy? This chapter will help you make responsible choices when buying and using health products and services.

## Health Products

Stop for a moment to think about the products that you use each day. Many of these are health products. What products do you use for physical health? Mental health? Social health? How do you know if you are making responsible decisions when you buy or use these products? Responsible decisions will help you buy the best products for your needs without paying the highest prices.

## 16:1  Who Is a Health Consumer?

*What is a health consumer?*

A **health consumer** is a person who buys or uses health products and health services. A **health product** is an item that improves your physical, mental, or social health. For example, shampoo is a health product. Shampoo improves your physical health by keeping your hair clean.

A **health service** is a person or a place that helps improve your physical, mental, or social health. When you have a dental checkup, your dentist is the person who improves your physical health. When you go to a physician's office, you are going to a place that provides services that improve your health.

## 16:2  Products for Physical Health

Products for physical health help keep your body healthy. There are many products you and others use for physical health. Some of these are listed below. Can you think of others?

| | | |
|---|---|---|
| toothpaste | bandages | mouthwash |
| dental floss | bath soap | sunscreen |
| tissues | shampoo | cotton swabs |
| cough syrup | eyeglasses | toothbrush |
| thermometer | hearing aid | nasal spray |

**FIGURE 16–1**. Many health products are available to maintain physical health.

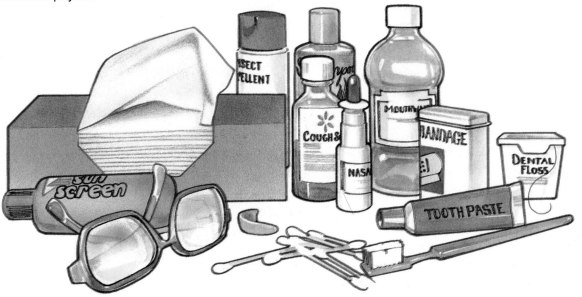

The following are some guidelines to help you make responsible decisions when buying health products.

- Examine the reasons why you are buying the product. It is helpful to make a list of the health products you plan to buy. Ask questions about each item.
    ◦ Do I need this product?
    ◦ Will I use it if I buy it?
    ◦ Do I have the money needed to buy it?
    ◦ Should I wait, save money, and buy something else?
- Compare the **unit price** of similar health products. The unit price is the cost of the product per ounce, gram, or other unit of measure. For example, suppose you are comparing the price of two different kinds of toothpastes. You would check to see the unit price per ounce. Suppose you were buying cotton swabs. You would want to check the price per swab.
- Compare the prices of health products sold in different quantities or weights. The **net weight** of a product is the weight of the contents of the product not including the container. Often, the unit price of the same product is lower when you buy a larger quantity. For example, the unit price for 4.6 oz of toothpaste might be less than the unit price for 2.2 oz of the same toothpaste.
- Read the labels of products to learn about ingredients, directions, and warnings. The **ingredients** are the substances in a product. For instance, you may want to buy a sunscreen. PABA is an ingredient used in sunscreens. It blocks out ultraviolet rays from the sun. It helps protect you from skin cancer. The list of ingredients will tell if PABA is in the sunscreen. If so, it will give the amount that is in the sunscreen. The **directions** are the instructions for using a product safely. You must follow the directions for the product to work as it should. The **warnings** are the explanations about possible side effects. Warnings may tell what to do if side effects occur and do not stop.

**FIGURE 16–2.** Comparisons of unit prices can be made to determine the best buy.

*What is net weight?*

*What are directions and warnings?*

*What is the difference between brand name products and generic products?*

- Learn who recommends different health products. Many health professionals and health associations examine products to help consumers make wise choices. For instance, the American Dental Association recommends certain dental products. These are often listed on the product containers.
- Compare brand name products with generic (juh NER ihk) products. A **brand name product** is a product in which the company name and advertising are used to influence you to buy the product. The cost for advertising increases the price of the product. A **generic product** is a product that has the same purpose and ingredients as a brand name product but usually does not cost as much. Less is spent on promoting the product. Suppose you are buying vitamins. A package labeled "multi-vitamin" with no brand name will probably cost less than a well known brand you see advertised.

*Why do people shop at discount stores?*

- Determine the best place to buy health products. There are many discount stores that sell health products. A **discount store** is a store that offers products at reduced prices. Discount stores sometimes are able to buy large quantities of certain items at lower prices. The discount stores are then able to pass the savings on to their customers. You may choose to shop at these stores to reduce the amount of money you spend.

**FIGURE 16–3.** Brand name products are frequently offered at sale prices.

## 16:3 Products for Mental Health

Products for mental health influence the way you think and feel. Let's examine three types of products you might buy or use and their possible effects on mental health.

*Books and magazines*   There are a variety of books and magazines you might buy and read. The ideas in books and magazines may affect your health. Suppose you read books and magazines that encourage you to think and help you learn. Challenging books and magazines help you exercise your mind. These books would have a positive effect on your mental health. Suppose you buy and read magazines that focus on violence. Reading this kind of magazine may have a harmful influence on your thoughts and actions.

*Movies, videotapes, and TV programs*   What you see on TV, videotapes, or in a movie will influence your thoughts and actions. A report from a subcommittee appointed by the United States Senate was issued recently. It reported that watching violent acts may have a harmful effect on you. When you choose movies, videotapes, and some TV programs, read the ratings. Ask your parents to discuss the ratings with you. These ratings are designed to help you choose movies and videotapes that may influence your thoughts and actions in ways that promote your mental health.

*Music*   Music may influence your moods as well as your thoughts and actions. Have you ever listened to a happy song that made you smile? Have you ever listened to a sad song that made you depressed?

The words in a song are important. These words may influence you. For example, you may have heard the words, "love means never having to say you're sorry." Think about those words for a moment. Are they true? Just because you love someone, it does not mean that you can forget to say you are sorry when you are wrong. Sometimes you begin to believe false statements when you hear them over and over again in a song. This may result in a negative influence on your mental health. Your actions also may influence the way others think about you.

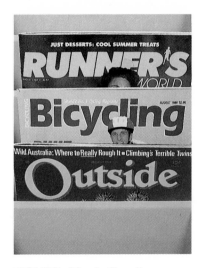

**FIGURE 16–4.** Reading informative materials that encourage a healthful lifestyle can contribute to your good health.

*How can ratings help you choose movies and videotapes?*

## ACTIVITY

### Make an Album Cover

Imagine you have been asked to help on a committee in your community that is promoting healthful living. An album has been produced including songs that describe areas such as healthful relationships, a drug-free lifestyle, and responsible decision making. You have been asked to design the album cover. Design the cover so it shows your message. Have a display of album covers in your class.

## 16:4 Products for Social Health

Products for social health influence the way you relate with others. Advertising often tries to make you think that some products will help you have good relationships. Many ads on TV try to convince you that some products help you be more attractive.

Perfumes, bath oils, and deodorants are examples of products for social health. A **deodorant** is a product used under the arms to control body odor. An **antiperspirant** is a product that controls body odor and perspiration. Use the guidelines you have studied in this chapter to make decisions about these products.

The way you dress also affects your social health. Advertisers often try to convince you that some clothing items will make you more attractive. **Designer labels** are special labels put on clothing to tell you who made the item. Wearing the same style of jeans without the designer label can help you be fashionable and save money. But what is most important for good social health is to keep a neat and clean appearance in order to feel good about yourself.

*What is the difference between a deodorant and an antiperspirant?*

**Think About It**

1. Why do some people buy generic brand products instead of brand name products?
2. Why do some young people try to convince their parents to buy clothes with designer labels?

252

# Health Services

Stop for a moment to think about the people and places that provide health services in your community. What people and places provide services for physical health, mental health, or social health?

## 16:5 What Are Health Services?

A health service can be provided by either a place or a person. To be a responsible health consumer, you need to know two other facts.

- Most health services located in a special place must meet certain standards. A **health standard** is a rule or code of behavior to protect health. For example, there are health standards for restaurants. These health standards state how foods must be prepared. They state that the restaurant equipment and workers must be neat and clean. The people who work at the restaurant cannot have diseases that might harm people who eat there. A **health inspector** is a person who checks to see that places that provide health services follow health standards. If a restaurant does not meet these standards, the management will need to take steps to meet them. If the standards are not met, the restaurant will be closed.

  *What is a health standard?*

- People who provide health services must also meet standards that assure you they can do their jobs correctly. Usually people in health related jobs need to have a certain number of years of general education. They may also need special training. After the special training or education has been completed, the person who will provide health service receives a license. The license is often displayed or the person carries it with him or her. There are people who have the job of checking to see that those who provide health services meet certain standards. They may check to see if a person has a current license to perform certain jobs.

**FIGURE 16–5.** Inspections help to assure that health standards are followed.

## 16:6 Services for Physical Health —————

There are many people and places in your community that provide services for physical health. You may be interested in a career that involves providing services to promote good physical health. There are many careers from which you can choose. There are many places where you might work. Table 16–1 describes some people and lists some places that provide services for physical health.

Table 16–1

| People and Places That Provide Services for Physical Health |
| :-- |
| **Some People Who Provide Services for Physical Health** |

1. A *pharmacist* prepares medications.
2. A *speech pathologist* (puh THAHL uh just) identifies and treats speech problems.
3. A *medical technologist* (tek NAHL uh just) helps a physician by doing certain tests in a lab.
4. A *dentist* examines and treats the teeth, mouth, and gums.
5. A *health educator* works to improve the knowledge, attitudes, and behaviors of people.
6. A *hospital attendant* helps hospital patients with daily activities.
7. A *medical doctor,* or physician, checks patients to prevent, diagnose, and treat illnesses.
8. A *dietitian* (di uh TIHSH un) helps others plan balanced, healthful meals and special diets.
9. A *nurse* cares for the sick and injured.
10. A *dental hygienist* cleans and flosses your teeth and assists the dentist.

| Some Places That Provide Services for Physical Health | |
| :-- | :-- |
| 1. rest home | 6. camp for people with disabilities |
| 2. speech clinic | 7. health office at school |
| 3. physician's office | 8. school for people who are blind |
| 4. hospital | 9. emergency room |
| 5. Red Cross | 10. local heart association |

## 16:7 Services for Mental Health

Some people choose careers that are concerned with mental health. These people want to help others understand personal thoughts, feelings, and actions.

A **social worker** is a person who helps people find resources to meet various personal needs. A **psychologist** (si KAHL uh just) is a person who treats people with mental illness or with problems of daily living. He or she may do psychological testing. A **psychiatrist** (suh KI uh trust) is a physician who treats mental illness or problems of daily living. A psychiatrist may prescribe medicines. A **school guidance counselor** is a person who has special training in helping young people make life choices.

Your community may have different places that provide services for mental health, such as a mental health clinic. Your school may have a psychologist. Many psychologists and psychiatrists have offices and also work at hospitals.

**FIGURE 16–6.** Health services that are private and confidential are available.

## 16:8 Services for Social Health

Many places provide the chance for you to improve your social health. These places provide a social health service. The people who work or help with these activities are also providing a health service.

Table 16–2

| Have You Used Services for Social Health? | |
|---|---|
| YWCA/YMCA | Big Brothers |
| YWHA/YMHA | Big Sisters |
| Boy Scouts | Indian Princesses |
| Girl Scouts | Indian Guides |
| Little League baseball | Campfire, Inc. |

When you take part in social activities, you learn about yourself and others. You may form new skills and make new friends. Taking part in services for social health helps you have a balanced lifestyle.

*Why is it healthful to participate in social activities?*

## 16:9 Making Wise Choices

People who write ads want you to buy and use their products or services. Be careful of ads that try to convince you to buy a product or service

*What are four ways ads are used to convince you to buy products and services?*

- to be more popular.
- because a famous athlete or actress uses it.
- to be able to get something free with it.
- to have something that everyone else has.

Some products and services are useless. A **quack** (KWAK) is a person who tries to sell you useless health products or services. Usually, these products and services do not improve health. They may be harmful if they prevent you from getting the right products and services. **Quackery** is the method a person uses to sell useless products and services. A quack will say or do things to try to help you make up your mind. Do not let statements made by quacks influence your choices.

*What is quackery?*

> **Think About It**

3. Why are health standards important?
4. Where may services for physical health be provided in a community?
5. How are a psychologist and a psychiatrist different?
6. How does a quack try to sell useless products and services?

## Life Skills

▶ Use guidelines to make responsible decisions when buying health products.
▶ Select books, magazines, movies, TV programs, and music that encourage positive, healthful behaviors.
▶ Select products for social behavior that help you have a neat and clean appearance.
▶ Participate in services for social health to learn about yourself, develop skills, and make friends.
▶ Evaluate advertisements before buying products.

# Chapter 16 Review

Summary

1. A health consumer buys and uses health products and services. *16:1*    Summary
2. Guidelines for buying health products include examining reasons, comparing unit prices, comparing prices for different quantities, reading labels, checking recommendations, comparing generic and brand name products, and determining the best place to buy a product. *16:2*
3. Examine products such as books, magazines, movies, TV programs, and music to decide if they have a positive effect on mental health. *16:3*
4. Purchase products for social health that help you have a neat and clean appearance. *16:4*
5. Most people and places that provide health services must meet certain standards. *16:5*
6. There are many careers for people interested in providing services for physical health and many places for these people to work. *16:6*
7. People who choose careers in mental health are interested in helping others understand their thoughts, feelings, and actions. *16:7*
8. Services for social health often include an opportunity to learn about yourself, develop skills, learn about others, and make new friends. *16:8*
9. Ads may try to sway you to buy a product or service you do not need, while quacks encourage you to buy something that is useless. *16:9*

---

*Complete each sentence with the correct word.*
*DO NOT WRITE IN THIS BOOK.*

Words
for Health

antiperspirant
deodorant
generic product
health consumer
health inspector
health product
health service
health standard
ingredients

psychiatrist
psychologist
quackery
school guidance
    counselor
social worker
unit price
warnings

1. A(n) _____ is a place or a person that helps improve your physical, mental, or social health.

2. _____ are explanations about possible side effects.
3. The _____ is the cost of the product per ounce, gram, or other unit of measure.
4. _____ is the method a person uses to sell useless products and services.
5. A(n) _____ is a person who buys or uses health products and health services.
6. A(n) _____ is a person who helps find resources to meet a variety of personal needs.
7. A(n) _____ is a product that controls body odor and perspiration.
8. A(n) _____ is a rule or code of behavior to protect health.
9. A(n) _____ is a physician who can treat mental health problems and prescribe medicines.
10. A(n) _____ is a product that has the same purpose as a brand name product but does not cost as much because less is spent on advertising and packaging.
11. A(n) _____ is a product used under the arms to control body odor.
12. A person who checks to see that places follow health standards is a(n) _____.
13. Shampoo is a(n) _____ because it improves your physical health.
14. _____ are the substances in a product.
15. A person who has special training in helping young people make life choices is a(n) _____.

## Reviewing Health

1. Who is a health consumer?
2. What are seven guidelines to help you make responsible decisions when buying products?
3. What is the difference between a brand name product and a generic product?
4. What did a recent report from a U.S. Senate subcommittee report about the effects of watching violence on TV or in the movies?
5. Why might a company put a designer label on clothing in a place where others will see it?
6. What might happen if a restaurant does not meet health standards?
7. What standards must people in health services meet?

8. What are five places where services for physical health might be provided?

9. What are four kinds of health professionals who provide services for mental health?

10. What are some examples of places that provide social health services?

11. Why might you participate in services for social health?

12. What are four ways that ads try to sway you to buy a product or service?

Using Life Skills

*Use the life skills from this chapter to respond to the following questions.*

*Situation:* You and a friend are trying to decide what to do on a Saturday afternoon. Your friend suggests going to a movie. The movie suggested is reported to contain violent scenes and has a rating that requires an adult to accompany young persons. Your friend says, "It is really scary, let's go. I know how we can sneak in without an adult."

1. Why are movies rated?
2. Why might it be healthful to avoid violent movies?
3. What would you tell your friend?

*Situation:* Suppose you are concerned about your skin. You would like to have clear skin throughout your teenage years. You read an ad in the back of a magazine about a medicated cream. The ad states that if this product is used at your age, "a special formula will change your skin so that you never have pimples." This cream is "so new that medical doctors have not discovered it."

1. What method is being used to sell the skin cream?
2. How would a responsible consumer react to this ad?

**Extending Health**

Select a book to read that will challenge your mind. Write a two page report describing new ideas you have learned. Include an ending that discusses how learning new ideas promotes your mental health.

# The Importance of Dental and Medical Care

The dentist and the assistant are part of the health care team. The health care team is made up of professionals who can help keep you healthy. What behaviors can you choose concerning your dental health that will promote good dental health?

# Chapter 17

*STUDENT OBJECTIVES:* You will be able to

● *discuss how a plan for dental care helps prevent tooth decay, gingivitis, and periodontal disease.*
● *explain why a physical examination is needed and what it includes.*

Your dentist and physician are professionals involved in helping with the care of your health. In this chapter, you will study about the services they provide. You will study about health habits they recommend. These health habits will help you maintain a high level of wellness.

## Dental Care

Your teeth perform many important functions. They

● chew the food you eat.
● help you form words as you speak.
● give your mouth and jaw shape.
● are an important part of your appearance.

### 17:1 A Plan for Dental Care

You and your parents have a shared responsibility for your dental care. With proper care, your teeth should last a lifetime.

*Who is responsible for your dental care?*

Your plan for dental health should include

- brushing and flossing teeth daily.
- following a healthful diet.
- using a fluoride toothpaste.
- having teeth cleaned and checked every six months.
- having cavities filled and crooked teeth straightened.
- wearing a safety belt in an automobile and a mouth protector in sports.
- following safety rules.

## 17:2   Tooth Decay

About 98 percent of all Americans will have tooth decay at some time during their lives. What causes tooth decay? How can tooth decay be prevented?

*What is plaque?*

**Plaque** (PLAK) is a sticky substance containing bacteria that is always forming on teeth. Plaque forms near the gumline as well as between your teeth. It can stick to the grooves and curves on your teeth.

Daily toothbrushing and flossing helps remove plaque. When plaque is not removed, it becomes hard. **Calculus** (KAL kyuh lus) is hardened plaque. Your dentist or dental hygienist can remove calculus during your regular dental examination and cleaning.

**FIGURE 17–1.** What is the difference between (a) a healthy tooth and (b) a decayed tooth?

a
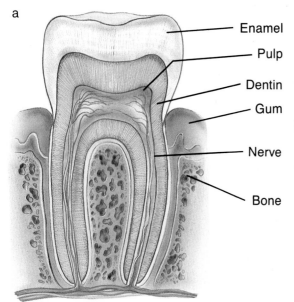

Enamel
Pulp
Dentin
Gum
Nerve
Bone

b
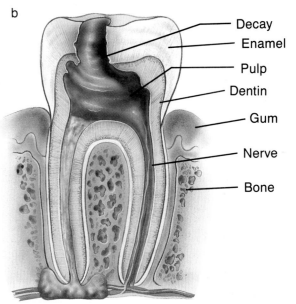

Decay
Enamel
Pulp
Dentin
Gum
Nerve
Bone

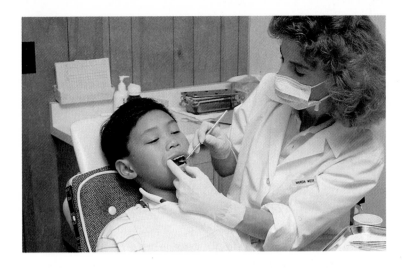

**FIGURE 17-2.** Regular dental checkups and daily brushing and flossing of your teeth is the best combination for cavity prevention.

Suppose you do not remove the plaque and calculus from your teeth. When you eat foods that contain sugar, the sugar and bacteria in plaque form an acid. The sticky plaque will hold this acid on your teeth and eventually will cause cavities. **Cavities** are holes in the enamel of a tooth caused by the acid.

When you have a dental checkup every six months, your dentist checks for cavities. He or she does this by carefully examining your teeth. Your dentist may take X rays to check for cavities inside or between teeth. A dentist is the only one who can repair a cavity. A **filling** is the material a dentist uses to repair the cavity in a tooth.

If a cavity is not filled, the bacteria from plaque may get into the dentin of the tooth. **Dentin** is the hard tissue that forms the body of the tooth. The bacteria can then destroy your whole tooth structure. From the dentin, the bacteria can get into the root and cause a serious dental disease.

*What might happen if a cavity is not filled?*

## 17:3 Periodontal Disease

**Peridontal** (per ee oh DAHNT ul) **disease** is a disease of the gums and other tissues that support the teeth. It is a disease that is usually painless and very common among adults. However, it may begin during childhood. Knowing how this disease begins can help you prevent it.

*What is periodontal disease?*

The first stage of periodontal disease is gingivitis (jihn juh VITE us). **Gingivitis** is a condition in which the gums are sore and bleed easily. Plaque around the gums is the main cause of gingivitis. Regular brushing and flossing will help prevent this condition. If you have gingivitis, your dentist can tell you what to do to make your gums healthy again.

Untreated gingivitis may lead to periodontal disease. This disease is more destructive than gingivitis. The plaque on the teeth hardens and forms calculus. If you do not have your teeth cleaned, more plaque forms on top of the calculus. Your gums will slowly separate from your teeth and make spaces or pockets. These pockets become filled with bacteria. If you do not go to the dentist for treatment, this disease will destroy the bones that support your teeth. Even healthy teeth will become loose. They may even fall out.

You can prevent tooth decay and periodontal disease by daily brushing and flossing. The correct procedures are shown in Figure 17–3.

*What may lead to periodontal disease?*

**FIGURE 17–3**. A correct technique for brushing and flossing is essential to dental health care.

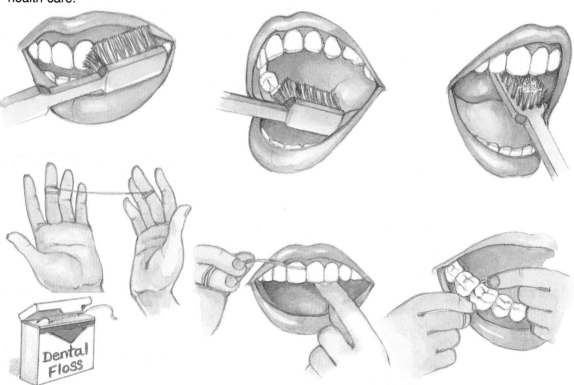

## 17:4   Fluoride and Diet

**Fluoride** (FLOOR ide) is a chemical that helps prevent tooth decay. Enamel is the outer, hard shell of the body of the tooth. Fluoride helps prevent decay by hardening the enamel. Fluoride may be added to drinking water, applied by the dentist, or obtained in toothpastes and mouthwashes. The American Dental Association recommends that everyone should have a source of fluoride for good dental health.

*How does fluoride help prevent tooth decay?*

Your diet also influences your dental health. You should be careful how much sugar you eat. Sugar and the bacteria in plaque combine to form the acid that makes cavities in your teeth. Reducing the amount of sugar you eat will help your dental health. When you get hungry for a snack, eat something low in sugar. Eat an apple instead of a cookie. Also try to avoid sweet snacks that stick to your teeth. When you do eat foods rich in sugar, brush your teeth as soon as possible to stop the effects of the sugar on your teeth.

Some foods help make your teeth and gums healthy. Calcium is a mineral that helps make teeth strong. Vitamin D is also needed for strong teeth. Both calcium and vitamin D are found in dairy products such as milk, yogurt, and ice cream. Vitamin C helps keep gums healthy. Vitamin C is found in citrus fruits such as oranges and lemons.

*What foods help make your teeth and gums healthy?*

## ACTIVITY
### Healthful Snacks

Form groups of four with classmates to plan a party for your class. Your party will feature snacks that promote healthy teeth and gums. What foods and beverages will you include?

**1.** How does tooth decay begin?
**2.** How can periodontal disease be prevented?
**3.** How does fluoride help prevent tooth decay?

**Think About It**

## Medical Care

An important factor will help you live a long and healthy life. This factor is having good medical care. Your medical care should include a physical examination at least every two years.

### 17:5   A Plan for Medical Care ————

**Life expectancy** (ihk SPEK tun see) is the number of years a person is expected to live. Many factors affect your life expectancy.

*What are some factors that affect life expectancy?*

- your health knowledge
- choosing healthful behaviors
- your heredity
- your environment
- the drugs you may have to take to keep you healthy

*What is a physical examination?*

A physician can help you make a plan to increase your life expectancy. The physician will ask questions to learn about your health. He or she will help you by giving you regular checkups. A **physical examination** is the checking of your body and the gathering of information about you and your family to determine your health status.

Sometimes a physician checks your body because you are ill. You may have symptoms of a disease. A symptom is a change in body functions that cannot be seen. For example, a headache is a symptom of flu. A physician examines you to make a diagnosis (di ihg NOH sus). A **diagnosis** is the identification of a disease based on symptoms.

It is also important to have a physician check your body when you are healthy, and you have no symptoms of illness. The physician wants you to remain healthy.

You will be asked many questions in order to gather facts for your health history. A **health history** is recorded information about your past health and your habits. Your parents may be questioned about you and your family. What illnesses have you had? What drugs have you taken when you were sick? Do you have any allergies? Your health history gives clues about your present health. Your health history may be helpful in diagnosing and treating a future illness.

*What is included in a health history?*

Your physician will keep your health record. A **health record** is a file in which information gathered from your health history and your checkups is kept. As you grow and develop, the physician will refer to your record and help you make a plan to stay healthy.

I. Personal Health History
   A. record of growth and development
   B. record of habits
II. Family Health History
   A. record of parents' habits
   B. blood relatives' medical history
III. Health Care
   A. dates and results of previous physicals
   B. eye examination
   C. hearing examination
   D. immunization history
   E. childhood diseases
   F. other diseases
IV. Health Facilities Used
   A. hospitalization record
   B. emergency care record
V. Health Insurance Policies

**FIGURE 17–5.** Information about your past health and habits may be helpful in treating future illnesses.

## 17:6   A Physical Examination ────────

When you go to a physician for a checkup, several procedures may be followed. These procedures are discussed in Table 17−1.

Table 17−1

| Procedures in a Physical Examination ||
| --- | --- |
| **Temperature** | **Height and Weight** |
| One of the easiest ways to learn if something is wrong with your body is to check your temperature. Normal temperature is around 37°C or 98.6°F. A **fever** is a body temperature that is higher than normal. It shows that the body is fighting an infection. | Your physician uses a height/weight graph to check your growth. The graph gives a range for your body build. The physician may talk about gaining or losing weight. |
| **Eyes** | **Ears** |
| Your physician checks your vision. An **ophthalmoscope** is an instrument used to shine light into your eye to see blood vessels and internal parts. The physician looks at your eyes for infections. | Your physician checks your hearing. An **otoscope** is an instrument used to examine the ear canal and eardrum. If there is a wax build-up, the physician will remove it. |
| **Nose** | **Mouth and Throat** |
| A **nasal speculum** is an instrument the physician uses to spread your nostrils to see if anything is blocking your breathing. The mucous membranes are the protective linings in your nose. If they are irritated, they are red and produce more mucus. | A **tongue depressor** is a stick used to hold your tongue down so the physician can see your mouth and throat. Post nasal drip is a heavy discharge that drains from the nose to the throat. It is a symptom of infection. |
| **Reflex Tests** | **Palpation or Feeling** |
| A reflex test, used to check your nerves, will cause certain movements or reflex actions. A reflex action occurs when a body part moves without being directed by the brain. | **Palpation** is a procedure in which the physician touches or feels your body to learn how it functions inside. This helps the physician check the size and location of organs. A check is made for firmness, softness, swelling, and pain. |

Table 17-1 *continued*

| Procedures in a Physical Examination | |
|---|---|
| **Percussion or Tapping** | **Auscultation or Listening** |
| **Percussion** is a procedure in which the physician taps on your chest, abdomen, or back with the fingers. The sounds that are made tell the physician what is happening in your body. Tapping on the back indicates the condition of the lungs. | **Auscultation** is a procedure in which the physician listens to sounds in your body. A stethoscope is an instrument that your physician uses to hear body sounds. The physician can listen to the heart beat and the valves of the heart open and close. The physician can also listen to the lungs. The physician is able to tell if air is getting to all parts of the lungs. |
| **Blood Pressure and Pulse** | **Blood Sample** |
| A **sphygmomanometer** is a special cuff that is used to measure blood pressure. Pressure is taken during the beat of the heart and also when the heart is filling with blood. There is a normal blood pressure for your age, sex, and body build. The physician also will hold your wrist and take your pulse. | A blood sample is drawn from one of your veins. Tests are used to determine if correct amounts of red and white blood cells are present. |

**4.** Why does the physician need your health history?

**5.** How does the physician check blood pressure?

> **Think About It**

# Life Skills

▶ Brush your teeth with fluoride toothpaste and floss daily.

▶ Have dental checkups every six months.

▶ Have X rays when recommended.

▶ Have a dentist repair cavities.

▶ Wear a safety belt in an automobile and a mouth protector during sports.

▶ Follow safety rules for sports to prevent dental injury.

▶ Have regular physical examinations.

▶ See a physician if you have symptoms of a disease.

# Health Highlights

## Braces

At Randy's six month dental checkup, the dentist noticed that Randy's teeth were crowded. He explained that teeth need room for good dental health. The dentist suggested that Randy have a checkup with an orthodontist (or thuh DAHNT ust). An orthodontist is a dentist who is trained to straighten teeth and to fit braces on teeth.

Dr. Berkowitz is an orthodontist. He examined Randy's teeth, jawbones, and facial muscles. After the short exam, the orthodontist told Randy's parents that Randy had an overbite that needed to be corrected. An overbite is a condition in which the upper front teeth stick out over the lower front teeth, when the mouth is closed. Dr. Berkowitz suggested that braces could correct the problem. Braces are tiny bands of metal or plastic that fit around or are bonded to teeth to hold them in place.

Randy had many questions. How long would he need to wear braces? Would it hurt when the orthodontist put the braces on his teeth? Dr. Berkowitz explained that Randy would need to wear braces for about two years. During that time, he would need to have them tightened at regular times. After two years, Randy would wear a retainer for another two years to keep the teeth from moving back to their original place.

Dr. Berkowitz assured Randy that putting the braces on the teeth is usually not painful. No injection is needed to numb the gums and mouth. Sometimes after the braces are tightened, the tissue surrounding the teeth will become tender. This may last a few days. Rinsing the mouth with warm salt water and taking aspirin will relieve the discomfort.

Dr. Berkowitz explained that teeth should last a lifetime. Many people think that braces are used just for appearance. They are actually needed to prevent tooth loss and problems with the mouth and jaw.

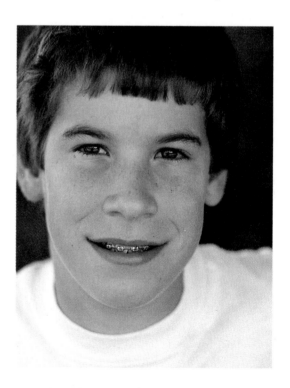

# Chapter 17 Review

**Summary**

1. Following a plan for dental care will help your teeth last a lifetime. *17:1*
2. Plaque and calculus on teeth can combine with sugar in foods to cause cavities. *17:2*
3. Tooth decay and periodontal disease can be prevented by daily brushing and flossing. *17:3*
4. Having a source of fluoride and eating foods with calcium and Vitamins D and C help keep teeth and gums healthy. *17:4*
5. During a physical examination, a physician checks your body and gathers information about you and your family. *17:5*
6. Procedures during a physical examination include checking temperature, height, weight, eyes, ears, nose, mouth, throat, reflexes, blood pressure, and pulse; palpation, percussion, and auscultation; and taking a blood sample. *17:6*

**Words for Health**

*Complete each sentence with the correct word.*
*DO NOT WRITE IN THIS BOOK.*

auscultation
calculus
cavities
dentin
diagnosis
fever
fluoride
gingivitis

health history
otoscope
percussion
periodontal disease
physical examination
plaque
sphygmomanometer

1. A(n) _____ is an instrument that is used to measure blood pressure.
2. A(n) _____ is a body temperature that is higher than normal.
3. _____ is a disease of the gums and other tissues that support the teeth.
4. _____ is a sticky substance on teeth that contains bacteria.
5. _____ is a procedure in which the physician listens to sounds in your body.
6. A(n) _____ is the process of identifying a disease based on symptoms.

7. _____ is hardened plaque.
8. _____ is a condition in which the gums are sore and bleed easily.
9. _____ is a chemical that helps prevent tooth decay.
10. A(n) _____ is the checking of your body and the gathering of information about you and your family to determine your health status.
11. A tapping procedure that a physician uses to check what is happening in the body is _____.
12. _____ is the hard tissue that forms the body of the tooth.
13. Acid causes holes, or _____, in the enamel of a tooth.
14. An instrument used to examine the ear is a(n) _____.
15. Your _____ is the recorded information about your past health and your habits.

**Reviewing Health**

1. What are eight life skills that should be included in a plan for dental care?
2. Why should wearing a safety belt in a car be included in a dental health plan?
3. Why must a dentist clean your teeth every six months?
4. How do cavities form in teeth?
5. Why must a cavity be filled?
6. What is gingivitis?
7. What happens when a person has periodontal disease?
8. How does fluoride help prevent tooth decay?
9. What are some sources of fluoride?
10. What foods keep teeth and gums healthy?
11. What are some factors that influence your life expectancy?
12. How does a physician make a diagnosis?
13. How might your physician use your health history?
14. What instruments does a physician use to check your eyes, ears, nose, and mouth and throat?
15. What does a physician learn from palpation?
16. Why might a physician want to draw a blood sample from one of your veins?

*Use the life skills from this chapter to respond to the following
questions.*

*Situation:* Your friend has a toothache. He does not visit the dentist for
regular checkups and is afraid to call the dentist about the toothache.

1. Why should your friend make an appointment with the dentist as soon
   as possible?
2. Why is it important for your friend to care for his teeth?
3. What would you tell your friend about making and following a plan for
   dental care?

*Situation:* You have not been ill, yet your parents make an appointment
for you with your family physician to have a physicial examination.

1. Why should a physical examination be given to a person who is not ill?
2. In what ways might a health history be useful?
3. What would you tell a friend who has never had a physical
   examination?

*Situation:* You have just visited your dentist for a checkup. Your dentist
suggests that you brush your teeth more often with a fluoride toothpaste
and floss each day. You decide to improve you dental health.

1. When do you plan to brush and floss your teeth each day?
2. What might happen if you do not brush and floss regularly?
3. How can you change your schedule to be certain that you have good
   dental health habits?

1. Research one of the following dental health specialties: public health
   dentist, periodontist, endodontist, oral surgeon, prosthodontist, or
   orthodontist. Write a report.
2. Research the use of fluoride. When did the use of fluoride become
   common? How has the use of fluoride affected dental health? Include
   ways you obtain fluoride.
3. Arrange with your physician to look at your health record and discuss
   it with him or her.

# Safety and First Aid

Did you know...

▶ very warm or cold temperatures can be harmful to your health?

▶ most injuries due to accidents could have been prevented?

# Giving Basic First Aid

Being the first one to find an injured or ill person can be a scary experience. But knowledge of first aid procedures can help you to become an effective care provider, and perhaps save someone's life. Could you assist an accident victim?

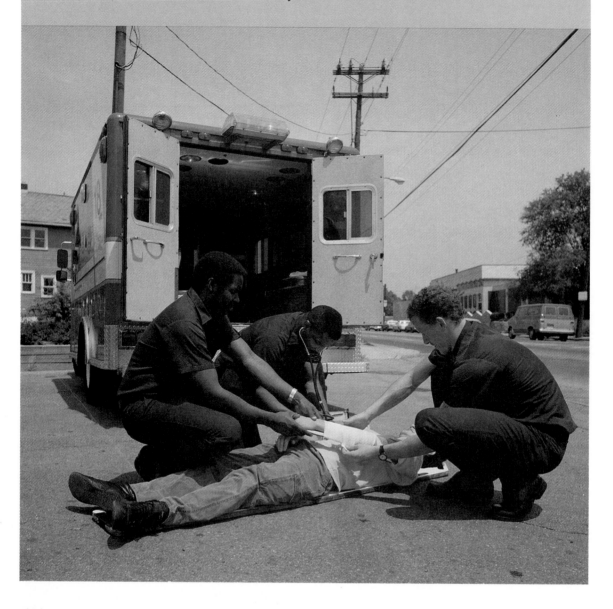

# Chapter 18

*STUDENT OBJECTIVES: You will be able to*

- *describe how to give first aid for breathing difficulties, bleeding, poisoning, shock, dislocations, fractures, and burns.*
- *describe first aid procedures for heat cramps, heat exhaustion, heatstroke, sunburn, frostbite, and hypothermia.*

At some time, you, or someone you know, may be injured. Injuries require quick care and treatment. When you know how to care for and treat injuries, you are promoting good health. You could help yourself or others who need care.

## Common First Aid Procedures

Suppose you are with a friend. Your friend falls and is injured. You want to help your friend. You must be able to think clearly to know what actions to take. Knowing first aid can help.

## 18:1 General First Aid Rules ——————

**First aid** is the immediate care given to a person who has been injured or suddenly becomes ill. It is normal to become nervous when faced with an emergency. Knowing first aid procedures will help you be prepared to help someone who is injured or ill.

- Be calm and think about actions to take.
- Get medical help by dialing the 9-1-1 emergency number or 0 for the operator.
- Encourage the injured person to help him or her remain calm.

**FIGURE 18-1.** (a)
Mouth-to-mouth rescue
breathing (b) Heimlich
maneuver

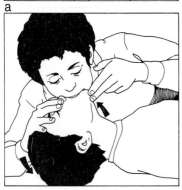

a

b

## 18:2   Helping a Person Breathe

Artificial respiration is a procedure used by one person to restore breathing in another person. One type of artificial respiration is mouth-to-mouth rescue breathing. The steps for rescue breathing are (a) open the airway by tilting the head and lifting the chin; check for breathing; (b) if the person is not breathing, pinch the victim's nose, seal the victim's mouth with yours and give two full breaths; (c) check the victim's pulse on the side of the neck nearest you; check for breathing; (d) if you find a pulse but no breathing, administer one breath every five seconds for an older child or adult.

Every year, many people die from choking. This may happen if a piece of food or other object becomes stuck in the throat. Many of these deaths could have been prevented if the Heimlich (HIME lihk) maneuver had been used. The **Heimlich maneuver** is a method in which the air is forced from the lungs to push out an object stuck in the throat.

How can you tell if a person has a blocked airway? Almost always, a person who is choking will grab at the throat. The lips may turn blue. The person will not be able to breathe, speak, or cough. When this happens, do the following:

- Call for help.

- Stand behind the person. Wrap your arms around this person's waist. Place the inside of your fist against the person's abdomen just below the lower ribs. Place your other hand over your fist. Press inward and upward on the person's abdomen. Do four quick upward thrusts. Anything in the airway should be forced out.

- Repeat this procedure if necessary.

Suppose you are alone and an object gets stuck in your throat. You can press your fist into your abdomen and give four quick upward thrusts. Another action is to lean over the back of a chair. Press your abdomen quickly and forcefully against the back of the chair. Either of these actions should force the object out of your airway.

## 18:3   Controlling Bleeding

Blood plays an important role in the body. It carries oxygen and nutrients to the cells. If a person gets cut and loses too much blood, cells may not receive enough nutrients and oxygen. Life may be threatened. It is important to give first aid to stop bleeding immediately.

The first way to stop bleeding is through the use of direct pressure. **Direct pressure** is force placed over a break in the skin to stop bleeding. This is done by placing a clean cloth over the cut and pressing down. If the cut is on a finger, raise the finger above the level of the heart. This slows the flow of blood to the finger. Often, this step is enough to stop bleeding. If bleeding does not stop, pressure should be applied to a supplying artery. A **supplying artery** is the main artery that carries blood to the affected limb. Applying pressure here stops blood flow within the limb. There are two places on the body where pressure on a supplying artery can be used. One place is under the arm. The other place is the inside of the leg near the top.  Which place should be pressed to stop bleeding from a finger?

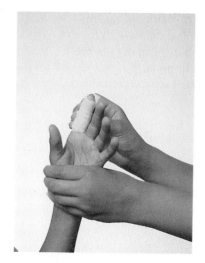

**FIGURE 18-2**. Direct pressure should be the first technique used to stop bleeding.

## 18:4   Poisoning

A **poison** is any product that can enter the body and cause illness. Poison can enter the body by swallowing, inhaling, injection, or absorption through the skin.

Suppose you see a person who has taken a poison and is still conscious. If the person can tell you what was taken, read the label on the container. Follow the first aid directions on the label. Get help from an adult. You can also call the local Poison Control Center. Be prepared to give as much information as possible about the kind of poison, when it was taken, and the amount taken. This information will help the person at the center advise you what to do.

Suppose the person who took poison is unconscious. Check that nothing is blocking the airway. Call an adult. If an adult is not near, call the Poison Control Center or 9-1-1. Do not try to get the person to vomit. Doing that may cause an unconscious person to choke.

*Where can you get help in treating a poison victim?*

## 18:5 Shock, Dislocations, Fractures, and Burns

How would you know if a person is in shock?

**Shock** is a condition in which the functions of body organs are slowed because of illness or injury. Any illness or injury can cause shock. A person in shock will have a lowered body temperature; the skin will feel cold. The pulse will be weak and difficult to find and breathing rate will be increased. If shock is not treated, a person can become unconscious and possibly die.

A person in shock should be kept lying down. Feet should be raised 8 to 12 inches above the level of the heart. However, if there is a head injury or a fracture to one or both legs, the feet should not be raised. The person should be covered with a blanket. This will help improve blood flow in the body. If the person is having difficulty breathing, raise the head and shoulders. Do not give the person anything to drink.

A dislocation is the movement of a bone away from its joint. The result of a dislocation is pain and swelling. To reduce the pain and swelling apply cold packs over the injured area. Keeping the body part still will also help reduce pain. Get medical help to correct the dislocation.

**FIGURE 18–3.** Treating a shock victim is often critical for his or her survival.

A **fracture** is a break or crack in a bone. The signs and symptoms of a fracture are similar to those for a dislocation. Suppose you have to give first aid to a person with a fracture. You should keep the fractured bone still. If the bone is broken and it moves, the surrounding tissue can be harmed. Place ice on the fracture to stop the swelling. Treat the person for shock. Always get medical help.

*What are the first aid procedures for a fracture?*

Burns also require immediate first aid treatment. There are three different kinds of burns: first-, second- and third-degree. A first-degree burn is the mildest kind and involves only the surface layers of the skin. In this type, the skin becomes red and is sore. Running cool water over a first-degree burn will ease the pain. A first-degree burn will heal in about six days.

A second-degree burn is more serious than a first-degree burn. The usual signs are a red blotched appearance, blisters, and swelling. First aid for a second-degree burn includes placing the injured body part in cool water. The burn should then be covered with a clean, dry dressing. Care should be taken not to break the blisters. Pathogens causing infection can easily enter the body through broken blisters.

A third-degree burn is the most serious kind of burn. Signs of a third-degree burn are deep tissue destruction, blackened skin, or loss of skin. First aid includes treatment for shock. The burn should be covered with a thick, sterile bandage. Burned hands and legs should be kept above the level of the heart. Burned body parts should not be put into cold water. To prevent further tissue and nerve damage, ice should not be applied to severe burns. However, cold packs may be applied to the person's face, hands, or feet. Immediate medical help is needed.

*What are the signs of third-degree burns?*

1. Why is choking dangerous?
2. Why should severe bleeding be treated immediately?
3. How might poison enter a person's body?
4. Why can shock be dangerous?
5. Why should a fractured bone be kept still?

**Think About It**

# First Aid for Heat and Cold

Many types of illnesses and injuries result from very warm or cold weather. Perhaps you have been in very cold or very warm weather for a long period of time. How did you feel? Did you want to get into a more comfortable temperature?

## 18:6 Heat Cramps

*What are heat cramps?*

**Heat cramps** are sharp muscle pains that may occur during long periods of physical activity. Heat cramps in the abdomen or leg muscles often occur during warm or hot weather. However, heat cramps can affect many different muscles in the body.

It is easy to know when you have a heat cramp. Suppose you get a heat cramp in the calf muscle. The calf muscle is in the back of the leg halfway between the knee and ankle. You would feel a sharp pain in the muscle. If you watch the muscle, you may see it contract or get smaller. You may also feel it get very hard. The exact cause of a heat cramp may not be known. Often it is caused by a lack of salt in the body. During long periods of exercise, salt is lost through sweat.

**FIGURE 18–4.** Heat cramps may be caused by a lack of salt in the body.

Heat cramps can be treated easily. It is important to rest the affected muscle. During rest, firm pressure with the hands or light massages will help the muscle relax. The heat cramp should disappear within a few minutes. It is also important to drink plenty of fluids when a muscle cramps. Sipping salt water every fifteen minutes for one hour will help. If a person gets active too soon after resting, the heat cramps may return.

Another way to relieve a heat cramp in the calf muscle is to do special stretching exercises. Sit on the ground. Extend the legs together in front of you. Keep the knees straight; point the toes or pull them toward the body. The pain should go away.

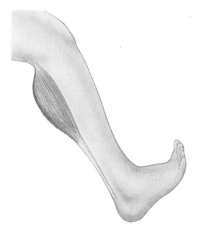

**FIGURE 18–5**. Massage can often relieve heat cramps.

## 18:7   Heat Exhaustion and Heatstroke

**Heat exhaustion** is a condition in which a person feels dizzy and tired from being in high temperatures for a long period of time. It is often caused by excess physical activity and extreme sweating while in a warm temperature. Persons who are not used to warm weather and who sweat heavily are affected most often.

A person with heat exhaustion will feel dizzy and have pale, cool, dry skin. The person's body temperature will either be normal or slightly above normal. First aid for heat exhaustion includes the following:

- Get to a cool place, lie down, and loosen clothing.
- Drink cool liquids. If possible, add salt to cool water and sip slowly.
- Sponge down with cold water.

These actions are usually enough to treat heat exhaustion. If a person does not feel better after being treated, medical help is needed.

**Heatstroke** is a sudden attack of illness from being in the sun or heat. The body is unable to sweat and cool itself. This causes the body temperature to rise as much as ten degrees above normal. A body temperature that high may destroy body tissue. Other signs and symptoms of heatstroke include hot, red, dry skin; headache; nausea; and weakness.

Heatstroke is a medical emergency. A person in this state should be taken to a hospital quickly. If not treated, heatstroke can result in death. First aid for heatstroke includes lowering body temperature. This can be done by moving the person into shade and sponging the skin with cool water.

Heat exhaustion and heatstroke can be prevented. Stay in cool places during hot, sunny weather. If signs and symptoms occur, stop all activity and rest.

*How can heat exhaustion and heatstroke be prevented?*

## 18:8  Sunburn

If you spend too much time in the sun, you may become sunburned. You can apply towels soaked in cool water to the sunburned area. This will reduce the pain. Taking cold showers can also be helpful. There are many products you can buy that may be used for reducing the pain. A pharmacist can help you choose the most effective product for your needs.

Severe cases of sunburn may result in second-degree burns. Blisters may appear and may fill with fluids. As with all second-degree burns, the blisters should not be broken. Pathogens may get into the body through the breaks in the skin. Medical care may be needed if severe sunburn covers a large area of the body.

**FIGURE 18–6**. Severe cases of sunburn may require medical attention.

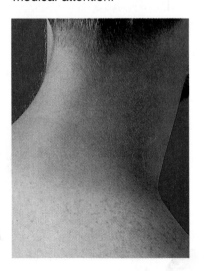

## 18:9  Frostbite and Hypothermia

**Frostbite** is damage to a body part due to freezing. The parts of the body most easily affected by frostbite are the ears, nose, toes, and fingers. The first sign of possible frostbite is pain. A tingling feeling may also be present. A person who has these symptoms should be moved into a warm area. When frostbite is present, the body part feels numb and looks waxy. Because the pain goes away, the person may not know he or she has frostbite. A white, cold spot may appear at the affected body part. A body part affected by frostbite should be placed in warm water. It should remain in the water for at least 20 minutes. Then it should be dried and kept warm. Get medical help as soon as possible.

**Hypothermia** (hi poh THUR mee uh) is a condition in which body temperature is lowered due to wind, cold, and dampness. Hypothermia can occur at temperatures as high as 50°F.

First aid for hypothermia includes warming the body. Move the person indoors and have him or her put on clean, dry clothing. Drinking hot fluids is helpful. Usually this is enough to treat hypothermia.

*What is the first aid treatment for hypothermia?*

Appropriate clothing in cold weather can help prevent hypothermia. Do not overdress, as this can cause sweating. Rather than wearing one heavy layer of clothing, wear several thin layers to be removed or worn as needed.

## ACTIVITY

### Preventing Hypothermia

Hypothermia can happen in many areas of the country. Write a list of ways you can prevent hypothermia. Focus on the type of clothing you might wear if you are going to be in cold weather. Visit a sporting goods store that sells clothing used for sports and camping. Interview a sales person. What kinds of clothing will help prevent hypothermia?

6. Why might a long distance runner get heat cramps?
7. Why is heatstroke extremely dangerous?
8. When does a sunburn require medical care?
9. Why may a person with frostbite not be aware of it?

**Think About It**

## Life Skills

► Know the basic rules of first aid.
► Know how to perform the Heimlich maneuver.
► Know how to use direct pressure to stop bleeding.
► Know the different kinds and treatments of burns.

# Health Highlights

## Lowering Body Temperature for Surgery

In recent years, physicians have been using lowered body temperature to aid them in some surgical procedures. In other words, physicians can place a person in hypothermia. Sometimes this can be helpful. Some physicians use this technique during special surgeries such as heart and brain surgeries. Lowered body temperature affects body systems. Blood pressure, heart rate, and breathing rate decrease. Blood flow is slowed. The tissues of the body need less oxygen when the body temperature is lowered. This helps keep body parts, such as the brain, from becoming harmed.

At some hospitals, physicians place babies in hypothermia. Suppose a baby needs open heart surgery. The physician can slow the flow of blood to the heart. The baby will receive a special injection to help it sleep. The baby is then placed in a special tub with ice. This lowers the body temperature. The physician can stop the heartbeat for a short time without harming the baby. Surgery can be performed. The heart is started again through gentle massage. When surgery ends, the baby is placed in warm water.

Hypothermia can also be used when a person needs brain surgery. The heart rate is lowered. The flow of blood to the brain is slowed enabling the physician to perform delicate surgery. A special machine is used to cool the blood in the body. The machine

that does this is called a heart-lung machine. The blood flows through the machine. The machine acts like a heart. It pumps cold blood, which flows more slowly through the body.

After surgery, the blood is warmed as it passes through the machine. The patient may also be placed in special blankets of warm water. This helps the body temperature return to normal. Through the use of hypothermia, delicate operations can be performed with less risk.

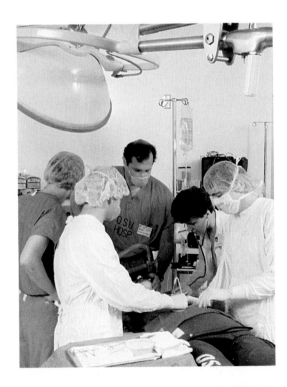

# Chapter 18 Review

**Summary**

1. Two general rules of first aid are to be calm and to get medical help. *18:1*
2. The Heimlich maneuver can be used to help a person who is choking. *18:2*
3. Direct pressure can be used in most cases to stop bleeding. *18:3*
4. A Poison Control Center can offer help to a person who needs to give first aid to a victim of poisoning. *18:4*
5. A person with any serious illness or injury should be treated for shock. *18:5*
6. A dislocation and fracture can be treated in similar ways. *18:5*
7. All types of burns should be treated, especially second- and third-degree burns. *18:5*
8. Heat cramps can often be relieved through massage. *18:6*
9. Signs of heatstroke include skin that is hot, red, and dry. *18:7*
10. Taking a cold shower can relieve pain due to sunburn. *18:8*
11. Frostbite most easily affects the nose, ears, toes, and fingers. *18:9*
12. Cold weather and wind can cause hypothermia. *18:9*

**Words for Health**

*Complete each sentence with the correct word.*
*DO NOT WRITE IN THIS BOOK.*

| | |
|---|---|
| direct pressure | heatstroke |
| first aid | Heimlich maneuver |
| fracture | hypothermia |
| frostbite | poison |
| heat cramps | shock |
| heat exhaustion | supplying artery |

1. Any substance that can harm the body after it enters the body is called a(n) _____.
2. _____ may have occurred if a finger feels numb and appears waxy.
3. Any break in a bone is a(n) _____.
4. Cold, dampness, and wind combine to lower body temperature and cause _____.
5. The main artery that carries blood to a limb is a(n) _____.

6. Any person who has a serious injury or illness should be treated for ____.

7. A procedure used to help a victim who has a blocked air passage is called the ____.

8. A person whose skin is pale, cool, and dry may be suffering from ____.

9. The quick care given to an injured person is called ____.

10. Most of the time, ____ can be used to stop bleeding.

11. A sudden attack of illness from being in the sun too long that causes a rise in body temperature is ____.

12. ____ are sharp muscle pains that may occur during long periods of physical activity.

## Reviewing Health

1. What are the general rules to follow in giving first aid?
2. What first aid steps should you take to help someone who is choking?
3. How can you help yourself if an object becomes stuck in your air passage?
4. What is the first step you would take to stop the bleeding from a break in the skin?
5. When should pressure to a supplying artery be used to stop bleeding?
6. How can you help a person who has taken a poison and is conscious? unconscious?
7. What are the signs of shock?
8. What are the first aid procedures for a fracture?
9. What are the signs of a second-degree burn?
10. What is the treatment for heat cramps?
11. What are the signs and symptoms of heat exhaustion?
12. What will happen if the body is unable to sweat?
13. Why should a person suffering from heatstroke be taken to a hospital immediately?
14. What can be done to relieve the pain of sunburn?
15. What are the first signs of possible frostbite?
16. What parts of the body are most easily affected by frostbite?

*Use the life skills from this chapter to respond to the following questions.*

*Situation:* You are having lunch with a friend. Both of you are eating hot dogs. You look at your friend and notice he has his hand to his throat and cannot talk.

1. What might you think is wrong with your friend?
2. What other evidence might make you think your friend needs help?
3. Describe the steps you would take to help your friend.

*Situation:* It is a sunny day and you and your friends have been out in the sun all day. One day later, one of your friends who was with you shows you a blister that has formed in a sunburned area. You notice your friend picking at the blister.

1. Why should your friend avoid picking at the blister?
2. What would you tell your friend to do to treat the blister?

*Situation:* While you and your friend are roller skating, she falls down on the sidewalk. You notice that her finger is bleeding.

1. What first aid procedure should you use to help your friend?
2. Why should your friend keep her finger raised?

1. Each student should identify one type of condition in which first aid is needed. Describe the first aid procedure and provide a picture or pictures of the procedure. The class can then put these pages together into a "First Aid Manual." One group can design and make a cover for the manual.
2. Make a list of the first aid supplies in your home. What supplies do you think you would need to have a complete first aid kit?
3. Visit an emergency squad headquarters and interview a paramedic. Ask what kind of training is needed for his or her job. Make a list of the most common types of medical emergencies to which he or she responds.
4. Contact your local Red Cross. Arrange to take a course in basic first aid. Demonstrate some procedures to the class.

# Safety in Your Environment

Unless we feel threatened, our safety is often taken for granted. However, with most injuries being due to accidents, actions should be taken by you to reduce your risks. Most accidents are avoidable, once you recognize the possibility of their occurrence.

# Chapter 19

**STUDENT OBJECTIVES:** *You will be able to*

- *describe how to keep safe in your environment.*
- *tell how to prevent injury from lightning, tornadoes, hurricanes, and earthquakes.*

People are safer when they learn ways to protect themselves. People can learn about safety in school or by reading newspapers. They can also learn about safety by watching special TV programs. And still, many people of all ages become injured each year. Accidents and crime are the leading causes of injuries to people your age. What can you do to keep safe in your environment?

## Safety Around You

If you read your local newspaper today, you will probably find a story that is related to safety. Perhaps there was a car accident. Maybe a house caught on fire or someone was injured because of a crime. Many possible accidents and injuries can easily be avoided. Some studies show that 80 percent or more of all accidents could have been prevented. To prevent or avoid accidents, it is important to understand their causes.

## 19:1 Causes of Accidents

When people are not safe, they can have accidents. Accidents are one of the leading causes of injuries and death to children. Have you ever had an accident? Perhaps you fell from your bike. Maybe you tripped over an object. You may have been doing something too fast. If you are aware of some of the causes of accidents, you can take steps to prevent them.

*Stress*  Stress is a leading cause of accidents. Have you ever tried to concentrate when you were under stress? It was probably difficult. Suppose you needed to repair something while standing on a ladder. You were concerned about a stressful event that occurred that day and found it hard to concentrate on the task. Your chances of losing your balance and falling were much greater under these circumstances. Studies show that people have more accidents when they are under stress.

*Age*  Very young children have accidents because their muscle control is not fully developed. Older people may have accidents because senses like seeing and hearing are not sharp. Even though persons your age are normally in good physical condition, they still have accidents. Accidents occur because people take needless risks. Accidents happen when people do not follow safety rules.

*How can stress cause accidents?*

**FIGURE 19–1**. Certain precautions can be taken to prevent an accident or at least reduce your chances of serious injury.

292

*Drugs*   Drugs, including alcohol, are a leading cause of accidents and death. Drugs affect a person's thinking and interfere with muscle control. The ability to make decisions and react quickly is reduced. More than half of all traffic accidents involve drugs.

*Illness*   When a person is ill, the risk of having an accident increases. Illness often makes a person tired. An ill person's senses are not as sharp. Medicine may cause a person to be less able to think clearly and react quickly. While taking medication, usual activities like riding a bike, may become risk behaviors.

FIGURE 19-2. The dangers of drinking and driving affect everyone.

## 19:2   Motor Vehicle Safety

While you are not old enough to drive a car, you still have a responsibility to be safe while riding in a car. Many people your age are injured each year in cars because they do not follow safety rules. Always wear lap and shoulder safety belts correctly. Do not distract the driver of the car. You should also follow safety rules when riding in a school bus.

Never accept a ride from a person who has been drinking alcohol. While this may be difficult at times, you have a right to be safe from someone who drinks and drives. Suppose you are at a friend's home and an adult offers to drive you home. However, the adult has been drinking. You can say, "NO. Thanks for the offer. I'll call home and have my older brother pick me up."  How else might you handle this situation?

All terrain vehicles (ATVs) have become popular with many people. Advertisements show these vehicles to be safe and fun. Yet many boys and girls your age have become injured or have died from ATV accidents. The driver of the ATV can easily lose control when riding over rough terrain. The ATV might then roll over and fall on the driver. New laws have been passed that provide training for people who buy ATVs. These laws also ban the sale of ATVs that have only three wheels. To remain safe on ATVs, wear protective gear like helmets and follow local laws.

*Why are ATVs dangerous?*

**FIGURE 19–3**. Following water safety rules lowers risk of injury.

*Why should you avoid jumping into the water to save a person who is in danger of drowning?*

## 19:3  Safety in the Water

Drowning is the second leading cause of accidental death to people your age. Following safety rules will lower the risk of injury while in the water. Always swim with at least one other person. Swim only where a lifeguard is on duty. If you are in a boat, always wear a life jacket.

Suppose you and a friend are at a pool. Your friend goes into the water. You hear your friend yelling for help. Your friend appears to be drowning. Do not jump into the water to save your friend. A drowning person panics. This person can pull you under. What should you do? Throw something that floats to your friend. If there is nothing available, hold out a long pole or branch that your friend can reach. Lie on the ground, flat on your stomach. Then extend the pole or branch. By lying in this position, you lower your risk of getting pulled into the water. If others are around, form a human chain while you use the pole.

## 19:4  Preventing Falls and Fires

Falls and fires are the leading causes of home accidents. Falls can easily be prevented. Be sure all walkways, especially stairs, are clear of objects. All parts of a home should be well-lighted. A secure ladder should be used correctly when reaching for something that is high.

There are many reasons that fires happen in a home. Cigarette smoking is a major cause of fires. Often a cigarette is not put out completely. It may fall from the ashtray onto furniture or the floor. People should never smoke in bed because they may fall asleep.

Many home fires are caused by overloading electrical circuits. Too many appliances may be connected to one outlet. Wires in an outlet can overheat. A fire can start in a wall and spread quickly before being detected.

Care should be taken when cooking. Suppose you put cooking oil in a pan and heat the oil by placing the burner on high. The oil may catch on fire and spread quickly. When cooking and using oil, do not leave the area. Do not cook using oil on high heat.

*What is a safety tip to follow when cooking with oil?*

## 19:5 Safety from Crime

One of the major health problems that young people face today is violent crime. Violent crimes are those in which a person receives physical harm. Many violent crimes can be prevented by using safe actions.

Sometimes, violent crimes occur in a home. There are ways you can be protected in your home. When alone, keep all doors and windows locked. If someone knocks on the door, do not open it unless you know who it is. Look through a peephole or ask who it is before opening the door.

**FIGURE 19–4.** Actions can be taken to help prevent crime.

Suppose you are babysitting. Never let anyone in the home unless you have been given specific instructions to do so. Be sure the people who have hired you to babysit leave a phone number where they can be reached. If someone tries to enter a home forcefully, call the police immediately. Dial 9-1-1 if your community uses this emergency phone number. When you dial this number, the address from which the call is placed shows up on a computer screen. Tell the person who answers what is happening. Help will be sent immediately. If the 9-1-1 number is not used in your community, dial the number 0. An operator will answer your call. Tell the operator there is an emergency and you need the police. You will be connected to the police immediately. Give the address where you are and tell what is happening.

Suppose you are home alone and you get a phone call from someone you do not know. This person asks for your parents. You might say, "My parents cannot come to the phone now. May I take a message?" Do not give a stranger your name or say your parents are not at home.

# ACTIVITY

## Analyzing Newspaper Events

Find five newspaper articles that describe accidents. Read and analyze these articles. On a piece of paper, describe how the accidents occurred. Tell about the kinds of injuries that resulted. Tell how you think these accidents could have been prevented.

## Think About It

1. How can your ability to handle stress help keep you safe?
2. Why should you say NO to accepting a ride from someone who has been drinking alcohol?
3. Why should you never swim alone?
4. Why is it important to have a well-lighted home?
5. Why should you know how to make an emergency phone call?

## Safety from Disasters

The disasters described in this part of the chapter cannot be prevented. However, the risk of injury that might result from these disasters can be lowered. It is important to know what action to take when a disaster strikes. Following the recommended safety tips may save your life and the lives of others in the event of a violent storm or earthquake.

## 19:6  Lightning

When people think of disasters in the environment, they most often think about hurricanes, tornadoes, or earthquakes. These disasters cause much damage to homes and property and can cause many deaths. For this reason they get most of the headlines in the news. These disasters can be dangerous, but the weather condition that causes more deaths than any other is lightning. Electrical storms occur in almost every area of the United States.

**Lightning** is an electrical discharge that travels from one cloud to another or between a cloud and Earth. Lightning results from certain changes in the atmosphere. Suppose you were standing under a tree during an electrical storm and lightning struck it. The electricity could travel from the tree to your body and into the ground. The electricity would burn and destroy body tissues. It might be powerful enough to cause serious injury or even death.

If you are outdoors during an electrical storm, hurry to try to get shelter indoors. If you remain outside, do not stand under tall objects that are outdoors, such as trees. Lightning is attracted to and strikes tall objects easily. The electricity from the lightning might then travel into your body.

Suppose you are running across a field when a storm was approaching. You could be the tallest object if you are in an open area. To help avoid being struck by lightning, you could roll into a ball on the ground. This would lower your body to the ground. The chances of your getting struck by lightning would be lessened.

*What is lightning?*

**FIGURE 19–5.** Shelter indoors should be taken during an electrical storm.

If you are swimming, get out of the water immediately. Lightning can travel easily through water.

Here are some other tips to keep you safe during an electrical storm.

*What are some safety tips to follow during an electrical storm?*

- Do not touch or stand near metal objects.
- Keep away from windows.
- Do not take a bath or shower while lightning is occurring in the area. Electricity can travel through metal pipes into water in a tub. The electricity will then pass through your body.
- Stay away from power lines and electrical towers.

## 19:7 Wind Storms

A **tornado** is a storm of whirling winds that forms over land and moves at very high speeds. Tornadoes are also called twisters. Although tornadoes can strike with little or no warning, they usually can be seen approaching. A **tornado warning** is an emergency announcement issued by the weather bureau when a tornado has been spotted. During a tornado warning, sirens will

**FIGURE 19–6.** Weather forecasters generally know when a tornado might develop.

sound. This means you are to take shelter immediately. At home, go to the center of your basement. If you have no basement, go to the lowest floor of the house. Lie on the floor in the center of the building away from windows. If possible, take cover under heavy furniture. If you cannot get indoors, lie flat on the ground.

Weather forecasters often know when a tornado might develop. A **tornado watch** is a message issued when weather conditions are right for a tornado to develop. When this happens, listen to the radio for instructions to protect yourself.

Remember that tornadoes are very powerful. They can knock down buildings and lift trees from the ground. Tornadoes can also lift cars into the air. Most injuries from tornadoes result from people being hit by objects flying in the air. You should always take tornado watches and warnings seriously. Take the necessary precautions and follow the instructions given to remain safe.

A **hurricane** is a storm with high winds and heavy rains that forms over water. To be considered a hurricane, winds must reach speeds of 74 miles per hour or higher. Hurricanes usually occur along the Gulf and Atlantic coasts. The destruction and injuries that result from hurricanes are caused by high winds and high tides that cause flooding.

You can protect yourself if a hurricane is approaching.

- Listen for radio and TV warnings about the hurricane issued by the weather bureau. People should leave their homes if they are advised to do so when a hurricane is approaching.
- Listen also for messages telling you directions for leaving the area safely.
- If advised to do so, shut off water and electricity in the home.
- Stay away from windows if you are in a building during a hurricane.
- Do not leave a building until the storm is over.
- Stay out of and away from coastal waters during a hurricane.

**FIGURE 19–7.** Hurricanes usually occur along the Gulf and Atlantic coasts.

*What is a hurricane?*

## 19:8　Earthquakes

An **earthquake** is movement below the surface of Earth that causes tremors on the surface. Tremors can cause trees to be uprooted and buildings to collapse. Most injuries are caused by the falling objects and fires. Fires can occur when natural gas lines or electrical wires are broken.

Earthquakes occur all around the world. In the United States, they occur most often on the West Coast. However, they can occur anywhere in the country.

Some earthquakes are more severe than others. Here are some safety tips to remember if you are in an area when an earthquake occurs.

- Stay calm. Do not panic.
- When indoors, take shelter under a desk or table. Keep away from objects that can fall on you. Stay away from windows.
- If you are in school, get under a desk.
- If you are outdoors, get away from buildings.
- Do not stand under any electrical wires or power lines if you are outdoors.

**Think About It**

6. Why should you avoid standing outside during an electrical storm?
7. Why should you stay away from windows if you are in a building during a hurricane?
8. Why are earthquakes dangerous?

# Life Skills

- ▶ Do not accept a ride from a driver who has been drinking alcohol.
- ▶ Always wear safety belts correctly when riding in a car.
- ▶ Do not overload electrical outlets.
- ▶ Know how to make an emergency telephone call.
- ▶ Avoid being outdoors during an electrical storm.
- ▶ Know how to protect yourself from injury due to tornadoes, hurricanes, and earthquakes.

# Chapter 19 Review

**Summary**

1. Stress, age, drugs, and illness commonly cause accidental injuries. *19:1*
2. There are rules for safety when riding in a car or on an ATV. *19:2*
3. Following water safety rules can help prevent drownings. *19:3*
4. Hazards that cause falls and fires can be easily prevented if people are more cautious. *19:4*
5. Following safety rules at home and knowing how to make emergency telephone calls are necessary when alone or babysitting. *19:5*
6. Injuries caused by lightning can be avoided by moving indoors during an electrical storm. *19:6*
7. Tornadoes and hurricanes are two kinds of wind storms that can cause great damage. *19:7*
8. Injuries due to tremors from earthquakes can be avoided by knowing rules for safety. *19:8*

**Words for Health**

*Complete each sentence with the correct word.*
*DO NOT WRITE IN THIS BOOK.*

earthquake
hurricane
lightning
tornado
tornado warning
tornado watch

1. A(n) _____ is a storm that forms over land in which there are swirling high winds.
2. An electrical charge that can travel between a cloud and Earth is called _____.
3. When weather conditions are right for a tornado to develop, a(n) _____ can be issued.
4. Heavy winds with rain near coastal areas may be indications of a(n) _____.
5. When a tornado has been spotted, a(n) _____ is issued.
6. In the United States, a(n) _____ can occur anywhere in the country.

**Reviewing Health**

1. How can stress be a cause of accidents?
2. How can age be a cause of accidents involving very young children and older people?
3. Why does illness increase the risk of having an accident?
4. What are two safety rules to follow when riding in a car?
5. What are two safety rules to follow when swimming?
6. How can falls in the home be prevented?
7. Why should people never smoke in bed?
8. Why should you avoid overloading electrical circuits?
9. How may cooking with oil be dangerous?
10. How can you help protect yourself in your home?
11. What are two emergency telephone numbers to use if you need help?
12. How can you keep safe during an electrical storm?
13. What are two kinds of wind storms and how do they differ?
14. What steps should you take upon hearing a signal for a tornado watch or a tornado warning?
15. How can you protect yourself in a hurricane?
16. What can you do to keep safe during an earthquake?

**Using Life Skills**

*Use the life skills from this chapter to respond to the following questions.*

*Situation:* You are at a party at a friend's house. You need a ride home. One choice is to go with a friend's sister who has offered you a ride. However, she has offered several others a ride and there will not be enough safety belts for everyone. Your other choice is to go with an adult who was also visiting. He does not live near you but has offered to take you home.

1. With which person should you accept a ride and why?
2. What other responsible choice can you make?

*Situation:* You are jogging when you notice a storm approaching. You see dark clouds and you suspect that there will be some lightning. You will soon be caught in the storm.

1. What plans might you make for shelter?
2. How can you best protect yourself from possible injury?

*Situation:* You and a friend are playing basketball in your driveway when you hear tornado sirens. Your friend tells you he is going to ride his bike home before the storm hits.

1. What would you suggest to your friend?
2. What steps should you and your friend take to protect yourselves from the storm?
3. What would you do if you were at a playground?

*Situation:* You are home alone and you hear a sound at the door. You look through the peephole but you don't recognize the person. He is trying to open the door. Your community does not have a 9-1-1 number.

1. Whom should you call for help?
2. What information should you give when you call?
3. What would you do until the police arrive?

## Extending Health

1. Imagine that you have been appointed safety director for a group of young boys and girls. Your job is to develop an exciting activity that would teach these children safety tips about riding in a car. Design your activity. You can draw pictures. You can develop songs about safety. Present your activity to the class.
2. Collect one current events article from a newspaper each day for one week. These articles should be related to injuries that resulted from accidents or weather-related storms. For each article, describe the type of accident that occurred, the conditions that may have caused the accident, and how you think the accident could have been prevented.
3. Find out if your state has a safety belt law and exactly what the law is. How many other states also have a safety belt law? Find out about other automobile safety features that have been developed or are being tested, such as air bags. Which of these features are currently being used by consumers?
4. Contact an agency that is concerned with disaster services. This agency may be associated with the American Red Cross, a church, or a government agency. Find out how the agency has helped people who have been struck by natural disasters, such as floods, hurricanes, and so on.

# Community and Environmental Health

Did you know . . .

▶ the effects of pollution are worldwide?

▶ we can stop the destruction of the ozone layer by controlling air pollution?

THRU HAZARDOUS CARGO CARRIERS

MUST USE

COLUMBUS BY-PASS

# Your Environment and Health

We each have a need to experience a healthful environment. It may be hiking by a mountain lake or walking down a busy street. But no environment can be preserved without a real attempt by each of us to control our pollution.

# Chapter 20

**STUDENT OBJECTIVES:** *You will be able to*

● *describe the causes and prevention of air, water, solid waste, and noise pollution, and the effects they have on health.*

● *describe the effects of pesticides, acid rain, radiation, and radon on health.*

Your environment is important to your health. You need clean air to breathe. You need clean water to drink. Breathing clean air and drinking clean water help keep you healthy. Air and water are only two parts of your environment. This chapter discusses these and other elements of your environment. It describes different ways your environment may be unsafe. This chapter will also tell you how you can keep healthy in your environment.

## Types of Pollution

Most likely you enjoy seeing a picture of a mountain scene. The air looks clear. The land looks clean. The plant life is thick and green. There is no trash present. This picture shows one kind of clean environment. It is the kind of environment in which most people enjoy living.

## 20:1   Air Pollution

**Pollution** is the presence of materials in the environment that are harmful to living things. Pollution may result from the burning of coal, oil, and gasoline. A **pollutant** is a harmful substance in the environment. Many pollutants in the air are poisonous. You may not always be able to see or smell them. However, they can harm your body.

*What is a pollutant?*

Your body uses the oxygen in the air that you breathe. Steps have been taken to improve the quality of that air. Cars are being made with antipollution devices that reduce the amount of harmful products released into the air.

For many years pollutants were released into the air from factories. Today, factories must meet clean air guidelines established by the Environmental Protection Agency (EPA). The **EPA** is a government agency that sets and enforces laws to prevent air, land, and water pollution. The EPA has been successful in reducing the amount of pollutants from factories.

*What does the EPA do?*

Everyone can help reduce air pollution. Try to walk, use public transportation, or ride a bike when possible. Fewer vehicles on the road will help reduce pollution from engine exhaust. Many communities encourage people to use car pools. A **car pool** is a system in which a group of people travel together in one car instead of using separate cars.

**FIGURE 20–1.** The combination of smoke and many different chemicals causes smog in a city.

## 20:2 Water Pollution

We use water every day for drinking, cooking, and washing. We eat fish that have lived in water. We even use water for activities such as swimming.

Sometimes water is made unsafe by pollution. For instance, industrial waste products from factories are sometimes dumped into waterways. Ships may spill oil and other wastes into the oceans. Water might also be polluted by heat. **Thermal pollution** is the presence of heated water from an industry dumped into a waterway. Heated water has less oxygen than cool or cold water. The combination of the raised temperature and reduced oxygen kills fish and harms other life in the water.

Sometimes water may be polluted by sewage. **Sewage** is waste material from homes and industries. Sewage can harm people because it contains pathogens. Many waterways have been made safer because EPA laws prohibit sewage from being dumped into them.

Most drinking water in the United States has been treated and purified in a water-treatment plant. In a water-treatment plant, the water from lakes and rivers passes through different kinds of filters that trap pathogens. Chemicals are then added to the water to kill any remaining pathogens. The cleaned water is then pumped through underground pipes into homes.

Some people get their drinking water from underground wells. Usually, this water is safe. However, harmful chemicals used on farm crops can soak into the groundwater. **Groundwater** is the natural supply of water from rain and snow that collects under Earth's surface. Groundwater supplies water for wells and springs. People can become ill from drinking polluted well water. For this reason, well water should be tested regularly to make sure it is safe to drink.

## 20:3 Solid Waste Pollution

Solid wastes are discarded waste products that threaten the environment. This includes trash and garbage. Garbage attracts flies, mosquitoes, and rats that may spread pathogens.

**FIGURE 20–2.** Oil from ships may pollute the oceans.

*What is the purpose of a water-treatment plant?*

Many cities control solid wastes by creating sanitary landfills. A **sanitary landfill** is an area where layers of solid wastes are dumped and covered with dirt. After the landfill is full, the land eventually may be made useful. Some sanitary landfills have been turned into recreational areas.

Some wastes are hazardous and are disposed of by being buried underground. **Hazardous wastes** are harmful substances that are difficult to discard safely. Hazardous wastes are stored and buried in special metal cans or drums. Occasionally, these wastes leak from their containers and enter the groundwater. Then this poses a serious threat to the health of people in the area.

Another way to treat solid wastes is through recycling. **Recycling** is the reusing of products. Products such as aluminum cans can be melted down and reused.

## 20:4 Noise Pollution

**Noise pollution** is the presence of sounds that are loud enough to harm a person's health. Examples of noise pollution are low-flying jets, loud music, and exploding firecrackers. Noise pollution can harm your health by causing a hearing loss.

A buzzing or humming may be present in your ears after hearing a loud noise. This is a sign of temporary hearing loss. If the nerves in the ears become damaged, the damage may be permanent. A **decibel** is the unit used to measure the loudness of sound. A whisper may be 20 decibels; a jet plane at takeoff may be 150 decibels. Being around sounds above 85 decibels for long periods of time can result in hearing loss.

You can reduce your risks of hearing loss caused by loud noise. Do not listen to loud music. Avoid being in places where there is loud noise.

**Think About It**

1. How does the EPA help protect you?
2. How can recycling reduce pollution?
3. Why should you avoid listening to loud music?

# Environmental Hazards

There are many different kinds of hazards in the environment. Hazards can be controlled so that they will not be harmful. You will study some hazards in this part of the chapter.

## 20:5  Pesticides

A **pesticide** (PES tuh side) is a poison that is used to kill some insects and other pests. Think about a fruit you have eaten. Most likely this fruit had been sprayed with a pesticide while it was growing. Pesticides can be helpful when they are used correctly. When used incorrectly, they may be harmful.

*What is a pesticide?*

Farmers use pesticides to save crops from insect destruction. Without pesticides, crops might be eaten by insects. However, some pesticides can harm people if they are swallowed. The government has laws concerning how these pesticides should be used. Some research shows that exposure to certain pesticides can cause cancer. Thus, while pesticides can be helpful, they can also be harmful.

You may have pesticides in your home that are used to kill garden or house pests. Since pesticides are poisons, they should be used and stored carefully. Do not use pesticides outdoors when the wind is blowing. The pesticide may be inhaled. Read the label on a pesticide container. It will list the ingredients and tell you how to use the pesticide safely.

*Why should the warning label on a pesticide be read before it is used?*

 ACTIVITY

### Understanding a Pesticide Label

Read the label on a pesticide container. Draw the pesticide label on a sheet of paper. Write the name of the product. Write the directions for safe use. Write what should be done if the pesticides gets into a person's body. Compare your label with those of your classmates. What did you learn from comparing the labels?

### 20:6 Acid Rain

**Acid rain** is rain that contains a high amount of acid. Acid rain forms when sulfur from burning fuels mixes with moisture in the air. The moisture then falls as acid rain. Acid rain is harmful. When it falls into rivers and lakes, plants and animals in the water are affected. Acid rain also destroys crops and trees.

*Why is it difficult to control acid rain?*

Acid rain is a worldwide problem that may not be easy to solve. One approach is to reduce air pollution caused by burning coal, gas, and oil. Acid rain can result from the use of coal as a fuel. The wind blows the pollution caused by the burning of coal to different countries. This is the reason controlling acid rain is not easy. People from all countries must work to solve the problem of acid rain.

### 20:7 Radiation

Radiation occurs naturally in the environment. **Radiation** is energy given off by atoms as light or particles. Radiation added to the environment or used incorrectly is a hazard to health.

One way radiation is added to the environment is the use of X rays. X rays are used to take pictures of inner body parts, such as bones. X rays are used by dentists to check teeth for cavities.

**FIGURE 20−3.** Radiation is produced in nuclear power plants.

Radiation can also be used to treat cancer. However, if not used correctly, X rays can cause cancer. Careful records, including dates of X rays received, will help prevent too much radiation from being used on a person.

Another way radiation is added to the environment is from nuclear power plants. Radiation is produced in these plants to help make electricity. In 1986, an explosion in a nuclear power plant in the Soviet Union released radiation into the air. People in the Soviet Union will continue to contract cancer for several years as a result of the exposure to the radiation.

The ultraviolet rays of the sun present another problem. **Ultraviolet rays** are harmful rays from the sun. Ultraviolet rays are filtered by the ozone layer. The **ozone layer** is the part of the atmosphere that filters out most of the sun's ultraviolet rays. Air pollution is causing the ozone layer to become thin above certain parts of Earth. Thus, the ultraviolet rays are not filtered as they should be. The result will be an increase in the number of cases of skin cancer.

*Why is the ozone layer important to health?*

To protect yourself from ultraviolet rays, avoid being in the sun too long and cover parts of your body that will be exposed. Do not use sunlamps or tanning booths. Both of these use ultraviolet rays.

4. Why is acid rain a worldwide problem?
5. Why is there more danger from ultraviolet rays now than in the past?

**Think About It**

## Life Skills

▶ Travel using public transportation, walking, or riding a bike when possible.
▶ Use all pesticides according to directions.
▶ Keep a record of the X rays you have had.

# Health Highlights

## Radon

Radon is a radioactive gas that occurs in nature. You cannot see, smell, or taste it. Radon results from a breakdown of uranium. It is found in soil or rocks that contain uranium.

Outdoors, radon is not a problem. It is not usually found in large amounts in any one area. However, indoors, radon can be a serious problem. Scientists believe that radon may be responsible for 5000 to 10 000 deaths each year by causing lung cancer. The risk of developing lung cancer from radon is closely linked with inhaling the gas. The greater the concentration of radon and the time exposed to it, the greater the risk of developing lung cancer.

How does radon cause lung cancer? When radon is inhaled, it gets trapped in the lungs. Because it is radioactive, it releases small bursts of energy that damage lung tissue.

How does radon get inside a home? Radon moves through small spaces in the soil under a house or other building. If there are cracks in a basement floor or wall, radon can leak into a building. This does not happen in every home. For example, two homes can be next to each other. One home can have a high level of radon while the other does not. To find out the amount of radon in a home, radon detectors are used. Radon testing is a simple and inexpensive procedure.

There are ways to protect your home from radon. Seal all cracks in a basement. This will stop radon from entering. Spend less time in places where radon may be present. For example, do not stay in a basement that tests for a high concentration of radon. When practical, keep windows open. Use fans to increase airflow through the house. This helps lower the concentration of radon in the house. If people in your family smoke, encourage them to stop. Inhaling tobacco smoke combined with exposure to radon increases the risk of lung cancer.

# Chapter 20 Review

**Summary**

1. The burning of harmful products such as coal and gasoline contributes to air pollution. *20:1*
2. Water pollution can result from many different kinds of pollutants, including sewage. *20:2*
3. Solid wastes can be buried in sanitary landfills. *20:3*
4. Buzzing and humming in the ears may be results of noise pollution. *20:4*
5. Pesticides can be both helpful and harmful. *20:5*
6. Acid rain is a worldwide problem that is difficult to control. *20:6*
7. Among the different forms of radiation are the sun's rays and X rays. *20:7*

**Words for Health**

*Complete each sentence below with the correct word.*
*DO NOT WRITE IN THIS BOOK.*

| | |
|---|---|
| acid rain | pesticide |
| car pool | pollutant |
| decibel | pollution |
| EPA | radiation |
| groundwater | recycling |
| hazardous wastes | sanitary landfill |
| noise pollution | sewage |
| ozone layer | thermal pollution |

1. The placing of heated water in a river or lake is an example of _____.

2. _____ can result from polluted air that travels from one country to another.

3. The _____ is a government agency that makes laws to protect people from pollution.

4. Reusing a product such as glass is an example of _____.

5. A(n) _____ is used to kill insects that can destroy crops.

6. You are protected from the sun's harmful rays by the _____ of the atmosphere.

7. Loud sounds in the environment are examples of _____

8. Harmful substances that are difficult to discard safely are called _____.

315

9. Anything in the environment that is harmful is called a(n) ____.
10. The loudness of sound is measured in ____.
11. ____ is energy given off by atoms as light or particles.
12. Water that soaks into the ground supplying wells and springs is ____.
13. ____ is the presence of materials in the environment that harm living things.
14. Waste material from homes and industries that contains pathogens is ____.
15. A(n) ____ is a place where layers of solid wastes are dumped and covered with dirt.

**Reviewing Health**

1. How does most air pollution occur?
2. What can you do to help reduce air pollution?
3. Why is thermal pollution harmful?
4. How is the dumping of sewage regulated?
5. Why should well water be tested?
6. What are some examples of solid wastes?
7. How can hazardous wastes become a problem after they are buried?
8. What are the signs of hearing loss due to exposure to loud noises?
9. How can pesticides be helpful?
10. Why should pesticides be used carefully?
11. How does acid rain form?
12. Why is acid rain a difficult problem to solve?
13. Why is the ozone layer of the atmosphere important?
14. What are some ways to protect yourself against radiation?

**Using Life Skills**

*Use the life skills from this chapter to respond to the following questions.*

*Situation:* You have been asked to go to the store by your parent. It is a nice day to be outdoors. You can either ride your bike or have someone drive you. The store is about one mile from your home.

1. Which way of travel would be most beneficial to your environment? Why?
2. How else might you choose to go to the store and yet not pollute the environment?

*Situation:* You are outdoors helping your mother and father with garden work. A can of bug spray is part of the garden supplies. You notice a lot of bugs on a bush. It is a windy day. The wind is traveling from west to east.

1. What precautions should you take if you use/or are in an area where bug spray is being used?
2. What should you tell your parents if you choose to spray the bugs?

*Situation:* Your soccer team is planning to play in a large tournament in a neighboring city. Many teams from different areas of the state and some from surrounding states will be involved. Your coach mentioned that you will need to arrive at the field early because parking will be a problem.

1. How might car pools be used in this situation?
2. What information would be needed to organize the families interested in this method of transportation?
3. What are some other occasions when using a car pool would be easy to use and give benefits to those involved?

**Extending Health**

1. Radon is a problem of great concern. You can find information about radon by calling or writing to your local health department. You can also get information from your local chapter of the American Lung Association. Write a one page report that describes what people can do to protect their home from radon.
2. Contact the Environmental Protection Agency in your state. Ask for information about the extent of pollution in your state and the regulations passed to control air, water, and land pollution. Report the information in the form of a newscast with visual aids. This could be done as a group activity with each person taking a different role in the newscast.

# Community Health Services

Many programs promoting health are made available by your community. You may already participate in one or more of these activities. What you may not be familiar with, however, is what is provided by your community to keep you safe and well.

**STUDENT OBJECTIVES:** *You will be able to*

● *identify the characteristics of community health agencies and services.*

● *describe the purpose and functions of hospitals.*

What might the American Cancer Society, the local health department, and a community hospital have in common? Each plays a role in helping you remain healthy. This chapter tells how health agencies and health professionals work to protect the health of people in a community.

## Health Departments and Agencies

The water in a community swimming pool is tested to make sure it is free of pathogens. This is one way people work to help others in the community remain in good health.

## 21:1  Health Departments ──────────

Every city has a health department that helps people. Some health departments are local. That is, they help people who live in a community, town, or city. Other health departments are statewide, serving people throughout the state. Nationwide health departments help people across the country. Each public health department is under the control of the local, state, or federal government.

People of different professions work in health departments. **Sanitarians** are people who inspect restaurants. They make sure the food that restaurants serve or sell is safe to eat. Sanitarians check certain functions in a restaurant. They make sure food is stored properly. They may check that water used to clean dishes is hot enough to kill any pathogens. They also make sure the restaurant and workers are clean.

Health educators work in health departments. **Health educators** are people who teach skills needed for healthful living. Health educators tell people about health problems. They may develop posters, booklets, and pamphlets that help people learn about certain diseases. They may give speeches to groups of people and conduct special classes about different health problems.

Health departments keep records about health and specific health concerns. They have information about certain diseases. The information is gathered by special workers who discover the ways diseases are spread. They use this information to control the spread of diseases through early detection.

Many health departments have clinics. A **clinic** is an area in a health department or hospital that offers medical assistance to people in a community.

**FIGURE 21–1.** Information about programs that promote health is available from the health education office in your community.

## 21:2  Voluntary Health Agencies ──────

A **voluntary health agency** is an agency that fights a specific health problem by raising money through donations. There are many agencies of this type. The American Lung Association fights diseases of the lungs. It offers classes to help people stop smoking and gives out information that tells the dangers of smoking. The American Lung Association also gives money to people who research problems about lung disease. It conducts summer camps for boys and girls who have asthma.

*What is an example of a voluntary health agency?*

The American Cancer Society is a voluntary agency that supports efforts to prevent cancer. The agency develops written material about the dangers of cancer. This agency provides speakers to inform people about cancer and grants funds to people who try to find cures for cancer. The American Cancer Society can help families of cancer patients. The agency will recommend other sources that may provide further help.

The American Heart Association is an agency that supports efforts to fight heart disease. Like the other agencies, it develops printed materials. These materials inform the public about ways to prevent heart disease. The agency sponsors classes to teach people CPR, a first aid procedure. The American Heart Association gives money to people who study ways to improve heart health.

There are many more voluntary health agencies that help people in your community. At some time, you may need to use a health agency. You can find the names of more of these in your local telephone book.

 ## ACTIVITY

### Health Agency Directory

Imagine that you have been asked to develop a directory of health agencies. Identify five different health agencies and make an advertisement about each. Draw pictures and write slogans, and a brief description of the services your agencies provide. Advertise the agencies in your directory.

**FIGURE 21–2.** In most communities, programs are provided to promote health.

## 21:3  Community Health and Fitness _____

Most likely you have been involved in a community program that promotes health through fitness. Have you ever been in a "Y" or an athletic club? There are many ways you can use these organizations. You can use different kinds of machines to build strong muscles. You might join classes in aerobic dancing. Lifetime sports, such as tennis or golf, may be learned.

Many communities have programs conducted through schools. After school hours, school buildings may be used to promote health. Health education classes or fitness classes, such as aerobic dancing, may be offered.

Colleges and universities may open facilities for public use. They may have tennis courts or organized family programs for recreation.

Many communities have park or recreation departments that may sponsor team sports for boys and girls. These sports might include little league baseball, basketball, and soccer.

What other agencies for fitness and health are located near your home? What services do they have? How can they be helpful to you?

*How can you keep fit through community health agencies?*

**Think About It**

1. What role does a health department play in helping you keep healthy?
2. How might the American Lung Association be helpful to a person who smokes?

## Hospitals

Have you ever needed medical treatment that could not be provided at your physician's office? If so, you may have had to use the services of a hospital.

### 21:4 Why People Go into Hospitals ———

A **hospital** is a place where people receive medical care, diagnosis, and treatment. A hospital is a part of the health services in your community.

There are many reasons to go into a hospital.

- A woman may go into a hospital to give birth. The hospital has special equipment for a safe birth. Most babies are born in hospitals.
- People may go into a hospital for treatment of a sudden illness or injury. Hospitals have special equipment to handle emergencies.
- People may go into hospitals when they need a specialist or close observation. For example, a person may have a kidney problem. This person may need a special machine to do the work usually done by the kidneys.
- People may go into a hospital when they do not know the cause of, or what to do for their illness. Special tests can be performed to diagnose health problems.

A person might become ill or injured at any time. He or she might need treatment late at night, during a weekend, or on a holiday. For this reason, hospitals are open 24 hours a day.

### 21:5 Physicians Who Work at a Hospital

Many different kinds of physicians work in a hospital. An **intern** is a graduate student who has completed medical school and is doing a year of further study at a hospital. This extra year of study is called an **internship.** A **resident** is a physician getting advanced training in special areas of medical care or surgery.

*What is a hospital?*

**FIGURE 21–3**. Physicians and nurses scrub their hands before surgery to reduce the risk of infection.

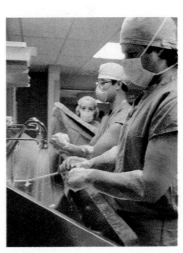

A **residency** is a period of advanced training in a special area of medical care. A physician doing his or her residency may study about heart health and heart problems. Upon completing training, the physician will be a heart specialist. A specialist is a physician who works in a particular area of medicine.

## 21:6   What Happens in a Hospital? ───────

Many people have a fear of hospitals. They are afraid because they are not sure what might happen in a hospital.

Suppose you needed hospital care. Your physician would call the hospital and make the first arrangements. You would then be told when to arrive at the hospital. Upon your arrival, you and your parents or guardian would go to a registration desk where information would be taken. This information might include your name, address, parents' name, and family physician's name. A plastic bracelet, used for identification, would be issued. It would be worn throughout your hospital stay.

You would be assigned a room. You might have a private room or share a room with other patients. Perhaps one, two, or three other people would share the room. Some tests may be done. Body temperature would be checked. A nurse may draw blood to be sent to a lab to be analyzed. Urine may also be collected and analyzed in a lab. A chest X ray may also be taken. This would tell the physician how healthy your lungs are. Blood pressure and heart rate might also be checked.

Many different activities could take place in the hospital. You might often hear messages over the loudspeaker. You would probably notice hospital personnel. Some of these nurses and physicians would regularly check on your health status. You would be receiving very good care.

Breakfast, lunch, and dinner would be served in your room. Often hospitals allow you to choose what you want to eat from a special menu. There would be times set aside for you to have visitors. Sometimes, visiting time is limited so you do not get too tired.

*What happens when a person first arrives at a hospital?*

**FIGURE 21-4**. Becoming familiar with a hospital setting helps to lessen fears associated with entering a hospital.

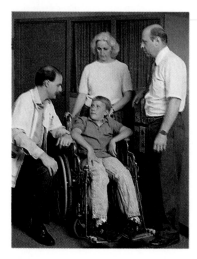

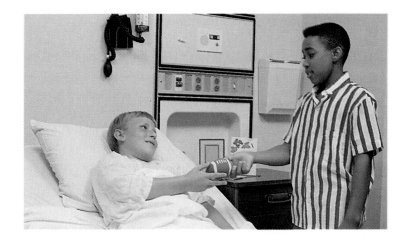

When in the hospital, you may be told about the tests or treatments you will receive. You should remember, that as a patient, you have the right to ask questions. Physicians and nurses are trained to provide you information concerning your health.

## 21:7  Parts of a Hospital

The **operating room** is the room in which surgery is performed. People who work in a hospital call it the O.R. People who work in the O.R. wear special clothes that are free of pathogens.

People in the O.R. wear masks that cover the lower half of their face and a cap to cover their hair. Before they enter the O.R., they scrub their hands, wrists, and arms with soap and water and put on sterile gloves. This helps prevent the patient from being infected by pathogens.

People who need surgery will usually be given an anesthetic (an us THET ihk) when they first enter the O.R. An **anesthetic** is a medicine that puts a patient to sleep and blocks pain. With the patient asleep, the surgeon can work more easily.

*What is an anesthetic?*

When surgery is finished, a patient is taken to a recovery room. The **recovery room** is a room where a person stays immediately after surgery. This person is watched by nurses for an hour or more, to be sure he or she begins to recover normally after surgery. Later, the person is taken back to his or her room in the hospital.

325

The **emergency room** is the area in the hospital where care is given to a person who has a sudden serious illness or injury. People who work in a hospital call this room the E.R.

Suppose a person is injured in a car accident. The rescue squad may take this person to the E.R. As soon as the person arrives at the E.R., treatment is started and a medical history taken. If the person cannot answer questions, someone with this person will do so. Treatment will be started immediately.

There are steps you should follow if you take someone to the E.R.

*When is treatment started in the emergency room?*

- Be calm and let the person know help is nearby.
- Be aware that others may be more seriously injured and thus need help first.
- Stay with the person until medical help arrives.
- Try to remember facts about the person's illness or injury.
- Remember information you are given.

There are urgent care centers in many communities. Physicians and nurses staff urgent care centers. If further care is needed a person is referred to a hospital. An urgent care center does not have many of the kinds of equipment found in a hospital.

**Think About It**

3. Why are hospitals always open?
4. Why are there different kinds of physicians who work in a hospital?
5. When you check into a hospital, why is information needed about you?
6. Why should you know what to do if you take a person to an emergency room?

# Life Skills

- ▶ Know how to use health services in your community.
- ▶ Be aware of what to do if you take someone to a hospital emergency room.

# Chapter 21 Review

**Summary**

1. Among the people who work in health departments in a community are sanitarians and health educators. *21:1*
2. Many different kinds of health agencies help fight diseases. *21:2*
3. You can exercise through many different health agencies in your community including Y's and physical fitness classes in schools. *21:3*
4. Treatment of illnesses and injuries are two of the reasons that people go to hospitals. *21:4*
5. Interns, residents, and specialists are among the different kinds of physicians in a hospital. *21:5*
6. Different people in a hospital will help patients with tasks such as checking in and the completion of medical tests. *21:6*
7. There are many different parts of a hospital including the recovery, operating, and emergency rooms. *21:7*

**Words for Health**

*Complete each sentence below with the correct word.*
*DO NOT WRITE IN THIS BOOK.*

| | |
|---|---|
| anesthetic | operating room |
| clinic | recovery room |
| emergency room | residency |
| health educators | resident |
| hospital | sanitarians |
| intern | specialist |
| internship | voluntary health agency |

1. _____ are people who work in a health agency to make sure restaurant food is safe to eat.
2. A(n) _____ is a physician who can treat specific problems such as heart disease.
3. After surgery, a patient will often be sent to the _____.
4. A(n) _____ is a place where a person who is ill or injured can receive medical care.
5. The American Lung Association is an example of a(n) _____.
6. A place in a hospital in which surgery is performed is the _____.
7. An area in a hospital or health agency that offers medical assistance to the community is called a(n) _____.

8. An extra year of study by a physician is called a(n) _____.
9. If you had a sudden injury that required quick medical attention, you might go to the _____ in a hospital.
10. A physician who gets advanced training in special areas of medicine is considered a(n) _____.
11. People who teach skills needed for healthful living are _____.
12. A(n) _____ is a medicine that puts a patient to sleep and blocks pain during surgery.

## Reviewing Health

1. What are the three kinds of public health departments and the function of each?
2. Why must sanitarians inspect restaurants?
3. What is the role of a health educator in a health agency?
4. Why is a clinic important to a community?
5. What are some examples of voluntary health agencies?
6. What are some services provided by voluntary health agencies?
7. How can agencies in your community help keep you physically fit?
8. What are two reasons why people might go to a hospital?
9. What are the different kinds of physicians who work in a hospital?
10. What happens when a person first enters a hospital?
11. What are some kinds of medical tests that are performed in a hospital?
12. What is the purpose of the recovery room in a hospital?
13. What do people who work in the operating room do to reduce the risk of pathogens in the surgery area?
14. What steps should you follow if you take someone to an emergency room?

## Using Life Skills

*Use the life skills from this chapter to respond to the following questions.*

*Situation:* Your friend is concerned about a relative who is ill. This relative has cancer. The family has very little money and does not know about services in the community that might be available.

1. What resources in your community might be able to help your friend?
2. How can you locate information about some of these resources?

*Situation:* You and a friend are riding bikes. Your friend falls and suffers a cut on his leg. The leg is bleeding heavily. There are no adults around, but you do notice you are a block away from a hospital.

**1.** To what part of the hospital should you take your friend?
**2.** What should you do when you get to this part of the hospital?

*Situation:* You and your family went to a restaurant for dinner. You and your sister chose the same meal from the menu. The rest of your family chose different items. That night, you and your sister became very ill. No other family member became ill.

**1.** What do you think might have happened?
**2.** What are some actions you might take?

*Situation:* Your friend is planning to be admitted into a hospital to have her tonsils out. She has never been to a hospital before and is very worried about what will be happening to her.

**1.** What might you suggest she do to prepare for her hospital stay?
**2.** How might you help her both before and after her surgery?

---

## Extending Health

**1.** Call a voluntary health agency in your community. Speak to someone who works there. Interview this person about his or her career. Find out information such as the job title this person holds, some of the activities involved in the job, and the kind of training needed to have this job.

**2.** There are many different kinds of medical specialists. Select five from this list and describe what each does.

| | |
|---|---|
| allergist | pediatrician |
| anesthesiologist | psychiatrist |
| endocrinologist | radiologist |
| ophthalmologist | thoracic surgeon |
| orthopedic surgeon | urologist |
| otologist | |

After selecting five, find the names of two other kinds of specialists, not listed and describe what they do.

**3.** Take a hospital tour. Observe the many different parts of the hospital and the various jobs done there. Record your observations.

# Glossary

## A

**abusive drinking:** drinking alcohol in a manner that is not responsible

**acid rain:** rain that contains a high amount of acid; forms when sulfur from burning fuels mixes with moisture in the air

**additive:** any chemical added to foods

**adolescence** (ad ul ES unts): the period of time between childhood and adulthood

**adopted child:** a child who permanently lives with parents in a family but who has different natural parents

**adrenaline** (uh DREN ul un): a hormone that raises blood pressure and causes the liver to release sugar into the bloodstream to provide extra energy

**aerobic** (er ROH bihk) **exercise:** a form of exercise that requires a continuous use of oxygen over an extended period of time

**aggressive behavior:** the use of words and/or actions that show disrespect toward others

**agility:** the ability to move with ease and speed

**Al-Anon:** an organization that helps family members of abusive drinkers

**Alateen:** a treatment organization for teenage children of abusive drinkers

**alcohol:** a depressant drug found in beer, wine, whiskey, wine coolers, and some other kinds of beverages

**Alcoholics Anonymous (AA):** an organization for abusive drinkers

**alcoholism:** a disease in which a person is chemically dependent on alcohol

**allergen:** a substance that causes an allergic reaction

**allergy:** a condition in which the body reacts to a food or substance in the environment

**anaerobic** (an uh ROH bihk) **exercise:** a form of exercise in which the body's demand for oxygen is greater than the supply

**anesthetic** (an us THET ihk): a medicine that puts a patient to sleep and blocks pain

**anger:** a strong, unfriendly feeling that usually occurs when a person's feelings are hurt

**anorexia nervosa** (an uh REK see uh · nur VOH suh): an emotional disorder in which a poor self-concept and an intense fear of being overweight result in starvation

**antibodies:** protein substances in blood that destroy pathogens

**antiperspirant:** a product that controls body odor and perspiration

**assertive behavior:** the practice of expressing your thoughts and feelings honestly

**asthma** (AZ muh): a condition that involves the closing or blocking of tubes in the respiratory system

**atherosclerosis** (ath uh roh skluh ROH sus): a disease in which fat deposits inside artery walls block blood flow

**auscultation** (aw skul TAY shun): a procedure in which a physician listens to sounds in your body

# B

**balance:** the ability to keep from falling

**beta-endorphins** (BAYT uh • en DOR fihnz): substances produced in the brain that relieve pain and promote feelings of pleasure and well-being

**blood alcohol level:** the amount of alcohol in a person's blood

**body composition:** the percentage of fat tissue and lean tissue in your body

**bulimia** (byew LIHM ee uh): an emotional disorder in which a poor self-concept and intense fear of being overweight result in secret heavy eating followed by starvation, self-induced vomiting, and the use of laxatives or diuretics

# C

**calculus** (KAL kyuh lus): hardened plaque

**Calorie:** a measure of the energy value of food

**cancer:** a disease in which abnormal body cells grow and multiply

**carbohydrates:** nutrients that are the main supply of energy for your body

**carbon monoxide:** a colorless and odorless gas that acts as a poison in the body

**carcinogen** (kar SIHN uh juhn): any substance that causes cancer

**cardiovascular fitness:** the condition of your heart and blood vessels

**cavities:** holes in the enamel of a tooth caused by acid

**cerebral** (SER uh brul) **palsy:** a nervous system disorder resulting in a loss of control of nerve and muscle movement

**chemotherapy** (kee moh THER uh pee): the use of chemicals to kill cancer cells

**chronic bronchitis** (KRAHN ihk • brahn KITE us): an inflammation of the bronchial tubes

**cilia** (SIHL ee uh): hair-like structures that trap dust and other particles that get into the air passage

**circulatory system:** the body system that consists of blood, blood vessels, and the heart

**cirrhosis** (suh ROH sus): a disease in which liver cells are destroyed due to the use of alcohol

**clinic:** an area in a health department or hospital that offers medical assistance to people in a community

**cocaine:** a stimulant obtained from the leaves of coca shrubs

**combination group:** a food group that contains ingredients from more than one of the four healthful food groups and supplies the same nutrients as the foods they contain

**communicable disease:** a disease that a person gets from contact with an infected person

**consumer:** a person who buys and uses products

**convalescent** (kahn vuh LES unt) **stage:** the period of time immediately following an illness when a person's body is still not as strong as before the illness

**cooling down:** a three to five minute period of reduced exercise

**coordination:** the ability to use body parts and senses together for movement

**crack:** an illegal drug made with cocaine and other unknown substances

**cruciferous** (krew SIHF uh rus) **vegetables:** vegetables in the cabbage family

**culture:** a blend of the influences on your life by people in your home, city, state, and nation

**curl-ups:** exercises that measure abdominal strength and endurance

# D

**decibel:** the unit used to measure the loudness of sound

**dehydration** (dee hi DRAY shun): a deficiency or lack of the amount of water needed for body processes

**dentin:** the hard tissue that forms the body of a tooth

**deodorant:** a product used under the arms to control body odor

**depressants:** a group of drugs that slow down the

functions of the body so they become slower than normal

**designer drugs:** drugs that imitate the effects of other drugs

**designer labels:** special labels put on clothing to tell you who made the item

**desirable weight:** a combination of the weight and body composition recommended for your age, sex, height, and body build

**diabetes** (di uh BEET us): a disease in which the body cannot use the sugar in foods in normal ways

**diagnosis** (di ihg NOH sus): the identification of a disease based on symptoms

**diaphragm** (DI uh fram): a muscle that separates the chest cavity from the abdomen

**digestive system:** the body system made of parts that help your body use food

**direct pressure:** a force placed over a break in the skin to stop bleeding

**dislocation:** an injury that occurs when a bone is forced away from a joint

**dissolution:** a legal way to end a marriage in which the couple decides the details of the agreement

**distress:** a harmful response to a stressor in which a person is unable to cope and to perform well

**diuretic** (di yuh RET ihk): a drug that causes the kidneys to release excess urine

**divorce:** a legal way to end a marriage in which a judge decides the details of the agreement

**drug:** any substance other than food that changes the way the body works

**drug abuse:** using a drug improperly and for no medical reason

**drug dependence:** a mental or physical need for a drug

**drug misuse:** using a drug improperly in the hopes of feeling better

**drug tolerance:** the change in the body's response to a drug so that larger and larger doses are needed for a desired effect

# E

**earthquake:** movement below the surface of Earth that causes tremors on the surface

**emotions:** the feelings you have in response to events and life situations

**enabler:** a person who takes actions that help someone continue a destructive behavior

**endocrine** (EN duh krun) **system:** the body system made up of glands that produce hormones

**enriched food:** a food to which vitamins have been added to replace vitamins lost during food processing

**environment:** everything that is around you and its influence on you

**EPA:** Environmental Protection Agency; a government agency that sets and enforces laws to prevent air, land, and water pollution

**epilepsy:** a condition in which nerve messages in the brain are disturbed for a brief time

**ethyl** (ETH ul) **alcohol:** a beverage made from the action of yeast cells on grains, fruits, and vegetables; grain alcohol

**eustress** (YOO strus): a helpful response to a stressor in which body changes help a person's performance

**extended family:** a family in which members from three generations live together

# F

**family:** a group of people who are related

**fats:** nutrients the body uses for energy and to help store some vitamins

**fat tissue:** the tissue that is found just beneath the skin and that surrounds the muscles and internal organs

**fetal alcohol syndrome (FAS):** a condition in which a baby is born with birth defects caused by the mother's drinking during pregnancy

**filling:** the material a dentist uses to repair a cavity in a tooth

**first aid:** the immediate care given to a person who has been injured or suddenly becomes ill

**fitness skills:** skills that can be used when participating in a variety of sports and games

**flexibility:** the ability to bend and move your body in many directions

**fluoride** (FLOOR ide): a chemical that helps prevent tooth decay

**fortified** (FOR tih fide) **food:** a food to which vitamins have been added

**foster child:** a child who temporarily lives with a family other than his or her own

**fracture:** a break or crack in a bone

**frostbite:** damage to a body part due to freezing

# G

**generic** (juh NER ihk) **product:** a product that has the same purpose and ingredients as a brand name product but usually does not cost as much

**gingivitis** (jihn juh VITE us): a condition in which the gums are sore and bleed easily

**grief:** the expression of sorrow

**groundwater:** the natural supply of water from rain and snow that collects under Earth's surface

# H

**hallucinogen** (huh LEWS un uh jun): an illegal drug that changes how a person's brain works

**hangover:** the sick feeling a person has the day after drinking too much

**hazardous wastes:** harmful substances that are difficult to discard safely

**health:** the state of your body and mind and how you get along with others

**health behavior contract:** a written guide that helps you make a plan to follow a life skill for good health

**health consumer:** a person who buys or uses health products and health services

**health educators:** people who teach skills needed for healthful living

**health history:** recorded information about your past health and your habits

**health inspector:** a person who checks to see that places that provide health services follow health standards

**health knowledge:** awareness of facts about health

**health product:** an item that improves your physical, mental, or social health

**health record:** a file in which information gathered from your health history and your checkups is kept

**health service:** a person or a place that helps improve your physical, mental, or social health

**health standard:** a rule or code of behavior to protect health

**healthful behaviors:** actions that increase the level of health for you and others

**heat cramps:** sharp muscle pains that may occur during long periods of physical activity

**heat exhaustion:** a condition in which a person feels dizzy and tired from being in high temperatures for a long period of time

**heatstroke:** a sudden attack of illness from being in the sun or heat

**Heimlich** (HIME lihk) **maneuver:** a method in which the air is forced from the lungs to push out an object stuck in the throat

**hemophilia** (hee muh FIHL ee uh): a disease in which a substance necessary for clotting is missing from the blood

**heredity** (huh RED ut ee): the passing of traits from one generation to another

**hormones:** chemicals that act as messengers to regulate body activities

**hurricane:** a storm, with high winds and heavy rain, that forms over water

**hypertension:** high blood pressure

**hypothermia** (hi poh THUR mee uh): a condition in which body temperature is lowered due to wind, cold, and dampness

# I

**immunity:** the body's protection from, or resistance to, disease

**incubation** (ihn kyuh BAY shun) **stage:** the period of time between a pathogen's first entry into the body and the first signs and symptoms

**infection:** a condition in which pathogens cause swelling and redness in an injured area

**ingredients:** the substances in a product

**integumentary** (ihn teg yuh MENT uh ree) **system:** the body system made of parts that cover the body

**intern:** a graduate student who has completed medical school and is doing further study at a hospital

**internship:** the extra year of study done by an intern

**intoxication:** the state of being drunk

**involuntary muscles:** muscles that you do not control

**isokinetic** (i suh kuh NET ihk) **exercise:** an exercise in which a weight is moved through an entire range of motion

**isometric** (i suh MET rihk) **exercise:** an exercise in which muscles are tightened for five to ten seconds without any movement of body parts

**isotonic** (i suh TAHN ihk) **exercise:** an exercise in which there is a muscle contraction that causes movement

# J

**joint:** a place where two bones meet

# L

**laxative:** a medicine that stimulates the digestive tract and produces a bowel movement

**lean tissue:** the tissue that consists of muscles, bones, cartilage, connective tissue, nerves, skin, and internal organs

**life expectancy** (ihk SPEC tun see): the number of years a person is expected to live

**life skill:** a healthful behavior to learn and practice throughout your life

**lifestyle:** the way in which you live

**lifetime sports:** activities in which you can participate for the rest of your life provided you stay in good health

**lightning:** an electrical discharge that travels from one cloud to another or between a cloud and Earth

**long-term goals:** goals to be achieved in the future

**loving person:** someone who is respectful, understanding, responsible, and self-disciplined

**low-calorie food:** food that contains less than 0.4 Calories per gram

# M

**mainstream smoke:** the smoke a person inhales and exhales from his or her cigarette

**marijuana** (mer uh WAHN uh): a drug made from the crushed leaves, flowers, seeds, and stems of the hemp plant

**maximum heart rate:** 220 minus your age

**melanin** (MEL uh nun): a substance that gives skin its color

**menstrual** (MEN strul) **cycle:** a monthly series of changes that occur in a female's body

**menstrual period:** the shedding of the lining of the uterus

**mental health:** the state of your mind and how you express your feelings

**metabolic** (met uh BAHL ihk) **rate:** the rate at which your body uses Calories

**metabolism** (muh TAB uh lihz um): the way your body uses food

**methyl** (METH ul) **alcohol:** a poisonous substance made from wood products and other substances

**mineral deficiency** (dih FIHSH un see): a lack of the amount of a certain mineral in the diet that is needed for good health

**minerals:** nutrients that regulate many of the chemical reactions in your body

**mucous** (MYEW kus) **membranes:** the linings of body openings; protect you by producing a sticky fluid that traps harmful products

**multiple sclerosis** (skluh ROH sus): a condition in which the covering of nerve fibers in the brain and spinal cord breaks down

**muscle soreness:** pain that results when you overuse muscles

**muscular dystrophy** (DIHS truh fee): an inherited disease in which the muscles lose their ability to function

**muscular endurance:** the ability to use the same muscles over a long period of time

**muscular strength:** the amount of force your muscles can produce

**muscular system:** the body system made up of all the muscles in your body

# N

**nasal speculum** (SPEK yuh lum): an instrument a physician uses to spread your nostrils to see if anything is blocking your breathing

**nervous system:** the body system for communication and control

**net quantity:** the amount of food not including the container

**net weight:** the weight of the contents of a product not including the container

**nicotine:** a colorless, oily stimulant in tobacco

**noise pollution:** the presence of sounds that are loud enough to harm a person's health

**noncommunicable disease:** a disease that is not caused by direct or indirect contact with a pathogen

**nonverbal behavior:** conduct without using words

**nutrients:** the chemical substances in food that the body uses for growth, repair of cells, and energy

# O

**one-mile walk/run:** an exercise to measure your level of cardiovascular fitness

**ophthalmoscope** (ahf THAL muh skohp): an instrument used to shine light into your eye to see blood vessels and internal parts

**opiates:** drugs made from the opium poppy plant

**otoscope** (OHT uh skohp): an instrument used to examine the ear canal and eardrum

**ovaries** (OHV reez): female reproductive glands that release ova

**over-the-counter (OTC) drugs:** drugs that can be bought without a physician's prescription

**overfat:** having too high a percentage of body fat compared to the percentage of lean tissue

**overweight:** weighing more than is recommended for a person's age, sex, height, and body build

**ozone layer:** the part of the atmosphere that filters out most of the sun's ultraviolet rays

# P

**palpation** (pal PAY shun): a procedure in which a physician touches or feels your body to learn how it functions inside

**pancreas** (PAN kree us): a large gland that produces insulin

**passive behavior:** the practice of not expressing ideas, opinions, and feelings

**pathogens:** harmful living organisms that cause communicable diseases

**peak stage:** the time during which signs and symptoms of a specific disease are present and may be identified

**peer pressure:** influence that people your age try to have on your decisions

**percussion:** a procedure in which a physician taps on your chest, abdomen, or back with the fingers

**periodontal** (per ee oh DAHNT ul) **disease:** a disease of the gums and other tissues that support the teeth

**personality:** the way a person feels, thinks, and acts

**pesticide** (PES tuh side): a poison that is used to kill some insects and other pests

**philosophy** (fuh LAHS uh fee) **of life:** a view of life or an attitude toward life and its purpose

**physical dependence:** a bodily need for a drug

**physical fitness:** the condition of your body as a result of a regular exercise program

**physical health:** the state of your body

**plaque** (PLAK): a sticky substance containing bacteria that is always forming on teeth

**plasma** (PLAZ muh): the liquid part of the blood

**platelets:** cells that help form clots

**pneumonia** (noo MOH nyuh): a lung infection with symptoms including a high fever, shortness of breath, chest pain, and coughing

**poison:** any product that can enter the body and cause illness

**pollutant:** a harmful substance in the environment

**pollution:** the presence of materials in the environment that are harmful to living things

**positive self-concept:** the good feeling you have about yourself most of the time

**posture:** the way you hold your body as you sit, stand, and move

**power:** the ability to combine strength with speed

**prescription drugs:** drugs that are ordered by a physician for a specific person

**preservative** (pree ZURV ut ihv): a chemical added to foods to prevent spoiling

**prodromal** (proh DROH mul) **stage:** the period of time when a person first begins to feel ill

**proof:** a word used to represent the amount of alcohol in a beverage

**proteins:** nutrients the body uses for the growth and repair of cells

**psychiatrist** (suh KI uh trust): a physician who treats mental illness or problems of daily living and who may prescribe medicines

**psychological** (si kuh LAHJ ih kul) **dependence:** the mental desire for a drug

**psychologist** (si KAHL uh just): a person who treats people with mental illness or with problems of daily living and who may do psychological testing

**puberty** (PYEW burt ee): the stage of development during which body changes occur that make males and females physically able to reproduce

**pulmonary emphysema** (PUL muh ner ee • em fuh SEE muh): a disease in which the alveoli in the lungs lose their ability to work

## Q

**quack** (KWAK): a person who tries to sell you useless health products or services

**quackery:** the method a person uses to sell useless products and services

## R

**radiation:** energy given off by atoms as light or particles

**reaction time:** the length of time you use to move after you see, hear, feel, or taste a signal

**recycling:** the reusing of products

**red blood cells:** cells that carry oxygen from the air in your lungs to the cells in your body

**reduced-calorie food:** a food that is at least one-third lower in Calories than similar foods

**reflex:** an involuntary response to changes inside or outside the body

**refusal skills:** ways to say NO to risk behaviors

**relationship:** the connection you have with another person

**residency:** for a physician, a period of advanced training in a special area of medical care

**resident:** a physician getting advanced training in special areas of medical care or surgery

**respectful:** showing you think other people are worthwhile

**respiratory system:** the body system that helps you use the air you breathe

**responsible:** trustworthy

**responsible decision-making model:** a list of steps you can use to help you make decisions

**responsible decisions:** decisions that result in actions that promote health for you and others

**Reye** (RI) **syndrome:** a serious disease that may damage the liver and brain

**risk behaviors:** actions that might be harmful to you or to others

**risk situations:** conditions that may harm your health

**role model:** a person whose behavior sets an example for others to follow

## S

**sanitarians:** people who inspect restaurants

**sanitary landfill:** an area where layers of solid wastes are dumped and covered with dirt

**saturated fats:** fats from dairy products and red meat

**scab:** dried blood that forms over a cut or injury to protect the opening to the body

**school guidance counselor:** a person who has special training in helping young people make life choices

**scrape:** a wearing away of the outer layers of the skin due to rubbing against a hard surface

**secondary sex characteristics:** the physical changes that occur during puberty in both males and females

**seizure:** the period during which there is a loss of mental and physical control

**self-centered behavior:** selfish behavior

**self-concept:** what you think and how you feel about yourself

**self-disciplined:** able to control your actions

**self-loving behavior:** behavior that shows concern and liking for oneself

**separation:** an agreement between a married couple to live apart but remain married while seeking to work out their problems

**seven dietary guidelines:** suggested guidelines for planning a diet to promote good health

**sewage:** waste material from homes and industries

**sex role:** the way you act as a result of your attitude about being male or female

**sexually transmitted diseases (STDs):** communicable diseases that are spread through sexual contact

**shock:** a condition in which the functions of body organs are slowed because of illness or injury

**short-term goals:** goals that are achieved in order to reach long-term goals

**sickle-cell anemia:** an inherited disease in which many red blood cells are curved instead of round

**side effect:** an unwanted result from a drug

**sidestream smoke:** the smoke a person inhales from someone else's cigarettes

**sign:** a visible change in the body

**skeletal system:** the body system made up of all the bones in the body

**smokeless tobacco:** tobacco that is placed inside the mouth and is not smoked

**social health:** the state of your relationships with others

**social worker:** a person who helps people find resources to meet various personal needs

**specialist:** a physician who works in a particular area of medicine

**speed:** the ability to move rapidly

**sphygmomanometer** (sfihg moh muh NAHM ut ur): a special cuff that is used to measure blood pressure

**sprain:** an injury to the tissue that connects bones at a joint

**stimulants:** drugs that speed up the functions of the body so they become faster than normal

**strength:** the areas in your life in which you do well

**stress:** the body's reaction to any physical, mental, or social demand

**stress management skills:** ways to reduce the harmful effects of the body changes caused by stress

**stressor:** anything that causes stress

**supplying artery:** the main artery that carries blood to a limb

**symptom:** a change in body function that cannot be seen

# T

**tar:** a thick, sticky substance that is produced from burning tobacco

**target heart rate:** a heart rate of 75 percent of the difference between your resting heart rate and your maximum heart rate plus your resting heart rate

**testes** (TES teez): male reproductive glands that produce sperm cells

**thermal pollution:** the presence of heated water dumped into a river or lake by an industry

**tongue depressor:** a stick used to hold your tongue down so a physician can see your mouth and throat

**tornado:** a storm of whirling winds that forms over land and moves at very high speeds

**tornado warning:** an emergency announcement issued by the weather bureau when a tornado has been spotted

**tornado watch:** a message issued when weather conditions are right for a tornado to develop

# U

**ultraviolet rays:** harmful rays from the sun

**underfat:** having too low a percentage of body fat

**understanding:** being aware of how another person feels or thinks

**underweight:** weighing less than is recommended for a person's age, sex, height, and body build

**United States Recommended Dietary Allowance (US RDA):** a list that suggests daily amounts of nutrients that should be included in a healthful diet

**unit price:** price per ounce or gram; can be used to compare prices on similar products

**unsaturated** (un SACH uh rayt ud) **fats:** fats from foods such as vegetables, nuts, seeds, poultry, and fish

**urinary** (YOOR uh ner ee) **system:** the body system that removes liquid wastes from the body

**uterus** (YEWT uh rus): the reproductive organ in which a developing baby grows

# V

**vaccine** (vak SEEN): a substance that contains weakened or dead pathogens that cause your body to produce antibodies

**value:** anything that is desirable or important to you

**vitamin deficiency:** a lack of the amount of one or more vitamins needed for good health

**vitamins:** nutrients that help regulate body processes and fight disease

**voluntary health agency:** an agency that fights a specific health problem by raising money through donations

**voluntary muscles:** muscles over which you have control

# W

**warming up:** three to five minutes of exercise to get muscles ready to do more work

**water:** a nutrient that helps with body processes such as digestion and the removal of waste products

**weight management:** a plan to maintain a person's ideal weight

**wellness:** the highest level of health you can reach

**white blood cells:** cells that help protect you by fighting pathogens that enter your body

**withdrawal:** a condition that develops when a drug that causes physical dependence is suddenly not available

# Index

## A

abusive drinking, 187, 189–190; **illus.,** 187, 189
acid rain, 312
additive, 108
adolescence, 86, 87–88, 122; **illus.,** 87
adopted child, 38
adrenal glands, 72
adrenaline, 26, 72
adulthood, 89; **illus.,** 89, 90
aerobic exercise, 142
aggressive behavior, 59, 60
agility, 140
AIDS, 221, 226
Al-Anon, 191
Alateen, 191
alcohol, 106, 180–181, 182, 183–192
**Alcoholics Anonymous (AA),** 190
alcoholism, 188, 189–191
allergy, 238
American Cancer Society, 110, 321
American Heart Association, 109, 321
American Lung Association, 321
anaerobic exercise, 142
anesthetic, 325
anorexia nervosa, 122, 123
antibodies, 217, 218
arteries, 75
assertive behavior, 59, 60, 205
asthma, 238; **illus.,** 238
atherosclerosis, 222
auscultation, table, 269

## B

balance, 140
balanced diet, illus., 101
behavior, 8, 51, 54
beta-endorphins, 135; illus., 135
blackout, 188
blood, 75, 76
blood alcohol level, 183, illus., 183
body composition, 116, 117, 137; illus., 116, 139

body fat, 116, 117
bones, 68
braces, 270
brand name product, 250; **illus.,** 250
bulimia, 124, 125; **illus.,** 125
burns, 281

## C

calculus, 262, 264
caliper, 117
Calorie, 118, 119, 121; **illus.,** 118; **table,** 118, 119
cancer, 8, 27, 110, 186, 200, 203, 224, 225; **illus.,** 224
capillaries, 75
carbohydrates, 101
carbon dioxide, 76
carbon monoxide, 199
carcinogen, 224
cardiovascular fitness, 137, 142
cavities, 263, 265
cerebral palsy, 231, 233, 234
chemical dependence, 168, 188
chemotherapy, 225
child abuse, 46
childhood, 84, 85–86; **illus.,** 85
chronic bronchitis, 201
cilia, 200, 217
circulatory system, 75, 76, 199; **illus.,** 75
cirrhosis, 186
clinic, 320
cocaine, 173, 174; **table,** 174
codeine, 173
combination group, 105
communicable diseases, 215, 216, 217–221
communication, 56, 58, 59; **illus.,** 59
consumer, 107; **illus.,** 107
control systems, 67
convalescent stage, 219
cooling down, 143
coordination, 140
crack, 174; **table,** 174
cruciferous vegetables, 110

# H

hallucinogen, 175
hazardous wastes, 310
health, 5, 6–8, 10–11, 13, 51, 90; illus., 8; table, 9
health behavior contract, 13; table, 14
health consumer, 248
health educators, 320
healthful behaviors, 7, 8, 11, 13
health history, 267; illus., 267
health inspector, 253
health knowledge, 8
health product, 248, 249–252
health record, 267
health service, 248, 253–255; table, 254, 255
health standard, 253; illus., 253
heart, 75
heart disease, 27, 75, 109, 117
heat cramps, 282; illus., 282, 283
heat exhaustion, 283, 284
heatstroke, 283, 284
Heimlich maneuver, 278; illus., 278
hemophilia, 236
heredity, 21
heroin, 173
hormones, 72
hospital, 323, 324–326; illus., 323, 324, 325
hypertension, 222, 223; illus., 222
hypothermia, 285, 286

# I

immune system, 27; illus., 27
immunity, 218
incubation stage, 218
infancy, 83–84, illus., 84
infection, 153
influenza (flu), 219
ingredients, 249
injuries, 153–157
insulin, 236, 237; illus., 236
integumentary system, 70; illus., 70
intern, 323
internship, 323
involuntary muscles, 69

isokinetic exercise, 141
isometric exercise, 141
isotonic exercise, 141

# J

joint, 68

# L

laxative, 123, 124
lean tissue, 116
life cycle, 83–91
life expectancy, 266
life skill, 13; illus., 13
lifestyle, 5; illus., 10
lifetime sports, 143; illus., 143
love, 24, 41; illus., 24
loving person, 41; illus., 41
low-calorie food, 108

# M

mainstream smoke, 204
manners, 56, 57; illus., 57
marijuana, 175, 176; illus., 175
maximum heart rate, 142
medical care, 266–269
melanin, 70
menstrual cycle, 87
menstrual period, 87
mental health, 5, 6, 7, 8, 19, 23, 120, 123, 134, 184, 251, 255; table, 7; illus., 23
metabolic rate, 119, 120, 121
metabolism, 119, 121
methyl alcohol, 182
mineral deficiency, 102
minerals, 102; table, 103
modified sit-ups, 138; illus., 139
morphine, 173
mouth protectors, 158
mucous membranes, 217
mucus, 201, 217; illus., 201
multiple sclerosis, 231, 232; illus., 232
muscle soreness, 155
muscular dystrophy, 231, 235; illus., 235

muscular endurance, 137
muscular strength, 137
muscular system, 67, 69; **illus.,** 69

# N

nasal speculum, **table,** 268
nervous system, 67, 71, 72; **illus.,** 71, 72
net quantity, 107
net weight, 249
neurons, 71, 72
nicotine, 198, 199, 201, 202
noise pollution, 310
noncommunicable disease, 222, 223–225
nonverbal behavior, 58
nonverbal communication, 58
nutrients, 74–75, 99, 100, 101–105; **illus.,**
  100, 101
nutrition, 96–110, 114–125, 135

# O

one-mile walk/run, 138; **illus.,** 139
operating room, 325
ophthalmoscope, **table,** 268
opiates, 173
osteoporosis, 92
otoscope, **table,** 268
ovaries, 72, 73, 87
overfat, 120
over-the-counter (OTC) drugs, 172, 173;
  **illus.,** 173
ozone layer, 313

# P

palpation, **table,** 268
pancreas, 236, 237
parents, 10, 38–39, 42–43; **illus.,** 43
passive behavior, 59, 60
pathogens, 27, 216, 217–218, 220; **illus.,**
  216, 217
peak stage, 218
peer pressure, 11, 59, 184
percussion, **table,** 269
periodontal disease, 263, 264
personality, 21; **illus.,** 21

pesticide, 311
pharmacist, 171; **illus.,** 167
philosophy of life, 22
Physical Best, 138
physical dependence, 168, 173, 198; **table,**
  174
physical examination, 266; **table,** 268–269
physical fitness, 132–133, 134, 135–144;
  **illus.,** 134, 135, 138, 139; **table,** 144
physical health, 5, 6, 7, 8, 120, 123, 248,
  254; **table,** 254
pituitary gland, 72–73
plaque, 262, 263–264
plasma, 75
platelets, 76
pneumonia, 219
poison, 279
pollutant, 308
pollution, 307, 308, 309–310; **illus.,** 309
positive self-concept, 19, 20–21; **illus.,** 20
posture, 138
power, 140
prescription drugs, 171, 172; **illus.,** 171,
  172; **table,** 172
preservatives, 108
President's Challenge, 138
prodromal stage, 218
progesterone, 73
proteins, 100
psychiatrist, 255
psychological dependence, 168, 173, 175;
  **table,** 174
psychologist, 255
puberty, 86, 87–88
pull-ups, 138; **illus.,** 139
pulmonary emphysema, 201

# Q

quack, 256
quackery, 256

# R

radiation, 312, 313; **illus.,** 312
reaction time, 140
recovery room, 325

traditional family, 37
transport system, 74

## U

ultraviolet rays, 313
underfat, 121
understanding, 41
underweight, 121
United States Recommended Dietary
    Allowance (US RDA), 103
unit price, 107, 249
unsaturated fats, 105, 106; illus., 105
urethra, 78
urinary system, 78
urine, 78
uterus, 87

## V

vaccine, 218; illus., 218
value, 22

veins, 75
venereal disease, 220
vitamin deficiency, 101
vitamins, 101, 116–117, table, 102
voluntary health agency, 321
voluntary muscles, 69
v-sit reach, 138; illus., 139

## W

warming up, 143
water safety, 294
weaknesses, 20, 21
weight management, 114–116, 117,
    118–125
wellness, 6, 7
Wellness Scale, 6, 7; illus., 7
white blood cells, 27, 76; illus., 27
withdrawal, 169, 173, 198

# PHOTO CREDITS

4 5 6 7 8 9 10 11 12 13 14 15—98 97 96 95 94 93 92 91 90